MARCUS CALDWELL

Battles of the Ages: World War I 1915

AF483266

Copyright © 2023 by Marcus Caldwell

All rights reserved. No part of this publication may be reproduced, stored or transmitted in any form or by any means, electronic, mechanical, photocopying, recording, scanning, or otherwise without written permission from the publisher. It is illegal to copy this book, post it to a website, or distribute it by any other means without permission.

First edition

Contents

Introduction

In the annals of human history, few years have been as pivotal and as devastating as 1915, the second year of the Great War. This period, known for its widespread and brutal conflict, was a time of groundbreaking military strategies, unprecedented human suffering, and significant changes in the world's geopolitical landscape.

The onset of 1915 brought little optimism for a swift end to the conflict that had consumed the globe since the summer of 1914. The initial enthusiasm seen across Europe, characterized by young men enlisting for what they believed would be a short and glorious campaign, had dissipated. Replacing it was the grim reality of trench warfare, a stalemate on the Western Front, and the realization that this war would be unlike any other in history.

The exploration of 1915 starts on the Western Front's battlefields, where the war had devolved into a deadly routine of trench warfare. The idyllic views of war vanished amidst the muddy, rat-infested trenches of Belgium and France. Soldiers faced not just the enemy, but also the relentless challenges of life on the front lines: extreme cold, mud, continuous artillery barrages, and the constant threat of gas attacks. The Battle of Neuve Chapelle in March, marking the British Army's first major offensive on the Western Front, set the tone for the brutal and costly battles that would ensue.

In the East, the situation was equally tragic, though markedly different. The Eastern Front saw a war of movement, with large armies engaging in vast battles over extensive territories. The Russian Empire, battling the forces of Germany and Austria-Hungary, experienced a significant shift in the balance of power during the Great Retreat of its armies in the summer of 1915.

1915 was not solely about land battles; it also marked the year when chemical weapons were used on a large scale, introducing a new and horrifying dimension to warfare. The Second Battle of Ypres, where German forces deployed chlorine gas against Allied troops, represented a shocking escalation in the brutality of war and had long-lasting effects.

This narrative delves into the personal stories of those who lived, fought, and died in 1915. From the generals orchestrating offensives to the soldiers in the trenches and civilians caught in the crossfire, their experiences and viewpoints add a human dimension to the vast scale of the war.

The technological advancements and tactical innovations of 1915 are also examined. The development of tanks, the increased use of aircraft for reconnaissance and combat, and the refinement of artillery tactics were instrumental in shaping the war's course.

Furthermore, 1915 saw the home front become crucial to the war effort. The mobilization of entire societies for war, with an unprecedented number of women entering the workforce and governments taking greater control over economies and information, transformed civilian life and laid the groundwork for the concept of total war.

As the events of 1915 are navigated, a homage is paid to those who endured the unthinkable and sacrificed their lives in hope of a better world. The legacy of 1915 is a complex tapestry of courage, tragedy, innovation, and transformation—a pivotal chapter in the story of World War I and the modern world.

I

Western Front

Battle of Neuve Chapelle

The tumultuous events of 1914 set the stage for a dramatic shift in the nature of warfare during the First World War. Initially characterized as encounter battles, these were a series of unforeseen actions where local commanders were compelled to make swift, reactive decisions. As the year progressed, the dynamic and fluid 'war of movement' gradually gave way to a protracted stalemate. This transition witnessed the formation of an extensive network of trenches, running from the Swiss Border to the Belgian Coast, a formidable stretch that came to be known as the Western Front.

This line of fortifications was separated by a daunting and infamous expanse known as No Man's Land. The trenches themselves were formidable barriers, fortified with layers of barbed wire, the relentless fire of machine guns, and the looming threat of heavy artillery. These defenses created an impervious barrier, effectively preventing either side from penetrating the other's lines. The mere act of peering above the parapet during daylight or attempting to traverse No Man's Land was tantamount to a death sentence, leaving both sides mired in a deadlock, unable to breach the enemy's defenses.

The winter of 1914/15 brought its own set of challenges, with troops on both sides enduring the harsh, cold conditions of living underground in muddy, waterlogged trenches. The frustration and hardship faced by these soldiers underscored a significant challenge for the Generals in 1915: devising a strategy to mobilize their troops from the trenches, across the perilous No

Man's Land, and into the enemy trenches, all while avoiding the deadly hail of machine gun fire and the devastating impact of shellfire.

The year 1915 opened with the French military contemplating offensive operations in Champagne and the Arras sector. Simultaneously, the British were formulating plans for an assault at Neuve Chapelle. Their objective was to capture the village and secure Aubers Ridge, a location of strategic importance. Holding Aubers Ridge would serve as a pivotal point for further operations aimed at capturing Lille, a city under German control that was being utilized as a major transport hub. This hub was integral to the German rail network, facilitating the movement of German forces along the Western Front. A successful breach of the German line in this sector would not only be a tactical victory but would also significantly disrupt the German communication and transport networks, potentially turning the tide of the war.

Field Marshal Sir John French, the Commander-in-Chief of the British Expeditionary Force (BEF), appointed General Sir Douglas Haig's First Army to lead the offensive at Neuve Chapelle. Although Haig had previously directed I Corps during the campaign of 1914, the Neuve Chapelle operation was his initial foray into managing a major attack as the commander of the First Army. Haig, along with his subordinate generals responsible for planning and organizing the operation, were products of a military education rooted in the Victorian era. Their training, primarily focused on colonial warfare, emphasized traditional strategies of advance and attack. However, these tactics proved largely ineffective with the cessation of the war of movement in 1914 and the onset of trench warfare. The static nature of trench warfare and the realities of modern industrialized war in 1915 posed new challenges, and the Neuve Chapelle operation represented their early efforts to devise strategies to break the stalemate.

Despite his Victorian military background, Haig demonstrated a willingness to embrace new technologies and innovative strategies. His approach to the challenges of advancing infantry across No Man's Land and breaching German lines incorporated several groundbreaking tactics. The Neuve Chapelle operation marked one of the first effective instances of coordinated infantry and artillery actions in a British offensive. This operation also featured the Royal Flying Corps, which played a crucial role. Although Haig initially had limited understanding of the potential military applications of aeroplanes, he was eager to explore their capabilities at Neuve Chapelle. Advancements in aerial reconnaissance, such as photographing enemy positions from the air, provided valuable intelligence. These aerial photographs facilitated the creation of detailed trench maps, offering ground commanders unprecedented insight into enemy targets prior to launching their attacks.

During the Battle of Neuve Chapelle, the Royal Flying Corps also participated in strategic bombing and artillery targeting. Observers from the corps directed artillery fire to targets behind German lines, marking a primitive yet significant step in the evolution of combined arms warfare. This innovative form of warfare, though in its nascent stages, would continue to develop and shape military tactics throughout the war.

The Neuve Chapelle operation in March 1915 was a groundbreaking moment in World War I, marking the first instance of a pre-planned artillery barrage by the British Army, featuring an unprecedented concentration of artillery firepower. This assault, which began at 7:30 a.m. on March 10th, lasted for 35 minutes and demonstrated the immense destructive capacity of concentrated artillery on a confined area. The strategy effectively breached the German trench system, previously deemed impregnable, primarily relying on the element of surprise to overwhelm and incapacitate the enemy forces.

Lieutenant Malcolm Kennedy of the 2nd Cameronian (Scottish Rifles) was present during this operation and provided a vivid description of the event. He recounted the overwhelming noise of the artillery barrage, likening it to the sound of numerous express trains rushing overhead, followed by the explosive impact of shells of various calibers on the German positions. Kennedy observed the chaos of the bombardment, with large chunks of earth and metal being hurled into the air and the distinctive yellow fumes of lyddite gas rising from the German trenches. His account highlighted the intensity and the transformative nature of this artillery strategy in the conflict.

As the artillery barrage shifted towards German positions beyond Neuve Chapelle at 8:05 a.m., the signal for the infantry to advance was given through a series of whistles. This moment marked the start of an attack by the IV Corps, led by Lieutenant-General Sir Henry Rawlinson, and the Indian Corps under Lieutenant General Sir James Willcocks. Their goal was to execute a convergent assault on a 2,000-yard front, aiming to seize the village of Neuve Chapelle before launching an attack on Aubers Ridge.

The effectiveness of the British artillery bombardment played a crucial role in this phase of the operation. It significantly subdued the German forces defending Neuve Chapelle, facilitating the advance of the British 8th Division infantry across No Man's Land and enabling them to capture the German trenches.

Sergeant William Siddons of the 2nd Middlesex Regiment was among the first wave of soldiers to advance. As they moved forward, the intensity of the close-quarters combat became evident. The British soldiers, described as fighting with exceptional ferocity, encountered a determined but psycho-logically shaken enemy, still reeling from the impact of the bombardment. Despite the heavy losses suffered by the British forces, the toll on the German defenders was described as considerable. The trenches were filled with casualties, showcasing the brutal nature of the conflict. Siddons' account, as reported in The Sunday Post on March 21, 1915, paints a vivid picture of the battle's ferocity and the significant human cost on both sides.

On March 10th, the British artillery bombardment, while largely successful, did not uniformly achieve its objectives across all sectors. Notably, in the area held by the 2nd Middlesex Regiment, the bombardment failed to sufficiently clear the German wire. This failure was attributed to several factors: the two 6-inch Howitzers assigned to this task arrived late on the afternoon before the attack, the artillery officers were not familiar with the terrain, and there was insufficient light to properly calibrate their guns.

As a result, soldiers from the left flank of the 2nd Middlesex Regiment and parts of the 2nd Cameronian (Scottish Rifles) found themselves entangled in the uncut wire, leading to heavy casualties. Brigadier General A. Holland, in his post-operation report, stressed the importance of artillery being close enough to their targets to guarantee wire cutting. He suggested a distance within 1,700 yards, noting that longer ranges might involve a greater element of chance. Holland emphasized that without assurance of wire being cut, attacks could result in severe losses.

Despite these challenges, the 8th Division succeeded in breaching the German trenches and entering the village of Neuve Chapelle, which had been reduced to ruins. The soldiers engaged in intense urban combat, searching for German soldiers who were taking shelter in underground cellars. They encountered the Indian Corps inside the village, who were engaged in a similar battle from the southwest. Remarkably, within just two hours of the attack's commencement, the objective of capturing Neuve Chapelle was achieved, demonstrating the tenacity and effectiveness of the Allied forces despite the initial setbacks.

Following the heavy losses sustained during the 1914 campaigns, the British Expeditionary Force (BEF) faced the daunting task of replenishing its ranks. The experienced officers, non-commissioned officers (NCOs), and soldiers lost in battle were not easily replaced. In response to this crisis, civilians heeded Field Marshal Earl Herbert Kitchener's call for volunteers, but equipping and training this new influx of troops was a monumental undertaking, one that would take two years to come to fruition.

In the early months of 1915, as Field Marshal Sir John French contemplated an assault on Neuve Chapelle, he was constrained by limited resources. The regular soldiers, rapidly deployed from colonial garrisons to Britain, formed the core of the 7th and 8th Divisions. However, these forces alone were insufficient for the task at hand. This predicament led the British Army to deploy Territorial soldiers, originally intended for home defense, and the Indian Army, a colonial force. These groups were the only fully trained units available within the British Empire at that time. Both the Territorial and Colonial soldiers, having been integrated into the front lines during the latter stages of the 1914 campaign, had already faced the harsh realities of war.

The BEF, therefore, became heavily reliant on the Territorial Army and the Indian Army to reinforce its ranks. Under the command of General Sir Douglas Haig, these diverse units formed the First Army, comprising IV Corps and the Indian Corps. Their combined efforts would play a crucial role in the success of the Neuve Chapelle operation in March 1915, demonstrating their effectiveness as combat soldiers.

Lieutenant-General Sir James Willcocks, in his official commendation, lauded the exemplary conduct and spirit of the troops involved in the Neuve Chapelle operation. He highlighted the commendable performance of the regulars, territorials, and Indian soldiers, noting their mutual dedication and bravery. Their collective effort was recognized and praised by both the Army Commander and the Field Marshal Commander-in-Chief, underlining the crucial role they played in this pivotal battle.

Lieutenant-General Sir James Willcocks notably acknowledged the exceptional performance of the Territorial units during the Neuve Chapelle operation. He commended their remarkable composure under fire, especially highlighting the 3rd London Regiment, which executed a direct attack and charge under challenging conditions that would have tested even the most seasoned veterans.

However, the success of the initial artillery bombardment on March 10th was not replicated in the subsequent days of the operation. A combination of insufficient munitions supplies and poor visibility due to morning mists hindered accurate targeting of German defenses. The lack of precise information on German positions and insufficient time for gun calibration also contributed to the difficulties on March 11th and 12th. This failure to capitalize on the initial capture of Neuve Chapelle led to a German counterattack on March 12th, signaling a return to the grueling trench warfare.

While IV and Indian Corps successfully captured Neuve Chapelle, the operation fell short of its broader objective to take Aubers Ridge. The feasibility of reaching the ridge on March 10th was questionable, given the presence of remaining German forces and the exhausted state of the British and Indian troops. Defending the ridge against fresh German reinforcements, especially with limited ammunition supplies, would have been a formidable challenge.

The heavy casualties at Neuve Chapelle underscored the grim reality of trench warfare in World War One. The battlefield was strewn with British, Indian, and German casualties, with recovery efforts in No Man's Land being perilously risky. German losses were significant, estimated at 108 officers and around 8,000 men, with the majority incurred by the 6th Bavarian Reserve Division during the counterattack on March 12th. Captured German soldiers, including 30 officers and 1,657 men, were transported to England, with some ending up in an internment camp near Dorchester.

The casualty toll for the British and Indian forces was also substantial, with Haig's First Army suffering a total of 11,652 casualties, including 544 officers and 11,108 men.

Despite not securing Aubers Ridge, demonstrated that German lines on the Western Front could be penetrated under certain conditions. A surprise attack following a brief, intense bombardment could effectively cut through enemy wire, level trenches, and demoralize the defenders. However, this operation also exposed the complexities and challenges of trench warfare, both in attack and defense, and highlighted issues in battlefield command and communications.

One significant problem encountered during the operation was the disruption of British communications by German artillery. The Germans were able to sever both exposed and buried telephone lines, critically impeding the British commanders' ability to assess and report on the battle's progress. With communications lines compromised, messages had to be relayed by runners and horse dispatch riders. These messengers often faced delays or failed to deliver updates due to the hazards of crossing battlefields under artillery fire. As a result, divisional headquarters frequently made decisions based on outdated information, leading to ineffective or misguided actions. This experience led to the establishment of a more regular system of messenger orderlies for communication between battalions and advanced brigade headquarters.

Another issue was the lack of coordination at the battalion level, with some units launching disjointed attacks unsupported by their flanks. Friendly fire incidents also occurred, with British shells mistakenly hitting their own troops. Despite breaching the German line at Neuve Chapelle, the British Expeditionary Force was unable to fully exploit this breakthrough due to resource limitations, poor communication, and a lack of cohesive action among brigades.

For General Sir Douglas Haig, commanding the First Army, the operation at Neuve Chapelle was a significant milestone in his career. While he partially achieved the operation's objectives—crossing No Man's Land, breaching German trenches, and capturing Neuve Chapelle—the failure to capture

Aubers Ridge meant the operation did not have a major strategic impact on the war. However, it set a precedent for future British offensive operations, integrating infantry, artillery, and aerial reconnaissance.

The role of the Royal Flying Corps was crucial, providing intelligence and aerial photographs of the battlefield. For the first time in warfare history, attacking forces could visually assess enemy positions beyond their immediate line of sight. The use of aerial reconnaissance for targeting railway hubs and communication lines also proved effective. Artillery was employed to soften enemy defenses before infantry assaults, supported by forward observation officers and aerial observers.

The operation not only demonstrated the offensive capabilities of the British Expeditionary Force (BEF) but also exerted significant pressure on German commanders. They were forced to redirect reinforcements from other critical fronts, including Ypres in the north and the battle at Notre Dame de Lorette, to counter the advances of the British First Army, which included the Indian Corps. This redeployment was a testament to the impact of the British offensive.

The success at Neuve Chapelle significantly raised the profile of General Sir Douglas Haig and the First Army. Haig was optimistic about the implications of this victory for future operations. In his assessment, he acknowledged the heavy losses but emphasized the strategic gains, expressing confidence in the British soldier's superiority and determination to win. Haig's belief that Neuve Chapelle was a precursor to greater victories reflected his conviction in the BEF's capabilities and the operation's role in advancing the war efforts.

This operation altered the perception of the British Army among both German and French military leaders. Previously seen as primarily a defensive force, the BEF's ability to break through enemy lines and capture and hold ground at Neuve Chapelle demonstrated its potency as an offensive force. This shift in perception bolstered the confidence of French commanders in the BEF, enhancing the collaboration between British and French forces. French General Joseph Joffre even sent his corps commanders to Haig's headquarters to learn from the First Army's tactics in breaching German defenses. By April 1915, Joffre was requesting a more prominent role for the British Army in joint offensives with the French, reflecting Britain's growing stature within the Allied coalition.

For Haig personally, the experience of commanding at Neuve Chapelle and overseeing subsequent operations in 1915 was instrumental in his development as a military leader. This experience positioned him as a leading candidate to succeed Field Marshal Sir John French as Commander-in-Chief later that year.

Although Haig's contributions to the Neuve Chapelle operation were not initially acknowledged in the post-operation report, recognition for his strategic planning came with Field Marshal Sir John French's dispatch on April 5, 1915. This acknowledgment further cemented Haig's reputation as a capable and effective military commander.

The success achieved by the British Expeditionary Force (BEF) at Neuve Chapelle, particularly by the 4th and Indian Corps, was recognized and commended by Field Marshal Sir John French. In a dispatch published in the London Gazette on April 14, 1915, he attributed the victory not only to the troops' exceptional bravery and resolve but also to the adept leadership of General Sir Douglas Haig, Commanding Officer of the First Army. French praised Haig's energy and skillful command, acknowledging him as a powerful and capable leader.

This victory also significantly altered Kaiser Wilhelm's perception of the BEF. Previously dismissive of the British forces, referring to them as a "contemptible little army," the Kaiser's attitude changed upon hearing of their success in capturing Neuve Chapelle. This operation proved the BEF's capability to launch effective offensive actions, dispelling the notion that they were merely a token force limited to defensive roles. The impact of the British offensive extended beyond the battlefield, causing a stir in Lille and prompting the relocation of German headquarters and military hospital to Tournai. Kaiser Wilhelm began to view Haig and the British forces as formidable opponents.

Brigadier-General John Charteris, in his biography of Field Marshal Earl Haig, recounted an anecdote illustrating the reach of the British Army's newfound reputation. According to Charteris, the Kaiser, in an interview with an American, had praised the British I Corps under Haig as the best in the world. Haig, however, humbly attributed this success to his staff and the training methods at Aldershot, rather than his own command in battle. This anecdote, while flattering, also contained a misapprehension, as Haig was in fact commanding the First Army, not the I Corps, during the Neuve Chapelle operation.

The operation served as a wake-up call to both British allies and German adversaries. It demonstrated that underestimating the BEF was a dangerous oversight. German commanders, who had previously stationed minimal forces opposite the British trenches, not expecting an offensive, were now compelled to reconsider their strategy. The British breakthrough and capture of Neuve Chapelle in March 1915 shocked the German command, leading them to realize the inadequacy of relying on a single line of defense. As a result, Germany had to fortify its positions by constructing secondary and tertiary defensive lines along the Western Front to maintain control of the territories captured in 1914 and solidify the stalemate.

In the aftermath the German defenses on the Western Front were notably reinforced, presenting greater challenges for future Allied offensives. The Germans not only maintained their initial trench lines but also constructed a secondary system, complete with its own barbed wire defenses and communication trenches, situated three thousand yards behind the first. This expansion transformed the Western Front into an even more daunting obstacle, as assaulting forces now faced the daunting task of breaching two fortified trench lines instead of one.

Reflecting on this development, the chroniclers of The Indian Corps in France, Lieutenant-Colonel Merewether and Sir Frederick Smith, speculated that the attack at Neuve Chapelle might have inadvertently prompted the Germans to bolster their trench system. This enhanced defense was evident in subsequent battles, such as Festubert and Loos in 1915 and on the Somme in 1916, complicating efforts to breach German lines.

While the initial day of the Neuve Chapelle operation on March 10, 1915, was successful in breaking through the German lines and capturing the village, the inability to capitalize on this advantage by advancing reserves and maintaining momentum ultimately led to the failure to capture Aubers Ridge. This shortcoming highlighted the challenges of maintaining an offensive push in trench warfare.

Despite its limited strategic impact on the overall situation of the Western Front, the Battle of Neuve Chapelle was significant in demonstrating the BEF's capacity to disrupt the stalemate of trench warfare and penetrate German defenses. The operation underscored the vulnerability of the German lines and showcased the potential for a breakthrough. The capture of Neuve Chapelle received wide media coverage and was celebrated as a significant victory, with nine Victoria Crosses awarded for actions during the battle.

The operation reinforced Field Marshal Sir John French's conviction that the Western Front was the crucial battleground for defeating Germany, countering arguments for diverting resources to other theaters like Gallipoli. It also bolstered the morale of the BEF, proving that trench warfare deadlock could be overcome.

Although the operation at Neuve Chapelle provided a tactical blueprint for future offensives, it also underscored the enduring challenges faced by all sides. Commanders continued to grapple with the formidable task of leading infantry across No Man's Land, navigating barbed wire, evading machine gun fire and artillery, and securing captured enemy trenches. Neuve Chapelle marked the beginning of a prolonged learning process for the Allied commanders. It would take three more years of intense conflict and immense sacrifices to develop a strategy capable of delivering a decisive victory over Germany.

Second Battle of Ypres

In the early 20th century, amidst the tumultuous backdrop of World War I, an innovative yet controversial idea emerged from the mind of Walther Nernst, a renowned German chemist. Nernst, who voluntarily served as a driver in the German army in 1914, witnessed firsthand the frustrating stalemates caused by trench warfare. Determined to break this deadlock, he approached Colonel Max Bauer, a key liaison officer between the German military and scientific communities, with a radical proposal: the use of tear gas in a surprise attack to clear enemy trenches.

Nernst's idea caught the attention of Fritz Haber, another prominent chemist, during a field test. However, Haber saw potential for a more drastic approach, suggesting the use of chlorine gas, which was heavier than air, to achieve a more profound impact. This idea was daring and untested, but it intrigued the German high command.

Erich von Falkenhayn, a high-ranking German commander, saw an opportunity in Haber's proposal. Falkenhayn planned to use this novel weapon as a diversionary tactic by his 4th Army. His strategy was to employ the gas to facilitate the withdrawal of Imperial German Army units to the Eastern Front, where they were needed to support Austria-Hungary in the significant Gorlice–Tarnów offensive against the Russian Empire.

The execution of this plan involved a meticulous and risky process. The Germans had to siphon liquid chlorine from cylinders to release the gas;

direct release was impossible as the valves would freeze. They hoped the wind would carry the lethal gas towards enemy lines. A staggering 5730 cylinders, the heftiest weighing 40 kilograms each, were transported and installed at the front line under the supervision of a team of scientists including Haber, Otto Hahn, James Franck, and Gustav Hertz. The operation was fraught with danger – cylinder breaches caused by shell fire led to casualties among the Germans, prompting some to use miners' oxygen breathing apparatus for protection.

The Ypres salient, with its strategic location following the canal and bulging eastward around the town, was chosen as the target for this unprecedented chemical attack. The area was defensively held by a diverse coalition of forces: the Belgian army controlled the northern line along the Yser, French divisions held the north end of the salient, while the eastern part was guarded by Canadian and British divisions. The Second Army, including the II Corps and V Corps, comprised various divisions such as the 1st, 2nd, 3rd Cavalry, and several infantry divisions, including the notable Northumbrian, Lahore, and 1st Canadian. This multi-national assembly of troops, entrenched in the Ypres salient, was unaware of the impending chemical onslaught that would soon redefine warfare and leave an indelible mark on military history.

On the afternoon of April 22, 1915, a pivotal moment in military history unfolded. At around 5:00 p.m., the German 4th Army initiated a ground-breaking and horrifying tactic in modern warfare. They released a massive 171 tons of chlorine gas over a 6.5-kilometer (4.0 miles) stretch of the battlefield. This toxic cloud was unleashed between the small hamlets of Langemark and Gravenstafel, targeting a section of the Allied line defended primarily by French Territorial and colonial troops, including Moroccan and Algerian soldiers from the 45th and 87th divisions.

The impact of this chemical onslaught was catastrophic. The French troops caught in the path of the advancing gas cloud suffered horrendous casualties, with estimates ranging from 2,000 to 3,000 affected, including 800 to 1,400 fatalities. The scene was one of utter chaos and desperation, as described by Colonel Henri Mordacq of the 90th Infantry Brigade. Soldiers, in a state of panic and agony, discarded their heavy gear, gasping for air, and some even collapsed on the ground in a futile struggle to breathe.

This gas attack created a substantial 6-kilometer gap in the French lines, left alarmingly undefended. German infantry cautiously advanced behind the lethal cloud, equipped with makeshift respiratory protection: cotton pads soaked in sodium thiosulfate solution. They managed to capture the villages of Langemark and Pilkem, establishing defensive positions there. Interestingly, the German forces could have moved towards Ypres with little resistance but chose to dig in instead. In this offensive, they captured around 2,000 prisoners and 51 artillery pieces.

The Canadian troops, positioned on the southern edge of the breach, recognized the smell of chlorine, likening it to the odor of their drinking water. The following day, they too faced a fierce chlorine gas attack from the Germans. The 13th Battalion of the Canadian Expeditionary Force (CEF) suffered particularly heavy casualties. Surrounded on three sides and with their left flank dangerously overextended following the collapse of the Algerian Division, they faced a dire situation.

In a valiant response to the devastating gas attack, the 10th Battalion of the 2nd Canadian Brigade was called upon for a critical counter-attack in the gap created by the German offensive. They prepared for action late in the evening of April 22nd. Joining them in this daring endeavor was the 16th Battalion (Canadian Scottish) from the 3rd Brigade. The two battalions, comprising over 800 soldiers, launched their attack in coordinated waves at 11:46 p.m.

Navigating through the night without prior reconnaissance, the battalions unexpectedly encountered various obstacles en route to their target. As they neared the woods, they faced intense small-arms fire. In a spontaneous and daring response, they initiated a bayonet charge. This fierce and impulsive attack successfully cleared the Germans from the area, which was once an oak plantation, but at a staggering casualty rate of 75%.

The British press struggled to grasp the full scope and nature of this attack. The Daily Mail reported on April 26, 1915, detailing how the Germans used sulphur chloride to create a dense, yellow cloud that incapacitated the French and Belgian troops. According to the report, the cloud caused severe disorientation and breathing difficulties, leading to a chaotic retreat. The newspaper noted the temporary effects of the sulphur on the wounded, mainly swelling of the eyes, but mistakenly believed that there was no permanent damage to sight.

Captain Alfred Oliver Pollard, in his 1932 memoir "The Memoirs of a VC," vividly described the horrific scene as dusk fell on the battlefield. He recounted how the German trenches released a deadly green cloud of chlorine gas, which swiftly spread towards the Allied lines. The soldiers, engulfed by this toxic cloud, suffered acutely, with many succumbing to the gas or enduring prolonged, agonizing deaths. Pollard's account highlighted the brutal reality of chemical warfare, noting the overwhelming smell of chlorine and its lethal effects.

The aftermath of this gas attack was grim. German reports acknowledged 200 gas casualties on their side, including 12 fatalities. In stark contrast, the Allies reported a much higher toll: approximately 5,000 soldiers killed and 15,000 wounded due to the gas attack.

In the days following this tragedy, the British received crucial advice from John Scott Haldane on countering the effects of chlorine gas—urinating on a cloth and breathing through it. Both sides, recognizing the horrifying potential of chemical warfare, began to develop more sophisticated and effective gas masks, marking a new, darker chapter in the history of warfare.

The quaint village of St. Julien, now known as Sint-Juliaan, was a peaceful backdrop in the rear of the 1st Canadian Division until the tragic events of April 22, 1915, when a poison-gas attack abruptly transformed it into a frontline battleground. A notable episode in the village's defense was the heroic actions of Lance Corporal Frederick Fisher from the 13th Battalion CEF's machine-gun detachment. Fisher bravely led a small group with a Colt machine gun, not once but twice, managing to hold back the advancing German troops and prevent them from breaking through St. Julien into the Canadian rear lines. Tragically, Fisher lost his life in combat the following day.

On the morning of April 24th, the Germans launched another devastating gas attack, this time targeting the newly reformed Canadian line just west of St. Julien. In a desperate attempt to mitigate the effects of the gas, the soldiers were advised to urinate on their handkerchiefs and use them to cover their noses and mouths. However, these rudimentary countermeasures proved inadequate against the potent chemical weapon, and the German forces eventually captured the village.

The following day witnessed the determined but ultimately unsuccessful counter-attack by the York and Durham Brigade units of the Northumberland Division. They were unable to fully secure their objectives but managed to establish a new defensive line closer to St. Julien. On April 26th, the 4th, 6th, and 7th Battalions of the Northumberland Brigade, the first Territorial brigade to engage in the conflict, launched an assault and temporarily secured a position in the village. Nevertheless, they were soon forced to retreat, suffering a staggering 1,954 casualties.

The 2nd Battalion Royal Dublin Fusiliers also played a significant role during this period, enduring relentless battles at Frezenberg and Bellewaarde. On April 24th, they faced a German gas attack near St. Julien, resulting in near annihilation of the battalion.

This period marked the first instance of the German Army using chlorine gas cylinders as a weapon of war. The attack took place in April 1915 against the French Army at Ypres. The gas, with its unusual pineapple and pepper scent, initially led French officers to believe it was a smokescreen for an infantry advance. However, as the yellow-green clouds reached the Allied trenches, the true nature of the attack became horrifyingly clear. Soldiers began to experience severe chest pains and a burning sensation in their throats, signaling the onset of the ghastly effects of chlorine gas.

Captain Francis Scrimger of the 2nd Canadian Field Ambulance, possibly acting on Lieutenant-Colonel George Gallie Nasmith's advice, may have been the one to recommend the use of urine to combat the effects of the gas attack. As the gas enveloped them, many soldiers realized the danger they were in and fled in panic. Within an hour of the attack's onset, a significant 1,500-yard gap had opened in the Allied line. The Germans, hesitant and fearful of the chlorine themselves, were slow to advance, giving Canadian and British forces a crucial window to regain their positions before the enemy could capitalize on the breach.

Following these initial chlorine gas attacks by the Germans, Allied troops were hastily provided with makeshift masks made from cotton pads soaked in urine. It was found that the urea in the urine could neutralize the chlorine. These pads, though rudimentary, were held over the soldiers' faces until the gas dissipated. Other troops opted for alternatives like handkerchiefs, socks, or flannel belts, dampened with a sodium bicarbonate solution, and tied over their mouths and noses. Fighting under these conditions was challenging, and efforts were soon underway to develop more effective protective measures against such attacks. By July 1915, more efficient gas masks and anti-asphyxiation respirators were distributed to the soldiers.

Private W. Hay of the Royal Scots, who arrived in Ypres shortly after the April 22nd attack, recounted the harrowing scene:

"We knew something was wrong. As we marched towards Ypres, we couldn't use the road because it was crowded with refugees. We used the railway line instead and saw people, both civilians and soldiers, in a terrible state along the roadside. They told us it was gas. We were unaware of what 'gas' meant. Arriving in Ypres, we found many Canadians dead from the gas attack the previous day. It was a traumatic and unforgettable sight, especially for someone as young as I was – only twenty at the time."

The French soldiers, caught off guard by this new form of warfare, suffered greatly. Some managed to escape, but many, unfamiliar with this novel threat, were overcome by the toxic fumes and perished. Those who survived experienced severe respiratory symptoms, coughing, and spitting blood due to the chlorine's corrosive effect on the mucous membranes. The corpses of the fallen turned black almost immediately. About 15 minutes after the gas release, German troops emerged from their trenches. Some advanced first, wearing masks to test if the air was breathable. Once deemed safe, they moved in large numbers to the area recently engulfed by gas, seizing the weapons of the dead. They showed no mercy, making no prisoners; any soldier not yet dead was left with a grim directive to "lie down to die better."

The German military strategy in May 1915 involved a significant repositioning of their artillery, with three army corps positioned opposite the 27th and 28th Divisions along the Frezenberg ridge. This tactical move set the stage for a major German offensive that commenced on May 8th. The initial phase of the attack saw a heavy bombardment of the 83rd Brigade, which was stationed on the forward slope of the ridge. Despite enduring severe shelling, the brigade managed to repel the first two waves of German infantry assaults. However, the relentless pressure of a third assault eventually forced the defenders to retreat.

This German advance, though successful in pushing back the 84th Brigade, was halted in part due to the resolute resistance of the neighboring 80th Brigade. Yet, the withdrawal of the 84th Brigade left a concerning 2-mile gap in the Allied line. This critical situation was addressed by the gallant counter-attacks of Princess Patricia's Canadian Light Infantry (PPCLI) and a strategic night maneuver by the 10th Brigade. The PPCLI, though greatly diminished in numbers from 700 to a mere 150, who were barely fit for further combat, played a crucial role in holding the line. This episode led to their enduring unofficial motto, "Holding up the whole damn line."

On May 24th, the Germans initiated another chemical warfare tactic, releasing a gas attack that severely impacted the area around Shell Trap Farm, particularly towards the northwest. Captain Thomas Leahy of the 2nd Royal Dublin Fusiliers recorded a chilling account of this event. His commanding officer, Lieutenant Colonel Arthur Loveband, had anticipated the gas attack and had pre-emptively warned all company officers. The Germans signaled the imminent gas release by firing red lights over their trench.

Captain Leahy recalled the urgency of the situation: "We had only just time to get our respirators on before the gas was over us."

Despite the overwhelming circumstances, the Royal Dublin Fusiliers, with support from the 9th Argyll and Sutherland Highlanders and amidst intense shellfire, managed to maintain control of their trenches until the end of the battle. The German forces, advancing under the protection of enfilade fire and in small groups, ultimately captured parts of the Battalion line by 2:30 p.m. Although the shelling ceased, rifle and machine gun fire continued to pose a significant threat, targeting any exposed soldiers until dusk.

As the battle near Ypres drew to a close, British forces were compelled to retreat, establishing a new defensive line approximately 3 miles closer to the city. This strategic withdrawal resulted in the tightening of the salient around Ypres. The city itself, subjected to relentless artillery bombardment, lay in ruins. The use of poison gas, although previously seen on the Eastern Front, caught the Allies off guard, leading to around 7,000 gas-related casualties. These victims were hastily transported to field ambulances and treated at casualty clearing stations. In the months of May and June alone, there were about 350 recorded British fatalities due to gas poisoning.

This grim turn of events accelerated the development and deployment of gas warfare tactics and countermeasures by both sides. Notably, the French and British forces used gas later that year during the Battle of Loos in September. On the defensive side, improvised respirators made from cotton waste pads treated with sodium hyposulphite, sodium bicarbonate, and glycerin were issued. However, their effectiveness was limited due to poor training, the use of makeshift devices, and the low quality of some imported items. By December 1915, the "P helmet," soaked in sodium phenate, was issued, followed by the PH helmet, effective against phosgene, in early 1916.

Field Marshal Sir John French, the Commander-in-Chief of the British Expeditionary Force, defended the French troops' reaction to the gas attacks, asserting that no blame should be attached to them. He highlighted their demonstrated bravery and steadfastness throughout the campaign and expressed his firm belief in their capability to withstand such an unexpected and treacherous assault, had it been possible for any troops.

The Canadian Division, though mounting a robust defense, suffered heavily, with 5,975 casualties by the time of its withdrawal on May 3rd. Unprepared for the type of warfare encountered on the Western Front, the division struggled with outdated linear tactics in the face of enemies armed with advanced rifles and machine guns. While the Canadian field artillery performed effectively, the deficiencies of the Ross rifle exacerbated their tactical challenges. The division received several thousand replacements soon after the battle.

The Battle of Second Ypres was a pivotal moment, marking the start of an extensive period of analysis and experimentation aimed at enhancing the effectiveness of Canadian infantry, artillery, and the coordination between them. Initially, a company was the smallest tactical unit in the infantry; by 1917, this would change to a section. Although the Canadians were later employed in offensive roles in 1915, these efforts were not markedly successful. The battle underscored the need for continual adaptation and improvement in military strategies and equipment.

Second Battle of Artois

In the pivotal month of March 1915, the landscape of World War I was marked by a crucial strategic dilemma. The astute French military leader, General Joseph Joffre, was acutely aware that any period of inactivity could potentially tip the scales in favor of the Germans. This concern led to a significant development in military strategy, largely influenced by General Ferdinand Foch, the then-commander of the Groupe Provisoire du Nord (GPN). Foch put forth a daring proposal for an offensive maneuver that would involve a coordinated "general action" on the Western Front. This action was envisioned to include not just the French forces but also their British allies. The primary aim was to disorient the German defenders and effectively immobilize their reserves.

This strategic proposal was more than a mere attack; it was a complex two-pronged approach. The first element was designed to create confusion and hold down German reserves, while the second, more crucial part, aimed at a decisive breakthrough in the German defenses. This breakthrough was targeted at a carefully chosen location - one where it was unlikely for the Germans to swiftly establish a new defensive line following a retreat. Joffre, recognizing the potential of this plan, approved it on 23 March. The ambitious objective set forth was the capture of Vimy Ridge, followed by an eastward push into the Douai plain.

However, the French army at this time faced significant challenges. They had not fully adapted to the demands of siege warfare, and there was a notable shortage of critical equipment, particularly in terms of heavy artillery. Moreover, synchronizing operations in Artois with the First Battle of Champagne, which concluded on 17 March, proved to be an insurmountable challenge. This situation sparked intense debate within the army, leading to the emergence of two distinct schools of thought. On one side were figures like Joffre, who advocated for a "continuous battle" approach, involving relentless attacks utilizing all available resources. On the other, leaders like Foch argued for a more "methodical battle" strategy, favoring a series of calculated attacks interspersed with periods for reorganization and consolidation.

The theoretical underpinnings of the French offensive in Artois were encapsulated in the document "But et conditions d'une action offensive d'ensemble" (Purpose and Conditions for Comprehensive Offensive Action), dated 16 April 1915. This document, a compilation of front-line reports and analyses since the onset of the war in 1914, detailed innovative military tactics. It outlined the systematic use of infiltration tactics, "rolling" barrages, and, notably, the first strategic employment of poison gas.

Despite Joffre's reservations about the British military's capabilities, he was keen on launching an offensive on the northern flank of the Tenth Army to compel the Germans to spread their defenses more thinly. A critical meeting on 29 March with Sir John French, commander of the British Expeditionary Force (BEF), and Herbert Kitchener, the Secretary of State for War, led to an agreement. It was decided that the IX Corps and XX Corps would be replaced at Ypres by British units, and on 1 April, French acquiesced to launch a simultaneous attack with the Tenth Army. However, mutual doubts lingered between the French and British forces, exacerbated by the events at Ypres on 22 April, where a German gas attack had devastatingly routed French troops. To secure British cooperation, Joffre was compelled to commit reserves to reinforce the Ypres front.

During the winter months, the German Army underwent significant structural changes. They expanded their forces by incorporating a large number of new recruits and restructured their divisions. The traditional twelve-battalion divisions, which were organized in a square format with two brigades each containing two regiments, were transformed into a more efficient triangular formation. This new structure consisted of a single brigade headquarters overseeing nine battalions divided into three regiments. The reorganization not only streamlined the divisions, making them smaller and more manageable, but also provided newly formed divisions with a core of experienced and well-trained troops. This restructuring allowed for easier redeployment of divisions from quieter sectors of the front without causing major disruptions.

On 3 March, a significant development occurred under the leadership of General Erich von Falkenhayn. He established the 11th Army, known as the Durchbruchsarmee or Breakthrough Army, which was intended to be the primary attacking force on the Western Front. By the end of March, Colonel Hans von Seeckt, the Chief of Staff of the 11th Army, proposed an ambitious offensive. This plan was to be executed between Arras and Albert, involving fourteen corps and a substantial artillery support of 150 heavy batteries. However, the situation on the Eastern Front, where the Austro-Hungarian Army was facing a potential collapse, led to a change in plans. In April, the planned offensive in the west was cancelled, and the 11th Army, along with other divisions from the Western Army (Westheer), was redirected to the east. Consequently, the initiative on the Western Front shifted to the Entente armies.

Meanwhile, the defensive systems of the German army in the west, which had been largely improvised since late 1914, were beginning to show vulnerabilities, especially against the increasing number of heavy French artillery. In response, the Westheer initiated a comprehensive construction of standard defense systems in the spring. A notable feature of this new system was the development of a secondary position, set behind a barrier of barbed wire and strategically placed far enough from the front line. This positioning was designed to force any attacker to halt and reposition their field artillery for effective range. The first line of defense was transformed into a more complex zone, featuring camouflaged strongpoints and concrete machine-gun nests located behind the front trenches.

The 6th Army was responsible for securing a 56-mile front, extending from Menin to south of Arras. This front was manned by thirteen divisions, with the 58th and 115th divisions kept in reserve by the Supreme Army Command (OHL). The 6th Army was equipped with 660 field guns and 150 heavy guns. The terrain posed unique challenges: west of Lille, the front line traversed a marshy plain in Flanders, while south of La Bassée, the land was intersected by a network of waterways and drainage ditches, complicating fortification efforts. Further west, near Lens, the strategically important high grounds of Vimy Ridge and the Lorette Spur offered commanding views over the surrounding areas. To the south, around Arras, the landscape was dominated by the ridge at Thilloy, overlooking the Scarpe river.

From January onward, French engineers in the Carency region undertook a massive and secretive tunneling operation. They burrowed a distance of approximately 1.5 miles, their goal being to place a staggering 30 long tons of explosives in underground galleries directly beneath the German positions. This was a bold and intricate part of their strategy.

The primary focus of the French offensive was centered around a key area stretching from the chapel on the Notre Dame de Lorette Spur, southward to the Labyrinthe. The Labyrinthe was an extensive network, covering an area of 2 square miles, consisting of a dense maze of trenches, tunnels, and dugouts. This network spanned across the Arras–Lens road north of Ecurie and Roclincourt. The Lorette Spur, a significant geographical feature, marked the southern boundary of the plain that extended north of the Béthune–La Bassée Canal. This area, about 6 miles in length, was partly wooded, especially towards the eastern end. The northern slopes of the ridge were relatively gentle, but the southern side presented a more challenging terrain with steep spurs interspersed by ravines. The region around Ablain St Nazaire was particularly strategic, featuring several prominent spurs including Spur Mathis, the Great Spur, Arabs' Spur, the Spur of the White Way, and the Spur of Souchez. These spurs offered commanding views and were critical to controlling the eastern edge of Ablain and the area between Ablain and Souchez. By 20 March, the French had advanced to the base of the Great Spur, and by 14 April, they had approached Ablain.

General d'Urbal assumed command of the Tenth Army on 2 April. This army was a formidable force, comprising six infantry corps, a cavalry corps, and three reserve divisions. The arrangement of the corps was strategically planned: X Corps, with the 19th and 20th divisions, was positioned on the right (southern) flank. To its left was the XVII Corps with the 34th and 33rd divisions, followed by the XX Corps, the XXXIII Corps, the XXI Corps, and finally the IX Corps which extended up to the British First Army, located 15 miles to the north. Notably, the IX Corps and XX Corps had been previously stationed in Flanders but were relocated south between 9 and 16 April. However, following the German gas attack at the Second Battle of Ypres, units including the IX Corps headquarters and the 18th, 152nd, and 153rd divisions were urgently dispatched back to Flanders.

The artillery power of the Tenth Army was significantly bolstered, with the heavy artillery count reaching 293 guns and field artillery comprising 1,075 guns. Despite this impressive arsenal, the French artillery faced challenges, as the production of ammunition had not scaled up adequately to meet the demands. This shortage, particularly of high explosive shells, coupled with the issue of poor quality ammunition, led to a significant number of premature detonations, hampering the effectiveness of the French artillery.

The Tenth Army was set to launch an attack across a 9.3-mile front, with the central assault spearheaded by the XVII, XX, and XXXIII corps over a 6.2-mile stretch. This main offensive was complemented by support attacks along the spur south of Bailleul-Sir-Berthoult and further assaults by the

XXI Corps, which deployed two divisions along the Notre-Dame de Lorette spur. The primary goal of this strategic operation was to seize control of Vimy Ridge and then quickly establish a strong defensive position to thwart any German counter-offensives aimed at reclaiming the strategic heights. Following the capture, reserve divisions and cavalry were poised to initiate a rapid advance from the ridge into the Douai plain.

General d'Urbal, leading the Tenth Army, initially proposed a concise, four-hour artillery bombardment, intending to catch the German defenders off guard. However, this plan was overridden by Generals Foch and Joffre, who, drawing from the experiences and lessons of previous offensives in the winter and early spring, particularly the St Mihiel offensive, advocated for a more prolonged, four-day bombardment. The execution of this plan faced a setback due to delays in the arrival of artillery, pushing the attack date from 1 May to 7 May. The bombardment commenced on 3 May, but adverse weather conditions, particularly poor visibility, necessitated extending the bombardment to six days.

On 8 May, the French artillery shifted to a destructive bombardment targeting the German front defenses, which suffered extensive damage. In the critical four hours leading up to the infantry assault, scheduled for 10:00 a.m., the entire artillery complement of the Tenth Army concentrated its fire on the German barbed wire defenses and both the primary and reserve trench lines. This intense preparatory bombardment was aimed at paving the way for the infantry's advance, ensuring the success of their attack.

Since the end of the war of movement in late 1914, the German defenses between Arras and Lens had been considerably strengthened. These improvements were made in the varied terrain of ridges, hollows, and ravines. The Germans had installed extensive barbed wire and chevaux-de-frise barriers in front of their positions. Additionally, a variety of defensive structures including tunnels, caves, trenches, cellars, and loopholed buildings had been fortified. The approaches to these defenses were carefully surveyed and registered by German artillery for maximum effectiveness.

The 6th Army of the German forces managed to retain most of the Lorette Spur plateau and all of the Spur of the White Way and Spur Souchez, despite local attacks by the French in March and April. As of 9 May, the French line was positioned approximately 1,100 yards west of the Chapel, extending to the summit of the Arabs' Spur, and then down towards the valley west of Ablain. The Germans had constructed five trench lines extending from the Arabs' Spur across the plateau to the road near Aix-Noulette. These trenches were heavily fortified with a combination of iron roofs, sandbags, concrete, and barbed wire.

The German defenses also included machine-gun nests built into the trench every 100 yards, along with small, fortified posts to bolster the defenders. One notable defense post was located northeast of the Chapel of Notre Dame de Lorette, equipped with dugouts over 50 feet deep. Artillery and machine-guns positioned in Ablain covered the southern slopes of the ridge, while those in Souchez guarded the eastern face of the spur. Additional guns hidden in Angres and Liévin, northeast of the plateau, controlled the approaches from the plain to the north and along the spur. The area below the southern side of the Lorette Spur, including Ablain, Souchez, and a sugar refinery along the banks of the St Nazaire stream, had been heavily fortified. This area also featured Mill Malon and marshes to the east of the sugar refinery.

To the south of Ablain, the terrain rose to wooded heights towards Carency. The village of Carency, situated in a hollow with houses grouped facing in all four cardinal directions, was protected by four lines of trenches. Each street and house in Carency had been fortified, connected by underground passages, and manned by four battalions of infantry and six companies of engineers. Field guns and machine-guns were strategically placed in gardens, orchards, and behind the church, making it nearly impossible to attack the village except from the south and east. Trenches linked Carency with Ablain and Souchez on the Béthune–Arras road.

Between Souchez and Arras, at the hamlet of La Targette, the Germans had constructed the White Works, a network of trenches concealing a fortress. East of La Targette was Neuville St Vaast, which had been transformed into an underground fortress. South of Neuville St Vaast, the Labyrinthe extended on both sides of the Arras–Lens road. This area featured tunnels and small strong points organized in a complex maze, with blank walls and sally ports allowing defenders to ambush attackers. These were linked by tunnels to Neuville St Vaast. The edge of the heights bounding the plain between the Scarpe and the Béthune–La-Bassée–Lille Canal lay about 2 miles east of the Labyrinthe and Neuville St Vaast.

Opposite the French Tenth Army, the German XIV Corps manned the front with the 29th and 28th divisions. To the south, the I Bavarian Reserve Corps held the line from Souchez to the south bank of the Scarpe at Arras, with the 5th and 1st Bavarian Reserve divisions.

After the British attack at Neuve Chapelle and subsequent local attacks since December 1914, only minor changes had occurred in the front line. However, by the end of April, signs of a larger impending attack and reports of new French units being formed suggested a more ambitious French offensive north of Arras. French artillery fire intensified in May, but cloudy and overcast weather conditions in Artois, coupled with French air superiority, limited German air reconnaissance and observation of the rear of the French Tenth Army. Infantry patrolling was also restricted, and the presence of the French XVII Corps was not detected until 8 May. On the same day, an attack was launched on the positions of the 28th Division west of Liévin by the French 43rd Division, which was eventually repulsed after heavy casualties on both sides.

The final phase of the bombardment began at 6:00 a.m., initially focusing on target registration for an hour. At 8:00 a.m., a pivotal moment occurred when mines in the Carency sector and the Lorette Spur were detonated. This was accompanied by an intense bombardment of the first two German positions, which continued until a brief ten-minute pause at 9:40 a.m. This pause was followed by an extremely intense, ten-minute hurricane bombardment. As the infantry commenced their attack, the nature of the bombardment shifted to a creeping barrage. The infantry assault officially began at 10:00 a.m. under bright, dry weather conditions. The XXI Corps, led by Chasseurs and supporting infantry, successfully captured three of the trench lines on the Lorette Spur, albeit with significant casualties.

However, a fortified post in the center of the German line remained in enemy hands, and German artillery near Angres launched a counter-bombardment on the lost trenches. Additionally, machine-gun fire from Ablain posed a significant challenge to the French infantry. The battle continued even after nightfall, with the French starting to entrench themselves. They managed to capture the German front trenches at Carency, but attempts to push further into the village were halted by heavy fire from a strong point to the east.

The XXI Corps made a notable advance of about 660 feet through the complex fortifications on the Lorette Spur, while the IX Corps nearby made only modest gains.

On the northern flank, the 70th Division of the XXXIII Corps attacked Ablain, Carency, Souchez, and key strong points like Bois 125 and the sugar refinery. The division reached the outskirts of these villages but had to retreat to a position 660 yards ahead of their starting line after the repulse of their right-hand regiment.

In the same corps area, the Division Marocaine launched an attack using two waves of lightly-equipped "shock troops". These troops quickly advanced, bypassing isolated German positions, leaving them for the following Nettoyeurs (cleaners) to handle. They found the German wire well-cut and by 11:30 a.m., had reached point 140 on Vimy Ridge, where they dug in after advancing over 4,300 yards.

Despite orders at 10:15 a.m. to send divisional reserves forward, the 18th Division, stationed 5 miles back to avoid German artillery, faced difficulty in advancing. The Division Marocaine, now in a narrow salient, came under heavy fire from all sides and was eventually forced off the ridge in the afternoon, although they managed to capture several guns, machine-guns, and about 1,500 German prisoners.

The 77th Division advanced to Givenchy-en-Gohelle, the cemetery at Souchez, and the Château de Carleul, capturing around 500 prisoners and thirty machine-guns. However, they were soon pushed back to the Souchez–Neuville road by German artillery fire and counter-attacks. The French infantry suffered heavy casualties and found their artillery support waning as the field artillery reached the limit of its range. The communication trenches between Carency and Souchez were blocked, isolating Carency except for the route via Ablain.

The 39th Division swiftly crossed the German trenches in front of La Targette, which housed two strong points with artillery. The rapidity of the French advance limited the German machine-gunners' ability to effectively engage, leading to the capture of the village by 11:15 a.m. Along with the village, 350 prisoners were taken. The area was quickly secured, and French field artillery units rushed forward to engage nearby German troops. The French then pressed on towards Neuville and advanced up the southern part of Vimy Ridge. However, the 11th Division on the right flank faced resistance from the defenders of the Labyrinthe. In the center, the French managed to establish a presence in houses at the southern end of Neuville and near the cemetery, capturing half of the village.

On the main front, the French artillery had effectively prepared the battlefield for the infantry. Creeping barrages pinned down the surviving German infantry, but in areas with fewer heavy guns and limited ammunition, the

French attacks faltered. The XVII Corps, expected to make a deeper advance, was halted by German machine-gun fire in no man's land, achieving only small footholds in the first position. Similarly, the X Corps infantry were stopped in no man's land. By nightfall, the Tenth Army had captured 3,000 prisoners, ten field guns, and fifty machine-guns. However, ammunition shortages and poor-quality shells (which caused 24 premature explosions in French guns compared to only four knocked out by German counter-battery fire) hindered the success of the XXXIII Corps.

On May 10, Joffre and Foch adjusted their strategy, acknowledging the limits of artillery support. D'Urbal's proposal for an attack south of Arras was rejected. Joffre ordered several cavalry divisions to move towards the Tenth Army area as a diversion. A feint attack north of the Lorette Spur towards Loos achieved a minor advance on the left before being halted by German artillery from Angres. Machine-gun fire from a German strong point near the chapel on the Lorette Spur inflicted heavy French casualties. An impending counter-attack from the sugar refinery between Ablain and Souchez led to a suspension of the French attack in that area. French artillery barrage fire prevented the German infantry from advancing, and the French troops moved down from the spur towards the Ablain ravine. The ongoing attack on Carency led to some German counter-attacks reclaiming parts of the communication trenches and tunnels connecting with Souchez. During the day, French forces stormed houses east of the village and captured a hollow south of the Carency–Souchez road.

There was a pause on the main front as the French infantry regrouped and the surviving German defenders recuperated. French gunners, uncertain of the positions of their infantry, were unable to conduct a preparatory bombardment and focused instead on shelling advancing German reserves and counter-battery fire. The most advanced French infantry, cut off by German barrage fire and suffering from water shortages, faced frequent counter-attacks, diminishing their capacity for further offensive actions, especially in units that had made the most progress. South of the XXXIII Corps, the 39th

Division attacked Neuville on orders from the corps commander, despite reservations from divisional and army commanders, and suffered heavy losses due to intense defensive fire. On the right, beyond the Arras–Béthune road, the Neuville cemetery was captured, and counter-attacks by German reserves from Douai and Lens were successfully repelled.

By 11 May, the Tenth Army was reorganized and ready for another general offensive. However, the Division Marocaine (DM) and the 77th Division, which were at the forefront, received minimal reinforcements and supplies. Despite the near impossibility of communication through the heavy German artillery fire, d'Urbal believed that any delay would further disadvantage the French as the German defense was rapidly strengthening. To the north, the 70th Division and the 13th Division of the XXI Corps made advances at Ablain, Carency, Bois 125, and along the Lorette Spur, effectively outflanking the German garrison in Ablain. The XXXIII Corps faced a massive volume of German artillery and small-arms fire, leading to their repulsion. The DM suffered 5,120 casualties since 9 May, and the 77th Division also made little progress due to German flanking fire. On the evening of 11 May, the French managed to capture the lower slopes of the Arabs' Spur in heavy fighting, and a German counter-attack from the Spur of the White Way was repelled.

During the night, the 13th and 43rd divisions captured the crest of the Lorette Spur, which deprived the Germans of their advantageous position on the ridge. However, German artillery in Angres and machine-guns in Ablain maintained constant fire on these new French positions.

On the same day, d'Urbal reinforced the XXXIII Corps and XX Corps with fresh divisions, preparing for an attack after a two-hour bombardment. The French succeeded in capturing the wood east of Carency, which overlooked and disrupted German communication trenches with Souchez. However, a German unit on a wooded hillock and infantry at a nearby stone quarry impeded further French advancement in the area. In Neuville, the XX Corps made slow progress, facing intense artillery fire. The IX Corps on the northern flank and the X and XVII corps on the southern flank conducted limited attacks, most of which were repulsed.

Further south, the French continued their attack on Neuville and the Labyrinthe, capturing the cemetery. General Pétain reported that the French were suffering increased casualties due to intensified German machine-gun and artillery fire. Consequently, d'Urbal directed that the German defenses at Souchez and Neuville must be secured before resuming the attack on Vimy Ridge. The XXI Corps was to continue its advance along the Lorette Spur, the XXXIII Corps aimed to capture Carency and then attack Souchez, while the XX Corps targeted Neuville.

Before dawn on 12 May, French Chasseurs attacked a strong point near the Chapel of Notre Dame de Lorette on the Lorette Spur. After intense hand-to-hand combat, they captured the strong point and the remains of the Chapel. Under German artillery fire at dawn, the French advanced towards the Spur of the White Way.

At Carency, French infantry, following a bombardment, captured the wooded hillock east of the village and eventually took the stone quarry to the west. Approximately 1,000 German soldiers surrendered by 5:30 p.m. The conditions on the plateau were dire due to shells unearthing the bodies of soldiers killed before the offensive. The French pushed from Carency towards Ablain, which unexpectedly caught fire during the German withdrawal. The French captured 2,000 prisoners, field artillery, and machine-guns in the area. A German counter-attack on the Spur of the White Way on 13 May was repelled. By 14 May, most of the Lorette Spur and Carency were under French control, but not the positions in between, which halted the XXXIII Corps' advance on Souchez. On 15 May, a French attack on the Spur of the White Way failed, and until 21 May, the French focused on consolidating their positions on the Lorette Spur, under continuous fire from German artillery in Angres and Liévin. The Germans maintained their hold on the east end of Ablain and recaptured the church and cemetery.

The British First Army, under the command of General Sir Douglas Haig, launched attacks on two segments of the German front line adjacent to the Neuve Chapelle battlefield. The southern attack was carried out by I Corps and the Indian Corps across a 2,400-yard front, starting from the Rue du Bois. In the north, IV Corps launched its assault on a 1,500-yard front opposite Fromelles. The objective was to create two breaches in the German defenses, spaced 6,000 yards apart, after which the infantry aimed to advance to Aubers Ridge, located about 3,000 yards beyond.

The preliminary bombardment for this operation commenced at 5:00 a.m. on 9 May and intensified significantly by 5:30 a.m. Ten minutes later, the British infantry initiated their attack, catching the German defenders by surprise. However, poor visibility due to smoke and dust, coupled with the less effective bombardment than anticipated, meant that many German machine-guns remained operational. The British shell-fire also fell short in several instances. Almost immediately, the German machine-gunners and artillery responded, causing heavy casualties among the advancing British infantry within the first ten minutes.

After achieving only minimal gains in the German first line, a second British assault was launched at 8:00 a.m., following a 45-minute bombardment. This attack too was repelled in no man's land by effective German defensive fire. Plans for a new attack around noon were postponed until about 5:00 p.m. Despite a heavy bombardment, the German machine-gun nests remained intact and effectively halted the British advance with flanking fire. An additional attack was contemplated for 8:00 p.m. to support the more successful French attack, but this was eventually cancelled as the feasibility of launching another offensive became doubtful.

The full extent of the British defeat was initially not realized due to communication challenges with the front line. The British forces incurred approximately 11,000 casualties. The Germans also suffered significant losses, and while their defensive position was heavily damaged, transforming it into a cratered landscape, German reserves were shifted from the British front to Vimy Ridge on 12 May.

Joffre and Foch met with General French on the same day to encourage him to resume the offensive, especially after the redeployment of German divisions to the south against the Tenth Army. French agreed to replace a French division south of La Bassée by 15 May.

Pétain proposed a joint attack on Souchez involving the divisions of the XXXIII and XXI Corps scheduled for 12 May, but this was dismissed due to the exhaustion of the XXI Corps divisions. Instead, Pétain planned three focused assaults against Carency, Bois 125, Ablain, and Souchez, alongside a similar attack in the south against Neuville. Joffre reinforced the Tenth Army with the III Corps but had to redirect some artillery to support the impending British attack at Festubert. Post-11 May, the French focused on consolidating their newly captured positions and advancing their logistical infrastructure, including hospitals, depots, rail lines, and headquarters. New artillery placements were prepared for operations aimed at securing bases de départ (jumping-off positions), while depleted units were rotated out and replacements integrated.

The assaults by parts of the 70th, 77th, and the 13th Divisions, which captured Bois 125, Carency, and the chapel on the Lorette Spur, left the German garrison in Ablain in a vulnerable position. This led to a German withdrawal on 12 May to a new defensive line. The remaining German troops on the Lorette Spur also retreated to maintain alignment with these new positions. The 70th Division cautiously followed the German retreat, and a combined attack by the 77th and 13th Divisions on the sugar refinery was planned. Engineers worked to rebuild trenches in anticipation of an assault on Souchez on 14 May.

At Neuville, the 11th Division and parts of the 39th Division launched another attack on 12 May despite the heavy losses incurred the previous day, including units suffering up to 50% casualties. The 39th Division's advance, spearheaded by a barrage of hand grenades and trench mortar bombs, was ultimately repelled. The 11th Division remained embroiled in Neuville and the Labyrinthe. General Nourrisson of the 39th Division opposed the continuation of large-scale attacks, but d'Urbal insisted they proceed as new defenses were established and fresh troops arrived. Subsequent large-scale assaults until 15 May resulted in mixed outcomes, with some limited successes but at high costs. A major general attack on 15 May ended in failure, hampered by inadequate artillery support, losses from German counter-battery fire, and poor quality of ammunition. The unchanged artillery tactics and reduced shell-fire density allowed German reinforcements to fortify their positions, effectively countering the French attack with concentrated machine-gun fire and heavy artillery bombardment.

On 18 May, d'Urbal requested the withdrawal of the XVII and X Corps by 24 May due to the high cost of their failed attacks. However, Foch overruled this, ordering a halt to rushed attacks and instead mandating an eight-day preparation period for a more thorough attack, reminiscent of the 9 May assault. In the meantime, focused local attacks were to be supported by massed artillery on limited objectives. Joffre concurred with Foch's intervention and instructed d'Urbal to limit operations to small-scale attacks targeting strategically important points. Up to 15 June, the French conducted numerous limited attacks on the flanks of the 77th and Moroccan divisions, employing consistent troops and tactics. On 23 May, the XXI Corps captured the remaining part of the Lorette Spur, followed by the 70th Division taking the Ablain cemetery on 27 May, and finally the sugar refinery on 31 May, rendering Souchez vulnerable to attacks from both the west and south. These narrowly focused attacks were significantly better supported by artillery.

In a dynamic update on May 20th, the General Headquarters (GQG) released an engaging revision of Note 5779, confirming that the initial April 16th strategy had proven successful in the face of unfolding events. This new iteration passionately advocates for a strategy of "continuous battle", underscoring the crucial need to advance reserves - a lesson sharply learned from the tactical hesitation on May 9th, when they were conservatively held back from the reach of German artillery.

The document provides a riveting analysis of German defensive tactics, spotlighting their innovative use of small, agile infantry units armed with a plethora of machine guns. These units, adept at firing from protected flanks and ensconced in deep, nearly impervious dug-outs, have set a new standard for defensive strategy. In response, French forces are now encouraged to mirror these formidable German positions.

Despite a resurgence of localized attacks, the Tenth Army faces a daunting challenge. While achieving modest successes within their material limits, they grapple with a severe depletion of experienced soldiers, a direct consequence of staggering French losses. The rigorous demands of Note 5779 for training and supplying replacement soldiers are stretching the Tenth Army's capacities to their limits. A bold attempt for a grand offensive by IX, XXI, and XXXIII corps between May 25th and 26th stumbled, largely due to the heightened prowess of German defenses, the elusive element of surprise, and the sheer lack of planning time and troop rest.

General Pétain offers a candid assessment of the current stalemate: German artillery, firing daily barrages, has rendered traditional infantry attacks nearly futile. The French strategy of varying bombardments for the element of surprise falls short against the fortified and ever-vigilant German artillery. The French counter-battery efforts, waiting to target German guns only after they reveal their positions, result in inefficient ammunition use. Pétain, envisioning alternative strategies, suggests a pivot towards detailed mapping of German rear areas and a systematic, continuous bombardment of their artillery placements. Yet, he acknowledges the grim reality of ammunition shortages, highlighting the impracticality of such ambitious plans.

On the evening of May 15th, Generals Foch and d'Urbal convened an important meeting, resulting in a pivotal decision: the ongoing offensive would be temporarily halted. This decision came after realizing that the assaults post-May 9th were not only hastily prepared but also increasingly ineffective. They resolved that before resuming the offensive, meticulous preparations, akin to those of the May 9th attack, were essential. Their strategy included capturing key "bases of departure" at Souchez and Neuville, setting the stage for a subsequent assault on Vimy Ridge, which Foch anticipated would require eight to ten days.

D'Urbal, acting on this new directive, called off an attack planned for May 16th. He instructed each corps to focus on capturing specific, limited objectives. The XXXIII Corps was assigned five targets before joining the Souchez offensive, and the XXI Corps had three objectives to secure in support of the same operation. The first of these targeted attacks was scheduled for May 17th, but unexpected rainstorms forced a postponement until May 20th and 21st. These operations were preceded by massive artillery bombardments, aiming to secure several hundred square meters of ground in each assault.

The afternoon of May 21st saw the French forces launch a strategic attack on the Spur of the White Way from multiple directions. Remarkably, a unit attacking from the Arabs' Spur swiftly captured their targets, and another group from the north successfully took over the main German communication trench, capturing the garrison. The attack from Ablain led to the capture of houses west of the church and severed the communication trench connecting the White Way with Souchez. This offensive resulted in the capture of 300 German prisoners and a field gun. A German counter-attack in the early hours of May 22nd was effectively repelled.

May 25th witnessed a coordinated assault by the IX, XXI, and XXXIII corps on limited objectives, following a day-long artillery bombardment. However, this effort saw minimal advancement. On May 28th, the French targeted the remaining German forces in Ablain, concentrated around the cemetery. An artillery barrage isolated the garrison, allowing the French infantry to attack and capture 400 prisoners. That night, a German contingent in the south of the church was neutralized, and the French seized a key strong point outside the village. By early May 29th, the French forces had overrun the remaining German positions at the church and rectory, at the cost of 200 casualties, primarily from artillery fire.

The French then advanced into the valley, capturing Mill Malon on May 31st and progressing through a communication trench to the sugar refinery, where they overpowered the German garrison as night fell. A German counter-attack at midnight initially pushed the French back, but a French artillery barrage and renewed infantry assaults on June 1st eventually secured the area, connecting it with Ablain through communication trenches. This area saw sporadic fighting from June to September. Despite continued efforts from May 25th to 28th, French attacks towards Andres failed.

D'Urbal, while continuing these limited-objective attacks, shifted the main artillery focus south to Neuville. A three-day bombardment commenced on June 2nd, and by June 6th, the French had captured the main road through Neuville amidst intense German small-arms and artillery fire. By June 11th, the French had made significant gains, advancing 550 yards on a 330-yard front.

In a strategic shift towards siege warfare, the British military adopted tactics involving limited but well-prepared attacks, supported by a substantial increase in artillery firepower. This approach aimed at capturing more ground while minimizing casualties. The renewed offensive near Festubert stretched from Port Arthur to Rue du Bois, marked by a nocturnal assault by three divisions at 11:30 pm on May 15th. This attack followed a meticulous three-day artillery bombardment, which saw 26,000 shells fired over a 5,000-yard front. The bombardment devastated the German breastwork, although numerous machine-gun posts and infantry dugouts beneath the second line of defenses remained intact.

The British offensive aimed for an advance of approximately 1,000 yards along La Quinque Rue road. On the right flank, a silent advance caught the surviving Germans off-guard, enabling the British to overrun the Wohngraben (support trench) and establish defensive positions. However, on the left, intense German return fire halted the British in no man's land. A subsequent attack at 3:15 a.m. by the 7th Division on the right achieved partial success, but at a heavy cost. The British managed to destroy and capture much of the German front line, but isolated German units entrenched in shell-holes impeded any further advance.

On May 16th, General Haig resumed the offensive with the Battle of Festubert, focusing on the right flank of the Aubers Ridge battlefield. British troops were instructed to secure local objectives only after consolidating their gains. By the morning of May 17th, the German 14th Division was compelled to fall back to a new line of defense situated about 0.75 miles behind their original front, connecting to the Stützpunktlinie (strongpoint line) at the rear. Consequently, British bombardments and assaults encountered merely small groups of German rearguards. The Quadrilateral, a key position, fell to the British around 10:15 a.m. on May 17th following a heavy bombardment, leading to the surrender of a large number of German troops. However, reinforced German defenses doubled their firepower, effectively repelling British attempts to advance further that afternoon. Adverse weather conditions, including low cloud and rain, obscured the battlefield, delaying British identification of the new German line for three days.

From May 18th to 25th, a series of attacks by four British divisions resulted in modest territorial gains. However, the newly captured positions were already targeted by German artillery, which maintained intense bombardment. This relentless shelling forced the British to retreat in some areas and inflicted heavy casualties. The offensive resulted in approximately 16,644 British casualties, compared to around 5,500 German losses. The fighting persisted until May 25th, focusing on local objectives and countering German reinforcements that were not available to confront the French forces further south.

The ambitious eight-day timeline General Foch anticipated for capturing strategic positions around the XXXIII Corps stretched into a grueling five-week endeavor. Although there were incremental gains, the Germans adeptly enhanced their defenses, exploiting the natural cover of dips and slopes. As German artillery reinforcements arrived, they were swiftly deployed along key attack routes, ready to open fire upon simple flare signals from the front lines. In contrast, the Tenth Army's artillery reinforcements only marginally bolstered their firepower, with setbacks from German counter-artillery, mechanical breakdowns, and premature detonations. The increase in infantry reinforcements was similarly slight, barely surpassing the rate of losses. For the second major offensive planned from June 16th to 18th, the artillery ammunition supply for the 355 heavy and 805 field guns was significantly larger, with 718,551 shells, a stark increase from the 265,430 shells used between May 3rd and 9th.

The preliminary bombardment, set to commence on June 10th, was strategically focused on specific areas to mask the impending infantry assault. On the day of the attack, artillery was tasked with demolishing overnight German repairs and engaging in counter-battery fire as a diversion. This tactic aimed to mislead the Germans and provide French infantry a window to cross no man's land before a German barrage could respond.

In parallel, a comprehensive Franco-British offensive was planned for early June, following the 16-mile front attack on May 9th. The French Second, Sixth, and Seventh armies, along with a British contingent near Zillebeke in Flanders, were to launch supporting attacks. The XXI Corps aimed to advance from the Lorette Spur towards Bois de Givenchy, the XX Corps to secure Neuville and the Labyrinthe, and the XXIII Corps to target Souchez, Château Carleul, Côte 119, and Givenchy-en-Gohelle. The IX

Corps, relocated between the XXXIII and XX Corps, was tasked with taking Vimy Ridge. Despite careful artillery observation and preparations, previous minor attacks by the IX Corps had seen limited success, with instances of infantry halting and refusing to advance, posing a risk to the XXXIII Corps.

On June 15th, the 17th Division commander, positioned on the right of the IX Corps, alerted General Curé that preparations fell short of Note 5779 standards, with jumping-off trenches being too far from the German lines and the infantry already fatigued. Across the Tenth Army, soldiers endured exhaustive digging sessions under German counter-bombardments. Moreover, the French artillery's accuracy was found wanting, as evidenced in a June 13th attack by the 70th Division on the sugar refinery, where the French artillery mistakenly bombarded their troops. Subsequent attacks only secured short stretches of trenches, with heavy reliance on reinforcements. Reports from the IX and XX Corps highlighted more precise French artillery fire, while the XXI Corps, thanks to its higher vantage point, had a clear view of German defenses. Maistre, the corps commander, had prioritized artillery observation as a specialized task, ensuring efficient coordination with infantry.

The Germans had strategically placed barbed wire 160 feet in front of their front line, a distance greater than anticipated. To overcome this, the French fired special bombardments to cut through the wire, and despite German counter-bombardments, patrols were sent to assess the results. On the front of the 43rd Division, it was noted that field artillery was merely displacing the wire instead of destroying it. However, the introduction of modern 155mm guns eventually created several gaps in the wire defenses.

On June 16th, visibility was poor early in the morning. The French heavy artillery started with a slow bombardment, which intensified around 12:15 p.m. A creeping barrage began moving in 160-foot bounds from the French line, accompanied by a second barrage starting at maximum range and creeping backwards in 82-foot bounds. Both barrages converged on Vimy

Ridge, transforming into a standing barrage to support the advancing French infantry. However, the IX Corps divisions discovered that the German defenses were largely intact, and the 17th Division was forced back to its original trenches due to heavy artillery and machine-gun fire. The 18th Division managed to capture the first German position, prompting a second attack in the afternoon.

The IX, XX, and XXXIII Corps used 10,000 shells filled with a mixture of poison gas and incendiary materials on targets including Neuville, Souchez, Angres, and German artillery positions. These shells, containing carbon disulfide and phosphorus, were designed to asphyxiate and burn simultaneously. This bombardment temporarily suppressed German artillery from 1:00 to 2:30 p.m. and ignited fires in Angres, though Souchez, already heavily bombarded, had little left to burn. The 17th Division advanced an additional 330 feet, but the 18th Division was stalled in no man's land. The 39th Division of the XX Corps, attempting a surprise advance, was repulsed.

In the XXXIII Corps area, the fresh DM units quickly overran the initial German defenses with minimal losses. However, as they pressed forward, they encountered well-protected German infantry in deep dugouts and flanking positions. The advance halted at Côte 119 due to heavy fire from Souchez. Supporting troops, delayed by crowded trenches filled with wounded and prisoners, arrived only by 8:00 p.m. German counter-attacks, heavily utilizing hand grenades, inflicted significant casualties.

To the north, the 77th and 70th divisions faced tough resistance in Souchez. Despite having double the artillery shells compared to May 9th, their effectiveness was limited by new German defenses on reverse slopes, immune to gun fire and only vulnerable to Howitzer fire, which were brought forward just twelve hours before the attack. The 159th Regiment was halted by uncut wire and heavy fire, while the 97th Regiment captured Souchez cemetery with fewer casualties. However, the repulse of the 159th Regiment exposed the flanks of the 97th Regiment and the adjacent DM, making an attack on Souchez village unfeasible. A subsequent attempt by the 159th Regiment at 4:00 p.m. was also immediately halted by German return fire.

In the sector controlled by the XXI Corps, the 70th Division faced a barrage of German artillery fire as the attack commenced, triggered by flare signals from the German front line. The 42nd BCP engaged in a fierce battle for part of Château Carleul, overcoming strong German resistance, but then halted to maintain alignment with the 77th Division on its right. The 360th and 237th regiments encountered a formidable wall of fire, halting their advance except on the far left flank, where the 13th Division had pushed forward by about 490 feet. The 48th Division, on the northern flank of the XXI Corps, managed to advance approximately 0.62 miles and capture its initial objectives within 25 minutes, albeit at a high cost. At the commencement of the attack, the 43rd Division on the left flank of the XXI Corps successfully detonated a mine under the German defenses opposite and swiftly occupied the crater, suffering minimal losses before the Germans could mount a counter-attack.

General d'Urbal, undeterred, ordered the offensive to continue on June 17th, focusing on the sectors held by the 77th Division and IX Corps, which flanked the XXXIII Corps. The most advanced positions of the DM had become untenable. However, the order to attack at 4:00 p.m. was postponed, leading to confusion and some units attacking prematurely. They found themselves pinned down in front of uncut wire and subjected to bombardment from both French and German artillery. Despite this, the 70th Division and other XXI Corps divisions on the northern flank managed to capture several German positions, though at great cost. The IX Corps, on the southern flank, faced an onslaught of artillery and machine-gun fire, making no progress.

On June 18th, d'Urbal shifted the Tenth Army's remaining offensive efforts against Vimy Ridge. The IX Corps was instructed to bypass the German defenses in Neuville. However, General Balfourier of the XX Corps refused to attack without support on the northern flank. The June 18th attack resulted in another setback, with the French infantry again confronting well-entrenched German positions on reverse slopes, invisible from the ground and undamaged. The uncut wire and vigilant German defenders inflicted heavy casualties on the French forces. General Foch eventually suspended the offensive, but d'Urbal persisted with piecemeal attacks for another week until General Joffre intervened and put an end to the offensive campaign.

During the Second Action of Givenchy, which took place on June 15th and 16th, the IV Corps of the British First Army, comprising the 7th, 51st, and Canadian divisions, launched an attack northwest of La Bassée. This offensive was preceded by a 60-hour bombardment, which was part of an effort to address a severe ammunition shortage. This strategy relied heavily on artillery observation and enhanced tactical reconnaissance by reinforced squadrons of the Royal Flying Corps (RFC). However, no suppressing fire was provided during the actual attack, and German forces were observed manning their front lines as the British advance began.

As the British troops moved forward, they were met with intense small-arms fire from the Germans. Despite this, the British succeeded in breaching the German front trench, leading to a fierce close-quarters battle with grenades. The British, however, found themselves isolated and under crossfire in no man's land, eventually being pushed back due to dwindling ammunition, with the last of them retreating at 4:00 a.m. A renewed attack on June 15th, utilizing all remaining artillery ammunition, was initially delayed by thick mist and reorganization challenges but proceeded at 4:45 p.m. This attack successfully captured the German front line, but progress was halted for consolidation. The British and Canadian troops, not pinned down in their trenches, were eventually forced to retreat by a German counter-attack at 8:00 p.m., leading to the cancellation of further assaults.

Simultaneously, the British Second Army initiated the First Attack on Bellewaarde on June 16th with the 3rd Division. They easily captured the German first line at 4:15 a.m. The subsequent waves, however, encountered their own artillery bombardment, obscured by mist and smoke, leading to friendly fire incidents. Despite this, they managed to reach the German second line. Three German counter-attacks were only able to push the 3rd Division back to the first line, largely due to a shortage of British ammunition. An attempt to capitalize on this initial success with support from a brigade of the 14th Division was hindered by German artillery fire. Less than two battalions of the 3rd Division advanced at 3:30 p.m. across an exposed slope and were met with heavy German resistance, resulting in significant casualties. By 6:00 p.m., the British had consolidated their position in the German front trench from the Menin road to Railway Wood, but they fell short of reaching Bellewaarde ridge and the key German observation posts along it.

General Joffre criticized the British for their "inaction," which, in his view, allowed the Germans to focus their resources against the Tenth Army more effectively.

In the Battle of Aubers Ridge, the British First Army launched an offensive to support the French operations further south. North of the La Bassée Canal, the British intensified their artillery fire against the German II Bavarian and XIX Saxon Corps. At 6:00 a.m., British forces initiated an attack against the 6th Bavarian Reserve Division, successfully breaching the first line north of Fromelles. However, the gains were temporary as the trenches were recaptured by the Germans in the evening. Further British assaults at Richbourg l'Avoué occasionally penetrated the German first line but ultimately failed to secure any lasting territorial gains. German forces, facing limited impact from these attacks, were soon redirected to reinforce the Arras front.

Meanwhile, the French artillery commenced an overnight bombardment on the German lines, pausing briefly before resuming at 6:00 a.m. with gradually intensifying fire. This bombardment targeted the fronts of the VII, XIV, and I Bavarian Reserve Corps. By mid-morning, the artillery fire reached its peak intensity, known as Trommelfeuer. The French used lulls in their bombardment as a tactic to draw German infantry out of shelter, only to resume the intense shelling unexpectedly. The German artillery response was notably sparse during this time.

The French infantry, having assembled undetected, commenced their advance following the detonation of several mines, achieving an element of surprise. The primary French assault at 11:00 a.m. targeted the left of the XIV Corps and the I Bavarian Reserve Corps, stretching from Lens to Arras. A simultaneous attack was launched against the center of the XIV Corps along the Béthune–Lens road but was repelled by a German counter-attack. The French 28th Division on the Lorette Spur suffered heavy losses and was pushed out of the front trenches, prompting the deployment of a battalion of Jäger in the evening. French attacks on the villages of Ablain-St Nazaire (Ablain) and Carency were met with staunch German resistance.

By noon, the French had captured approximately 2.5 miles of the German front defenses and penetrated up to 1.9 miles deep in some areas. In the sector held by the I Bavarian Reserve Corps under General Karl von Fasbender, the 5th Bavarian Reserve Division, led by General Kress von Kressenstein south of Carency, was forced back to a line from Cabaret Rouge to Neuville St Vaast (Neuville). French forces advanced towards artillery positions around Givenchy-en-Gohelle (Givenchy), where German reinforcements arrived around noon, halting further French progress. To the south, the 1st Bavarian Reserve Division, commanded by Lieutenant-General Göringer, successfully repulsed French forces in close combat and then managed to flank French troops who had breached the lines at La Targette.

Crown Prince Rupprecht requested additional support from General Falken-hayn, leading to the deployment of two divisions from the OHL reserve. The 115th Division, under Major-General von Kleist, moved behind the 5th Bavarian Reserve Division, while the 58th Division, led by Lieutenant-General von Gersdorf, joined the 6th Army reserve and moved closer to Lens.

Additional artillery units from the OHL reserve were also brought forward to bolster the German defenses.

On the southern edge of the breakthrough, French forces were gradually making progress through the complex trench network known as the Labyrinthe. North of Ecurie, the Bavarian Reserve Infantry Regiment 12 managed to secure additional ground, effectively hindering the French from expanding their breakthrough. In Neuville St Vaast, a counter-offensive led by a battalion of the Bavarian Reserve Infantry Regiment 10 successfully recaptured the eastern part of the village, along with several previously lost field guns. An improvised defensive line was established between Neuville and La Folie to the north, enabling German forces to flank the French troops further north with crossfire. The Bavarian Infantry Regiment 7, brought up from reserve, launched a counter-attack against the French on Vimy Ridge, pushing them back from the strategic positions of Hill 145 and Hill 119 by 1:00 p.m. Meanwhile, the 28th Division was forced out of its first position at the eastern end of the Lorette Spur.

By the afternoon, the left flank of the XIV Corps near Carency was exposed. Crown Prince Rupprecht planned to deploy the remnants of the 5th Bavarian Reserve Division and the 115th Division for a counter-assault to reclaim lost ground. However, the 115th Division was redirected to defend the right flank of the I Bavarian Reserve Corps, and the 5th Bavarian Reserve Division was deemed too depleted for an offensive. German troops managed a counter-attack at Souchez, regaining some territory before being halted by heavy French artillery fire around 8:00 p.m. Despite the intense fighting, Rupprecht remained confident that the four German divisions could repel the twelve French divisions. The OHL dispatched the 117th Division to Douai, and Rupprecht assigned two regiments of the 58th Division to support the I Bavarian Reserve Corps in the Souchez counter-attack. Additional artillery support was positioned east of Vimy Ridge.

During the night, a French assault captured the front trenches along the

Béthune–Lens road. Lieutenant-General von Haenisch deployed the last corps reserve to the 29th Division, who successfully reclaimed the trenches in a morning counter-attack. South-west of Carency, the trench leading to Souchez was lost, leaving Carency nearly encircled. Rupprecht and Haenisch decided against a retreat, opting instead for a counter-attack from Souchez to Neuville with the I Bavarian Reserve Corps and the 58th and 115th divisions. At 4:00 p.m., French forces launched attacks on the Lorette Spur and at Carency but failed to dislodge the defenders. The German counter-attack, spearheaded by the 58th Division with support from parts of the 115th Division, initially made progress but was eventually stalled by French defensive fire. The situation became critical for the 28th Division headquarters, which began to fear the potential collapse of the line between Ablain and Carency.

On May 10th, the I Bavarian Reserve Division withstood intense French assaults, particularly at Neuville on its right flank. Despite support from parts of the IV Corps and the 115th Division, the German counter-attacks only managed to reclaim small portions of the village. The following day, General Fasbender, concerned about the sustainability of the line stretching from Ablain to Carency, requested additional reinforcements. In response, Falkenhayn dispatched the 117th Division and relocated the VIII Corps headquarters, along with the 16th Division, to Douai as a new OHL reserve.

To prevent a strategic withdrawal that would result in losing the Lorette Spur, Crown Prince Rupprecht convened a meeting with corps commanders and issued a directive to hold positions, bolstered by the relative calm from the French on the morning of May 11th. However, the French attacks that afternoon, though aggressive, were poorly coordinated and resulted in heavy casualties. A captured French order indicated their intent to make a maximum effort to break through the German lines, prompting the allocation of a regiment from the 117th Division to the 6th Army as a precautionary measure. Additionally, part of the 58th Division was repositioned nearer to the 28th Division on the Lorette Spur.

On May 11th, Falkenhayn ordered Rupprecht not to retreat under any circumstances, leaving him the discretion to decide between offensive and defensive strategies. Rupprecht, however, deemed a counter-attack unfeasible. The following day, two regiments from the 117th Division were assigned to the I Bavarian Reserve Corps to fortify Neuville. Reinforcements intended for the OHL reserve behind the 6th Army were absorbed, and part of the 15th Division was dispatched to Douai as a new OHL reserve. Falkenhayn also proposed establishing a special headquarters for coordinating counter-attacks.

This move by Falkenhayn, coupled with the arrival of two liaison officers from OHL to assess the feasibility of a counter-attack by the most threatened corps, seemed to undermine the authority of the 6th Army HQ. Rupprecht interpreted this as an indirect criticism of Karl von Fassbender, commander of the I Bavarian Reserve Corps, and expressed his dissatisfaction, blaming Falkenhayn for not heeding earlier calls for reinforcements.

On June 13th, Rupprecht reiterated his orders to the XIV Corps to hold Carency. Haenisch sent engineers to construct a reserve trench behind the left flank of the 28th Division. The pressure on the Lorette Spur from the French had lessened, allowing a regiment from the 58th Division to recapture trenches on the northern slope. However, a counter-attack at Carency was not feasible, and the I Bavarian Reserve Corps focused on defending the line stretching from Souchez to Neuville and St Laurent, which faced renewed French assaults in the afternoon.

Counter-attacks successfully sealed gaps on either side of Hill 123, but a persistent gap between a depression known as Artilleriemulde, north of the Lorette Spur, and Souchez remained open, leaving Carency nearly encircled. The defenses to the west and south of Carency, lost on May 9th, continued to be eroded by relentless French assaults. On the morning of May 12th, a massive French bombardment with 23,000 shells targeted the remaining German positions north of the village, effectively isolating the survivors and leading to the village's capture over the subsequent two days. While French offensives in the north started to wane on May 13th due to rainstorms turning the battlefield into a muddy quagmire, a fierce bombardment erupted on Souchez at 2:00 p.m. on May 15th, lasting until 6:00 p.m., although no infantry assault followed.

In response to these developments, Crown Prince Rupprecht established Armee–Gruppe Fasbender late on May 12th to oversee operations in the XIV and I Bavarian Reserve Corps areas. This group was tasked with maintaining current positions and forming a defensive line from Carency to Neuville. A counter-attack at the cemetery south of Souchez faltered without support from Carency, which fell to a French attack at dusk, posing a significant threat to the German line. Haenish promptly ordered the shelling of the village and directed the 28th Division to establish a new line stretching from the Lorette Spur to Ablain church and Souchez. Additional reinforcements, including a battalion from the 117th Division, were dispatched to the 28th Division, with a regiment from the 16th Division moved to Lens as a replacement.

By June 13th, the right flank of the 28th Division still controlled the northern slope of the Lorette Spur, but the line around the Lorette Chapel had been lost from Schlammulde (Muddy Hollow) to the Ablain track. The French had captured most of Ablain, but further advances were halted in fierce, costly skirmishes. A temporary lull ensued, except for a minor French attack at Neuville.

Rupprecht evaluated several divisions, including the 29th, 28th, and 5th Bavarian Reserve Divisions, as depleted or exhausted, with the 1st Bavarian Reserve Division, 58th, and 115th Divisions also suffering severe damage. From May 9th to 13th, approximately 20,000 casualties were incurred. Rupprecht appealed for more reinforcements to replace the depleted divisions, prompting Falkenhayn to start reallocating units from other Western Front areas. General Ewald von Lochow, commander of the III Corps, was appointed to oversee the incoming units to the 6th Army.

The relief of the 28th Division by the 117th Division commenced on the night of May 13th to 14th, and the remnants of the 5th Bavarian Reserve Division were relieved during the day. General Julius Riemann, commander of the VIII Corps, took command of the 16th, 58th, 115th, and parts of the 15th divisions from Souchez to Neuville. This reinforcement effort significantly depleted the OHL reserve, leading to a refusal of further requests from Rupprecht, who subsequently expressed his concerns to the Kaiser.

North of the Lorette Spur and within the area of the 1st Bavarian Reserve Division, much of the original front line remained intact. The XIV Corps, north of the Carency stream, maintained positions in parts of the front line in Schlammulde, along Barrikadenweg (Barricade Way), and at the eastern end of Ablain. South of the stream, the defensive line was held by a combination of the 58th and 115th divisions, remnants of the 5th Bavarian Reserve Division, and a regiment from the 52nd Reserve Infantry Brigade. In reserve, the 16th Division, commanded by Lieutenant-General Fuchs, was prepared to occupy a front stretching from Souchez to Hill 123, spanning 1.2 miles. Additionally, the 15th Division and the new 1st Trench Mortar Battalion had arrived in the 6th Army sector.

General Lochow, who took command from May 14th to June 12th, focused on reorganizing intermixed units and rotating exhausted troops into reserve. Artillery command in each area was centralized, enhancing the effectiveness of barrage fire, counter-battery attacks, and crossfire into adjacent sectors. The 5th Bavarian Reserve and 58th Divisions were relieved by the 16th Division, and three distinct corps sectors were established: the XIV Corps on the right with the 117th Division and 85th Reserve Brigade; the VIII Corps, comprising the 115th and 58th divisions from the Carency stream to the Arras–Lens road; and the 1st Bavarian Reserve Corps, including the 1st Bavarian Reserve Division and 52nd Infantry Brigade, stretching from the road to the Scarpe river.

Lochow's plan for a counter-attack by the XIV Corps aimed at regaining control of the Lorette Spur, conducted from May 15th to 17th, only succeeded in depleting the 117th Division, necessitating its withdrawal. Air reconnaissance detected significant French troop and artillery movements to Doullens station, indicating the continuation of the French offensive. A proposed counter-attack towards Ecurie to disrupt French artillery was abandoned due to troop shortages. The only feasible attack location was Neuville, where troops could assemble discreetly with effective artillery support. The 15th Division, led by Major-General Vollbrecht and reinforced by elements of the 115th Division, launched an assault at 8:30 p.m. on May 22nd. Despite support from the 1st Trench Mortar Battalion and flamethrowers, the attack failed with heavy losses.

To the south, the battle for the Labyrinthe persisted, with frequent attempts to recapture the central first position and relieve the right flank, which was surrounded on three sides. The Bavarian Reserve Infantry Brigade 2 mounted a counter-attack towards the Lossow-Arkaden, advancing about 490 feet before being repulsed. French assaults in the opposite direction, occurring up to six times daily, also largely failed, except for some gains on the Thélus road on the evening of May 11th. Newly arrived German reinforcements were quickly deployed to halt the French progress towards Thélus.

On the British front, an attack was launched on the night of May 15th/16th, south of Neuve Chapelle. By May 20th, the British had advanced approximately 1.9 miles, drawing in German reinforcements. These reinforcements managed to repel British attacks over the Estaires–La Bassée road from May 20th to 21st.

The French offensive had significantly weakened the 6th German Army, depleting all the fresh units it had received from the OHL reserve in France. The 2nd Guard Reserve Division, originally designated for the VII Corps opposite the British, had to be redirected due to the intense pressure from French supporting attacks beyond Artois, even before these units could rest.

This left only the fatigued 111th, 123rd, and 8th Bavarian Reserve Divisions in the OHL reserve. Despite this strain, the artillery strength of the 6th Army had increased substantially, growing from 100 heavy howitzers and 74 heavy guns to 209 heavy howitzers and 98 heavy guns by May 22nd, with a sufficient supply of ammunition. From May 9th to 19th, the 6th Army had expended a massive amount of artillery shells: 508,000 field artillery and 105,000 heavy shells. On May 19th, Krafft von Delmensingen, the Chief of Staff of the 6th Army, was replaced by Colonel von Wenge and reassigned to Italy with the newly formed Alpenkorps.

In the Lorette Spur region, the 117th Division was deployed on May 18th to relieve the 28th Division, extending from the Schlammulde (Muddy Hollow) to Ablain and the southern end of Souchez. The trenches in this area were in poor condition, many demolished and those near the river were flooded. Supply deliveries were erratic, as field kitchens were positioned far back to evade shellfire. The remaining defenses, improvised between attacks, were vulnerable, with some directly overlooked by French positions. A significant French attack on May 21st pushed the German defenders back, and a counter-attack to reclaim the position failed, leading to the establishment of a new defensive line along a track at Ablain's northern edge. Trenches dug towards the Lorette Spur offered some flank protection. The II Battalion, Infantry Regiment 157, heavily depleted in the fighting, was reinforced with units from six different regiments. Persistent French assaults gradually pushed back the remaining defenders, but the strategic importance of the area north-west of Souchez necessitated continuous German reinforcements between late May and June 7th.

Following several days of minor engagements, the French infantry launched an attack from the Lorette Spur to the Scarpe at 4:00 p.m. South of Ecurie, French troop movements were detected and bombarded, halting their advance in no man's land. In the north, the French gained several footholds, which were only recaptured overnight. Lochow called for more reinforcements, leading to the IV Corps south of Arras, with the 8th and 7th

Divisions, being replaced by two exhausted divisions. The 111th Division took over from the 8th Division, and the 58th Division relieved the 115th Division at Neuville. French attacks from May 25th to 26th, stretching from Liévin to Souchez, initially captured German trenches but then lost them to German counter-attacks. By May 27th, the Germans had lost Ablain cemetery and adjacent trenches, making the village's defense untenable. On May 28th, they retreated to a line around the sugar refinery west of Souchez. Despite ongoing local skirmishes, a French assault on May 29th along the road from Aix-Noulette to Souchez was repelled by the Reserve Infantry Brigade 85. Lochow suspected this attack was a diversion, and indeed, the French launched a larger offensive further south the next day.

On May 30th, the French artillery intensified its bombardment in the southern sector, extending into the area of the VIII Corps. This was followed by an attack at 5:00 p.m., stretching from Souchez to Roclincourt, which the Germans eventually repelled. Late on May 31st, German trenches between Angres, the Carency stream, and the sugar refinery were captured by the French, and despite numerous counter-attacks, only the trenches to the north were retaken on June 1st. That evening, a French offensive from Neuville to Tsingtao Trench succeeded, posing a serious threat to the German control over the Labyrinthe. In response, Lochow appointed Fasbinder to command with the 58th Division and shifted the 15th Division to Neuville.

Meanwhile, British diversionary attacks near Givenchy-lez-la-Bassée continued into early June, leading to heavy losses for both the VII and XIX corps. Within Armee-Gruppe Lochow, the struggle for the Labyrinthe persisted, and from June 4th to 6th, Neuville faced repeated French assaults. After a French attack on June 8th, German defenders were forced to withdraw to an eastern trench. The French attacks on the Lorette Spur, coordinated with those at Neuville, drained the XIV Corps troops, necessitating their replacement with the 7th and 8th divisions of IV Corps, which were initially reserved for a counter-offensive.

To the south, the French had fortified their position in the Neuville cemetery, using it as a base for further assaults on Neuville, thereby endangering the German hold on the Labyrinthe. By June 7th, German defenses in Neuville began to falter, despite high command orders to hold the area at all costs. Officers of the 58th Division sought permission to withdraw from the village, but were only granted the liberty to make a temporary, limited retreat for the purpose of organizing a counter-attack. On June 8th, the northwest part of Neuville fell, and the last defenders of Infantry Regiment 160 were mistakenly shelled by their own artillery. The 15th Division dispatched a battalion to counter-attack a French salient near the Lossow-Arkade in the Labyrinthe, supported by grenade teams and flamethrowers. This attack failed, though some ground and the Tsingtau-Graben at the Labyrinthe were regained. French attacks continued, and in the early hours of June 11th, a counter-offensive by the 1st Bavarian Reserve Division recaptured a trench.

German intelligence noted French preparations for another widespread assault and moved substantial artillery ammunition to the front. On June 10th, the 15th Division's senior gunner anticipated a French attack from Vimy to La Folie, Thélus, and Neuville St Vaast, which, if successful, could lead to the loss of the German artillery positions around Vimy and La Folie. Unable to launch a preemptive strike, German forces at Roclincourt watched as French troops sapped within 200 feet of their lines. The ensuing French bombardment increased in intensity until 11:30 a.m., when an explosion occurred, and French infantry broke through the German defenses. German soldiers quickly formed flanking barricades and a blocking position to contain the French incursion. German artillery relentlessly shelled the captured area and no man's land to hinder French reinforcements. Subsequent counter-attacks by reserved German troops eventually ousted the French from their footholds, but at a considerable cost in casualties.

On June 7th, General Falkenhayn convened a meeting with the commanders of the 6th Army and acknowledged their assessment that only with the infusion of fresh troops could the 6th Army's positions be maintained.

Consequently, the 5th and 123rd Divisions were dispatched to reinforce the 6th Army, and the XIX Saxon Corps was replaced by the IV Corps on June 14th. The 117th Division, having been stationed at the Lorette Spur, was moved beyond the Béthune–Lens road for rest. Meanwhile, the 7th Division (under Lieutenant-General Riedel) and the 8th Division (led by Major-General von Hanstein) were entrenched in deteriorating positions around Liévin and Angres, unable to conduct repairs at night due to French searchlights exposing their movements.

The area of Schlammulde, south of the Aix-Noulette–Souchez road, although somewhat shielded from French artillery, was littered with corpses, creating a distressing environment for the German troops who were unable to bury the dead. Efforts continued to close a 980-foot gap towards a switch trench leading to the sugar refinery and Souchez. Additional fortifications were constructed near the Château in Souchez, while the 16th Division used a lull in attacks to repair defenses from Souchez to Hill 123. The trenches held by the 5th Division (commanded by Major-General von Gabain) remained in poor condition.

In the I Bavarian Reserve Corps sector, the 58th Division still controlled much of the Labyrinthe, while to the south, the 1st Bavarian Reserve Division and the exhausted 52nd Reserve Infantry Brigade, though in the original front line, faced severely damaged trenches. German artillery had been restructured into divisional groups, and batteries south of the Scarpe River were providing flanking fire on French artillery positions to the north. New trench lines were being constructed from Loos to Lens, Vimy, and Thélus, with plans for an additional line east of Lens towards Oppy and Feuchy, strategically positioned to diminish any tactical advantage the French might gain from capturing Vimy Ridge.

By June 14th, signs of another impending French attack were evident, with active French reconnaissance from Angres to Neuville and escalating artillery fire. The intensity of the shelling, including super-heavy shells capable of penetrating concrete shelters, wreaked havoc on German command posts and staging areas. On the morning of June 16th, much of the German wire defenses were cut, trenches destroyed, and the infantry had sustained heavy casualties. At noon, the French launched an attack from Liévin to the Scarpe, with the German artillery largely silenced by counter-battery fire and under constant surveillance from unchallenged French aircraft.

In a late-evening offensive on June 16th, the French used smoke screens to reach and establish footholds in the forward German positions. German counter-attacks later that night recaptured one foothold and captured 205 prisoners, but the French maintained another foothold under heavy artillery cover. By nightfall, the French had solidified their positions in the trenches of the 7th Division at Liévin and Angres. The German survivors in the Schlammulde, between Angres and the chapel at Notre Dame de Lorette, were pushed back. Intense urban combat ensued in Souchez, and in the area held by the 16th Division, where a 0.62-mile stretch of the front line was lost. Some French units even reached German artillery positions, beyond which there were no prepared trench defenses.

In the south against the 5th Division, French attacks initially faltered, but they managed to break through the 58th Division at the Labyrinthe and adjacent areas. Overnight, Armee-Gruppe Lochow's counter-attacks enabled the 7th Division to retake trenches at Liévin and Angres, although they were unsuccessful southwest and at Schlammulde. The 8th Division recaptured the second Lorette switch line, and the 16th Division cleared some isolated French advances but could not secure the area south of Souchez due to intense artillery fire. A continuous barrage (Dauerfeur) over the breakthrough area hindered further French progression, except near the churchyard at Souchez. By dawn, the Labyrinthe had been recaptured, and around 700 French prisoners were taken.

The 6th Army, in a precarious state, received VI Corps reinforcements as they arrived. On June 17th, a renewed French attack penetrated the 5th

Division defenses but was eventually repulsed. A French advance along the Aix-Noulette–Souchez road rendered Schlammulde untenable, and it was abandoned; Marokkanerwäldchen (Moroccan Copse) on the Arras–Béthune road was also lost. The 16th Division, suffering heavy losses, was replaced by the 11th Division from the VI Corps, while the 58th Division remained due to a lack of replacements. In response to this crisis, the OHL allocated the 15th Division and the 123rd Division. The 12th Division of the VI Corps and the 187th Infantry Brigade were rushed north, the 53rd Reserve Division relieved the 3rd Bavarian Division, which then replaced the 58th Division. Thirteen additional heavy batteries were sent to support the 6th Army.

Armee-Gruppe Lochow, now comprising the IV Corps headquarters, the 117th and 123rd Saxon divisions on the right, and the 7th and 8th divisions on the left with the 3rd Ersatz Brigade in reserve, held the northern sector. The VIII Corps managed the central area with the 11th and 5th divisions, soon to be joined by the 12th Division on the northern flank, and the 6th Division in 6th Army reserve upon arrival. The southern sector was held by the 3rd Bavarian, 1st Bavarian, and 5th Bavarian Reserve divisions, with plans to withdraw the 15th and 16th divisions.

The French attacks on June 18th were less intense, raising German hopes that the offensive was winding down. However, the OHL's order to thin out defenses to create a new strategic reserve was contested by the 6th Army headquarters and Lochow, who argued that it was premature. Lochow, on June 24th, anticipated more attacks and stressed the necessity for ongoing fresh division reinforcements, also highlighting the high number of casualties. Attempts to restore the front positions continued until the end of June, but the Germans failed to recapture the Lorette Spur, with French artillery maintaining pressure from Angres to Souchez. The 12th Division was brought in as reinforcement, and French attacks on June 25th and 27th were successfully countered.

In the old 16th Division area south of Souchez, the 11th Division gradually regained lost ground from the June 16th attack. The struggle at the Labyrinthe persisted until June 24th, when the 3rd Bavarian Division reestablished the previous front line. The depleted 52nd Reserve Infantry Brigade was relieved on June 25th, and on June 28th, Armee-Gruppe Lochow was disbanded and replaced by the VI Corps headquarters under General Kurt von Pritzelwitz. The Arras front remained critical for the German Western Front, leading Falkenhayn to initially plan for Eastern Front reinforcements. However, Rupprecht asserted that the 6th Army could hold its position without additional forces, resulting in the cancellation of these deployments. Throughout July, minor skirmishes occurred around Souchez, but the French offensive did not resume. In August, there was a reorganization of the Western Army, with more units moving into reserve and a comprehensive trench digging program initiated along the entire Western Front.

Major Hermann von der Lieth-Thomsen, appointed as the Chief of Field Air Forces on March 11, initiated a significant expansion of the Imperial German Flying Corps. This included the formation of five new air units in Germany, the deployment of replacements, and the rapid introduction of the new Fokker E.I aircraft. To enhance coordination with ground forces, a staff officer for aviation was appointed to each army. By April, armed C-class aircraft began arriving at front-line units. These aircraft observed increased activity behind the French Tenth Army lines, leading to more C-class aircraft being allocated to the 6th Army from quieter Western Front sectors.

On May 9th, French aircraft targeted the 6th Army headquarters at La Madeleine en Lille and railway stations in the area, causing minimal damage. By May 19th, German aerial reconnaissance reported large concentrations of artillery and troop movements at Doullens station, indicating a potential large-scale French offensive.

Simultaneously, the French conducted secondary attacks along the Western Front, intending to pin down German reserves. This was part of a broader strategy to support the main effort at Arras. Notably, the Second Army attacked a German salient near Serre, making modest territorial gains but incurring significant casualties on both sides.

In the south-east, the First Army's operations at the Saint-Mihiel salient from early May to late June involved intense fighting, with the 9th Division being pushed back but later regaining ground, especially near Les Éparges. These operations yielded only minor territorial gains for the French, with heavy casualties.

In Lorraine, the Army Detachment of Lorraine made some progress in June, advancing on a wide front but also suffering substantial losses. In early July, the III Bavarian Corps successfully counter-attacked near Apremont, capturing French trenches and withstanding subsequent French assaults.

The Seventh Army's offensive west of Colmar from early May to late June resulted in the capture of strategic heights and the village of Metzeral, though at considerable cost. Further attempts to capture key positions like the Lingekopf saw mixed success, with ongoing local skirmishes continuing into August.

Overall, these supporting French attacks, while less extensive than the Tenth Army's operations in Artois, still resulted in significant casualties, emphasizing the high human cost of the conflict.

On May 9th, a significant French offensive saw five corps launch an attack against two German divisions across a 16-mile front, achieving a notable advance of 2.5 miles at the sector held by the 5th Bavarian Reserve Division between the Lorette Spur and La Targette. The 77th Division and the DM of the XXXIII Corps made significant inroads between Carency and Neuville, overcoming Landwehr Regiment 39 and seizing Hill 145, the highest point on Vimy Ridge. However, these gains were countered by effective local German counter-attacks, particularly by the Bavarian Infantry Regiment 7, which had been rapidly deployed from reserve.

From May 9th to 12th, the French Tenth Army made substantial progress, marking the largest advance since the onset of trench warfare. This was largely due to the implementation of new tactics, which posed significant challenges for the German defenders. Despite initial successes, the extent and speed of the French plans proved too ambitious, constrained by material limitations and the state of French munitions production. German artillery and flanking fire from Souchez and Neuville eventually forced the XXXIII Corps off Vimy Ridge. Nevertheless, the French had reclaimed a significant area of about 6.2 square miles before the offensive was halted.

General Foch, in an early August report, analyzed the reasons behind the inability to maintain control of Hill 145. He pointed out that the reserves of the XXXIII Corps and the Tenth Army were positioned too far from the frontlines and not deployed according to a well-conceived reinforcement plan. The reserves' delayed and staggered arrival, coupled with the failed supporting attack by the British First Army at the Battle of Aubers Ridge on May 9th, compounded the difficulties. The subsequent British offensive at the Battle of Festubert, starting on May 16th, managed to capture the village and advance about 1.9 miles.

During this period, the British Second Army was engaged in the Second Battle of Ypres against the German 4th Army from April 21st to May 25th, diverting resources from the First Army. Post-May 11th, the French Tenth Army shifted to conducting localized, methodical attacks to secure tactically important grounds in preparation for another major attempt to capture Vimy Ridge. However, the loss of experienced soldiers had significantly diminished the effectiveness of the first-class French divisions. The inconsistent application of the tactics outlined in Note 5779 further exacerbated the situation, especially as inexperienced replacement troops struggled to sustain the offensive momentum.

The French effort in June to seize Vimy Ridge with a set-piece attack, despite a series of local attacks on the flanks of the XXXIII Corps and the successful capture of the Lorette Spur, ended in an expensive failure. French tactics remained largely unchanged from May, and the relentless local attacks provided no opportunity for essential training or strategic revisions. Mid-June amendments to Note 5779 brought only minor adjustments, with an emphasis on the role of cavalry in mobile warfare, as mentioned in the amendment of June 18th. However, these changes couldn't keep pace with the rapid adaptations in German defenses, which by June had rendered the French May tactics outdated.

The persistent German control of Souchez and Neuville created a significant obstacle for the French, preventing them from capturing Vimy Ridge. The defenses of these villages proved too strong to be quickly overcome. An original strategy of sequential attacks might have been more successful in eliminating Souchez and Neuville as barriers, but the material limitations facing the French in the spring of 1915 meant that Foch's plan could not be fully executed.

By September, Foch reflected on the Germans' rapid response from May 9th to 18th, noting their swift reinforcement deployments, construction of new defensive lines, and the introduction of additional heavy artillery. From May 18th, German artillery barrages consistently dominated the Tenth Army front, severely hampering the French in consolidating captured positions and planning further offensives. Even the shift from continuous combat to more methodical, intermittent attacks resulted in less territorial gain, fewer prisoners captured, and higher French casualties.

Foch concluded that a breakthrough was unlikely until the German forces in France were significantly more depleted. He advocated for smaller, step-by-step attacks using methodical and economical approaches. This perspective was echoed by Fayolle, who critiqued the notion of continuous battle as a "grand illusion" and criticized Foch and d'Urbal for their unrealistic expectations. This period also saw André Laffargue, an artillery officer, write "Étude sur l'attaque dans le période actuelle de la guerre," reflecting a growing trend towards artillery-focused tactics and the concept of infantry infiltration.

From June 10th to 16th, the French artillery fired a staggering 497,122 shells, yet this bombardment proved less effective than the 265,430 rounds fired earlier from May 3rd to 9th. The German forces effectively countered with their own heavy artillery barrage, approximately 100,000 shells, which effectively halted the French infantry assault and obstructed the movement of supporting troops. Attempts by the French to replicate the surprise element of the May 9th attack were unsuccessful, as German counter-barrages quickly responded, often within two minutes of the French infantry's advance.

The battles in mid-June highlighted the limited impact of counter-battery and neutralizing fire, as well as adjustments in artillery-fire patterns and timing, particularly when German wire defenses remained intact at the onset of an infantry advance. German field defenses were significantly reinforced and expanded in complexity during this offensive, accompanied by a more active and better-equipped German artillery presence.

The new German defenses, situated on ground visible from the Lorette Spur, were more challenging and expensive to defend, making Vimy Ridge more susceptible to attack. The French army leadership perceived the initial success on May 9th, particularly the capture of Vimy Ridge, as an indicator that a breakthrough was achievable with better organization, informing their planning for subsequent offensives in Artois and Champagne. Pétain noted that the May 9th attack demonstrated the potential for a breakthrough, achievable through meticulous preparation of communication and jumping-off trenches, and assembly positions, along with thorough reconnaissance and heavy artillery bombardment of German defenses. He emphasized the importance of maintaining momentum with closely following reserve troops and advocated for attacks across open country rather than getting mired in battles over obstacles like villages and woods. The attack should be broad-fronted to outflank resistance centers and disperse German defensive firepower.

In response, the German analysis of the battle, compiled in a June 1915 memorandum, led to a renewed focus on creating deeper infantry shelters, impervious to heavy artillery, and constructing additional defensive positions behind the front line. These measures were intended to slow enemy advances and delay subsequent attacks by forcing attackers to reposition their artillery. Following the capture of a copy of Note 5779 by the Germans on the Artois front in June, there was an immediate directive for intensive construction of reserve positions as robust as front-line defenses. Much of the new German trench work on the Western Front was strategically located on reverse slopes, hidden from ground observation and vulnerable only to howitzer fire. By the time the French offensive resumed in September 1915, these defensive changes had rendered French attack methods outdated, leading to heavy French casualties on such slopes, in front of uncut wires, and against undamaged secondary positions.

Battle of Loos

In the early months of 1915, the French military, rejuvenated by an influx of 200,000 new recruits since October 1914, found itself in a position of relative strength against the German forces in the Western Front. General Joseph Joffre, the French Commander-in-Chief, recognized this strategic advantage and was eager to capitalize on it. He envisioned a series of bold offensives aimed at breaking through the entrenched German lines, leveraging the current numerical superiority of the French Army.

The plan was ambitious, involving three coordinated attacks, although eventually only two materialized. The primary focus was on a large-scale offensive in the Champagne region, aimed at capturing vast open territories and pushing the German forces back. Simultaneously, another assault was planned in Artois, targeting the crucial rail networks between Douai and Noyon, which were vital for German logistics. Joffre calculated that a successful advance of merely 20 miles in this region would compel the Germans to withdraw.

Meanwhile, the British Expeditionary Force (BEF), under the command of Sir John French, was also drawn into these grand plans. On June 4, 1915, the British were requested to extend their front by an additional 22 miles near the River Somme. This maneuver was crucial in freeing up French reserves for the impending offensive. Furthermore, the BEF was invited to join the renewed offensive in Artois alongside the French Tenth Army. Despite the challenges and the heavy commitments in other theatres like Gallipoli, Sir

John French agreed to this proposal. He directed Sir Douglas Haig, leading the First Army, to craft a detailed strategy for the attack, which was to occur south of the previous failed attempts at Aubers and Festubert.

In this grand scheme, the BEF, despite being the junior partner in the conflict, was entrusted with a significant role. Joffre specifically urged Sir John French to launch a powerful offensive north of the French Tenth Army, between Loos and La Bassée. This area was deemed to offer particularly favorable conditions for an attack. Thus, amidst growing strength and strategic planning, the stage was set for a series of offensives that would mark a pivotal chapter in the First World War, as allies coordinated in an attempt to break the deadlock on the Western Front.

The Loos battlefield, located just north of the industrial town of Lens in north-east France, is characterized by its uniformly flat terrain, punctuated by slag heaps associated with the region's coal mining industry. In 1915, the landscape was marked by mining villages, collieries, and industrial structures, posing a significant challenge to any attacking force. Although the area has seen some changes since then, with a decline in mining activities and alterations in the size and presence of slag heaps and pit-heads, it still retains much of its historical character.

In 1915, a major Franco-British offensive was planned against the German Sixth Army. Under the supervision of General Foch, this offensive would involve both the French Tenth Army and the British First Army, attacking along a 20-mile front stretching from Arras to La Bassée. While the entire front would be subjected to artillery bombardment, a central 4000-yard section facing Liévin and Lens was to be excluded from direct assault. The French Tenth Army, positioned to the south, was set to deploy 17 infantry divisions supported by 420 heavy guns, with two cavalry divisions on standby to exploit any breakthrough. To the north, the British First Army, comprising six divisions from I and IV Corps and equipped with 70 heavy guns, was also prepared with two cavalry corps (Indian and III) to advance the attack.

The operation's goals were ambitious, with the cavalry aiming to reach Ath and Mons in Belgium, some 50 miles away. Joffre's strategy was straight-forward yet aggressive: a continuous four-day artillery bombardment, culminating in a four-hour intense shelling, followed by a massive infantry assault. The infantry were to be deployed in depth, with each division placing no more than half of two brigades in the front line, and a steady stream of reinforcements ready to follow.

In addition to the main assault, Sir John French planned subsidiary attacks near Ypres by the Second Army and north of the La Bassée canal by the First Army. Approximately 75,000 British infantry were designated for the initial attack. Lessons learned from previous engagements at Neuve Chapelle and Festubert highlighted the dangers of attacking on a narrow front due to concentrated enemy fire. Consequently, the First Army expanded its attack front, deploying all six divisions of I and IV Corps. However, this broader front presented a challenge due to insufficient heavy artillery. To mitigate this, the British decided to use smoke barrages for concealment and, for the first time, chlorine gas, to compensate for the lighter artillery. Details of the plan, especially regarding the use of gas, were kept under strict secrecy, with codewords like 'accessory' used in orders.

The pivotal takeaway from the Spring offensive emphasized the critical role of heavy artillery, particularly high-explosive shells, in breaking enemy defenses and creating openings for infantry to penetrate enemy lines. The upcoming assaults were to traverse open terrain, visible from elevated positions. To counter this, it was crucial to use smoke screens to shield the infantry from machine guns that might withstand even the most intense bombardments. While the preliminary bombardment eliminated the element of surprise regarding the location of the battle, efforts were made to maintain some unpredictability in the timing of the attack.

In the strategic layout, the General Reserve divisions were positioned north and south of Lillers, awaiting orders from the Commander-in-Chief. This reserve included the 1st, 2nd, and 3rd Cavalry Divisions and the XI Corps, comprising the Guards, 21st, and 24th Divisions, the latter two being recent arrivals in France and inexperienced in trench warfare. These units began their movement from St. Omer on September 20th, undertaking nightly marches exceeding 20 miles.

Sir John French directed Sir Douglas Haig to formulate the attack plan, assuring him that two reserve divisions would be at his disposal when needed. Haig's strategy involved utilizing the 21st and 24th Divisions as an immediate reserve, which allowed him to deploy all six of his frontline divisions in the assault. He reassured his Corps commanders of the availability of ample reserves to reinforce or capitalize on any successes.

However, by September 18th, Haig discovered that French intended to keep the reserves at Lillers, about 16 miles from the frontline. Haig protested, referencing the lessons from Neuve Chapelle and Festubert where quick reinforcement was crucial. General Foch suggested a closer reserve distance of 2000 yards. French, mindful of the scarce resources in manpower, munitions, and equipment since Neuve Chapelle, did not consent but ordered that the 21st and 24th Divisions be positioned at Noeux-les-Mines and Beuvry by dawn on the assault day, with the Guards Division following.

On September 24th, the reserve divisions were instructed to carry extra rations and greatcoats for their march to the battle area, starting at 7 pm that night, in anticipation of potential delays in receiving supplies.

The medical infrastructure set up for the First Army at Loos was extensive. It included 16 Advanced Dressing Stations, 15 Main Dressing Stations, and 13 Casualty Clearing Stations located in various strategic locations. These facilities had a combined capacity for over 11,500 casualties at any given time. Additionally, 17 ambulance trains, barges, and road transport were arranged to evacuate the wounded towards the coast, preparing to handle up to 40,000 casualties.

The Royal Flying Corps was tasked with bombing missions targeting German railways and communication lines, in addition to their crucial artillery reconnaissance missions.

Air reconnaissance missions had disclosed significant fortifications in the German defenses within the targeted attack zone. These enhancements were not limited to the front line, which had been expanded, reinforced, and equipped with numerous machine-gun redoubts and extensive barbed wire barriers. The Germans had also meticulously established strong second and third lines of defense. Notably, the second line was strategically positioned on a reverse slope, making it invisible from the British lines. The barbed wire protecting this second line, measuring 15 yards in depth, was not only more robust than that in no man's land but was also made from a new, tougher design that the British infantry's wire-cutters couldn't breach. Furthermore, this wire lay beyond the range of British field artillery, implying that unless the first line was breached and the artillery moved forward, the wire would remain unscathed. This situation suggested that even if the British managed to advance their artillery, the Germans would likely have sufficient time to reinforce their positions, making the breakthrough as per Joffre's comprehensive plan an extremely daunting prospect.

Intelligence reports indicated that the target area was held by the German 117th Division, a reconstituted 3-Regiment unit after heavy losses at Vimy in the Spring, and the 14th Division, familiar adversaries from Neuve Chapelle, with two of their four regiments stationed south of the canal. The 2nd Guard Division and 8th Division were identified as reserves, positioned within 12 miles of the front. British intelligence had accurately pinpointed all enemy units in the vicinity.

In England, speculation and rumors about this 'Big Push' had been circulating for weeks prior to the attack. With little in the way of strategic deception, the preparations near the battlefront were conspicuously apparent. The only unknowns to the enemy were the exact date and time of the attack, and once the preliminary bombardment commenced, it was clear that the assault was imminent.

On September 21, 1915, the British began bombarding German positions, continuing relentlessly into the morning of the planned assault. Observation was hindered by weather conditions, including chalk dust clouds and later, mist. Feint attacks were employed, using dummy troops and other ruses, to keep German forces engaged.

The weather on September 23 turned unfavorable with a violent thunderstorm, complicating artillery observation, yet the bombardment persisted. By September 24, despite unhelpful weather and quietened enemy artillery, German wire entanglements and defenses largely remained intact. That evening, two reserve divisions commenced a delayed 7-mile march to the battlefront. Sir John French's move to Chateau Philomel hampered communication, relying on the public French telephone system.

At 9:00 pm, weather reports suggested improving conditions for a westerly wind, crucial for the planned gas release. By 10:00 pm, assault brigades took positions in front-line trenches, with some troops in shallow trenches close to the enemy. Meanwhile, unaware to the British, the German troops were largely unaffected by the bombardment.

On the morning of September 25, weather reports indicated less favorable conditions, but Haig ordered the release of gas at 5:50 am, followed by the infantry attack. Despite slight wind improvements, the gas moved slowly and inconsistently. At 6:00 am, the exhausted reserve divisions completed assembly, while a diversionary attack at Givenchy led to significant British casualties with little gain.

At 6:30 am, the main assault began. Early reports showed promising advances, and Haig ordered reserves to move forward. By 7:05 am, British artillery shifted to target German communication trenches.

From 7:05 am to noon, the IV Corps, particularly the 47th (2nd London) Division, encountered varied success. The gas and smoke effectively concealed their advance, leading to the capture of initial German positions. However, they faced stiff resistance, particularly from German machine guns and counter-attacks. The 1/20 Londons captured the Chalk Pit and the 140th Brigade secured the Double Crassier, but the 1/19th Londons suffered heavy casualties, with their advance into Loos being chaotic and costly.

The centre 15th (Scottish) Division in this particular sector of the battlefield, the gas cloud's failure to advance as planned caused significant issues. The infantry, initially shielded by the gas and smoke for only 40 yards of their 200-yard advance, became exposed to German machine-gun and artillery fire, resulting in numerous casualties. Despite these challenges, the British troops managed to clear the German front lines and take control of Loos village by 8:00 am. Progress continued on the left flank, reaching the La Bassee-Lens road by 9:15 am, prompting calls for reserve support.

However, disorientation among the advancing units led to a deviation from the original plan. Many soldiers, lacking clear directions and leadership, mistakenly headed towards Hill 70 instead of their intended leftward objective. This error left the 1/9 Black Watch without expected flank support, forcing them to halt. The bulk of the infantry, now on Hill 70, faced German retreat but soon encountered crossfire from German second-line defenses, halting their advance by 10:30 am. Artillery support requests resulted in misdirected bombardments, and about 200 men, joined by reinforcements, entrenched themselves behind Hill 70's crest line. By 11:30 am, despite the British threat, the Germans had reinforced their positions, and Lens was evacuated in anticipation of a potential Scottish advance.

Meanwhile, the 1st Division's advance was impeded by British gas drifting back into their trenches, causing early casualties. The 2nd Brigade encountered undamaged enemy wire and heavy German fire, leading to stalled progress and exposed troops in no man's land. The 1st Brigade fared better, pushing through to Gun Trench despite heavy losses. The 1/Camerons advanced towards Hulluch, awaiting the 2nd Brigade, which was repeatedly repelled by intense German fire.

By 9:10 am, additional support was ordered, but communication failures delayed its arrival. Frontal assaults by the 1/14th London Regiment and 1/9th King's faced severe gunfire, resulting in heavy casualties. The 2/Royal Munster Fusiliers, advancing overground due to overcrowded trenches, suffered near annihilation. Ultimately, the attack in this sector ground to a halt under the weight of German defensive fire.

In the I Corps sector, the 7th Division encountered mixed effectiveness with the gas cloud, leading to local variations in its deployment. Many soldiers, struggling with their gas helmets in the cloud, removed them and suffered from gas exposure. The 20th Brigade, especially the 8/Devonshire, faced heavy losses due to German shelling and machine-gun fire, with the wire in their sector only partially cleared. In contrast, the 2/Gordon Highlanders made better progress, moving towards Gun Trench and Hulluch.

The 22nd Brigade experienced severe casualties, with the 1/South Stafford-shire and 2/Royal Warwicks losing about 70% of their strength before reaching German lines. Despite this, they managed to capture the German support line by 7:30 am. Artillery support was quickly brought up, with two RFA batteries firing near Notre-Dame de la Consolation by 9:00 am. The leading men crossed the Lens Road south of Vermelles-Hulluch road, disrupting German reinforcements. Support battalions, including the 1/6/Gordon Highlanders and 2/Border, faced heavy fire, limiting their advance. However, by 9:30 am, with reinforcements from the 2/Queens, the 22nd Brigade had captured Hulluch Quarries, with further advances halted due to lack of support.

The 21st Brigade, moving up from Vermelles, also faced challenges in penetrating uncut wire under fire from Cite St Elie, leading to a halt in and around Gun Trench and the Quarries. Divisional artillery was directed to shell Cite St Elie and its defenses until 4:00 pm.

The central 9th (Scottish) Division's task was to assault the Hohenzollern Redoubt and Fosse 8, key enemy observation posts. Despite casualties during the initial advance through gas and smoke, they successfully breached well-cut wire and quickly took control of the front face of the Redoubt. The 7/Seaforths pushed towards Fosse 8 soon after 7:00 am, advancing beyond the rear of the redoubt.

Thirty minutes after their initial advance, the 7/Seaforths regrouped in the flooded Corons Trench. The 5/Camerons, despite crossfire from Mad Point, reached the front face of the Hohenzollern Redoubt and joined the Seaforths by 7:45 am. However, the 8/Black Watch, reinforcing from reserve, incurred heavy casualties from Mad Point. Realizing further advancement was impossible due to failures on their left, the Brigade prepared for counterattacks under continuous enemy shelling.

The 8/Gordon Highlanders, moving south of the Dump, managed to reach Pekin Trench, 1000 yards ahead of the consolidating units at the Redoubt. The 27th Brigade's support efforts were mixed: the 12/Royal Scots reached Pekin Trench with minimal losses, while the 11/Royal Scots got entangled in wire and suffered heavy machine-gun casualties. The 10/Argyll & Sutherland Highlanders halted at Fosse Alley upon hearing Pekin Trench was heavily defended.

Four guns from No 7 Mountain Battery RGA were moved to support the Redoubt by 10:30 am. The 28th Brigade, on the division's left front, faced severe challenges. Gas drifting back into trenches caused havoc, with German artillery targeting the crowded front lines. The 6/KOSB advanced to uncut enemy wire but were decimated by machine-gun fire from Strong Point and Mad Point. The 10/HLI faced similar fate from Railway Redoubt's crossfire, with successive ranks also suffering heavy losses.

At 11:15 am, orders were given to renew the attack at 12:15 pm, but the preparatory bombardment proved ineffective against the German defenses near Auchy. The 9/Scottish Rifles and half of the 11/HLI faced severe losses in the renewed attack, unable to even reach the German wire. By 1:30 pm, the Brigade halted further attacks and reorganized for defense.

The 2nd Division's attack along the La Bassee canal was entirely unsuccessful, resulting in high casualties. Its objective was to protect the 9th Division's right flank from fire or counterattacks from the canal area. However, the terrain, already cratered from mine warfare, proved disadvantageous. The 19th Brigade's advance, preceded by mines detonated by the 173rd Tunnelling Company, RE, was further hampered by gas drifting back into trenches. Forced to navigate around craters, the infantry became easy targets for concentrated enemy machine-gun fire.

By 9:00 am, it became apparent that the 19th Brigade would not make progress, leading to orders for withdrawal to the original front lines. The 1/Middlesex, unable to retreat from no man's land, sought cover until nightfall. A small group of the 2/Argyll & Sutherland Highlanders occupied an empty German trench, but only 11 survived by night, with the rest killed or captured.

Adjacent to this Brigade, the 6th Brigade faced issues with the gas release. An RE officer, concerned about poor wind conditions, was initially reluctant but eventually released the gas at 6:00 am, causing delays. The dense gas incapacitated 130 men of the 2/South Staffordshire. The 1/King's found uncut wire, and their advance was halted, except for a South Staffordshire group that reached Embankment Redoubt but was repelled by German grenades. Despite renewed bombardments at 9:00 am, German strongpoints remained active, leading the 19th and 6th Brigades to halt further advances by 9:45 am.

North of the canal, the 5th Brigade's attack was impaired by gas drifting from the south, causing friendly casualties. The attack's failure was compounded by the 6th Brigade's inability to suppress Embankment Redoubt, rendering the 1/9th HLI's attempt to capture Tortoise Redoubt extremely difficult. The leading platoons were decimated, and the attack was called off.

Regarding reserves, at 8:45 am, Haig messaged French, indicating that all reserve units of I and IV Corps were deployed and urged the release of XI Corps. French signaled XI Corps at 9:30 am but did not place them under First Army orders until their arrival in the trenches. By noon, they were still navigating through damaged communication trenches, crowded with wounded men, stretcher bearers, and traffic, all under shellfire. Optimistic early reports led First Army to order the 3rd Cavalry Division to Corons de Rutoire by 10:30 am, ready to advance once Cite St Auguste fell.

By noon on September 25, 1915, despite significant losses and the ineffective use of gas, there was still optimism. The British had breached enemy lines in several areas, but uncertainty about further German defenses and reactions remained. Poor flying conditions limited reconnaissance, and few prisoners were captured. The 47th and 15th Divisions had taken Loos but faced potential counterattacks on Hill 70. Signs of German withdrawal were evident near Loos and Lens. The 7th Division was near Hulluch, and the 9th Division was advancing at the Hohenzollern Redoubt and Fosse 8. However, attacks by the left of the 9th Division and the 2nd Division had failed, halting further ambitions in those areas.

By early afternoon, the reserve XI Corps was finally under Haig's command, but its late arrival forced a piecemeal deployment rather than a unified action. The 47th (London) Division consolidated its positions, preparing for potential counterattacks from the south. The 15th (Scottish) Division, despite capturing Loos, faced difficulties with men pinned down on Hill 70 and delayed artillery support. A German counterattack recaptured Hill 70.

At noon, the French Tenth Army began its bombardment south of Lens, with an infantry attack following at 12:45 am. This new threat caused German commanders to shift reserves, halting further counterattacks against the British. The 46th Brigade reinforced its left flank, weakened by the 1st Division's failure to advance, establishing a line from Chalk Pit Wood to Chalet Wood. The 45th Brigade's attempt to recapture Hill 70 was hindered by lack of artillery support, leading them to dig in at Loos. Supply lines were severely disrupted by debris and casualties.

By 3:00 pm, battalions from the 21st Division were ordered to reinforce Loos and potentially retake Hill 70. However, they faced intense shrapnel and machine-gun fire, suffering heavy casualties and exhaustion. By nightfall, both divisions were consolidating positions between the old German first and second lines, with the enemy regaining control of Hill 70. A German night attack against the 7/Royal Scots Fusiliers was repelled.

In the Hulluch area, the 1st Division's attack was halted by intense enemy fire. The 2nd Brigade, reinforced by the 1/Gloucesters, shifted south to flank the enemy, leveraging the 15th Division's success. The 2/Welch crossed no man's land with minimal losses, finding the 2/Royal Munster Fusiliers heavily battered. They positioned themselves against the enemy's defense line. Despite a counter-attack on the 1st Brigade, the Welch, by 2.30pm, had nearly encircled 400 German soldiers of the 157th Regiment, leading to their surrender. The brigade advanced but was reduced to 1,500 men due to losses, reaching the Lens road near Bois Hugo by 5.20pm. However, a significant gap remained in the line.

Concurrently, the First Army's reserve 3rd Cavalry Division was held back by Major-General Briggs due to unfavorable conditions, contrary to the Army's belief. Haig ordered two reserve infantry divisions to advance between Hulluch and Cite St Auguste, unaware of the enemy's resilience. Delays and darkness hampered the advance, with many soldiers perishing before receiving revised orders to halt.

In the Auchy area, the 9th (Scottish) Division secured enemy trenches around the Hohenzollern Redoubt, Fosse 8, and Pekin Trench. Reinforcements and artillery were deployed to support Fosse 8. However, the German forces regained ground with superior grenade tactics, forcing a British withdrawal to a new front line at Fosse Alley. The advanced field batteries retreated to their initial positions.

By nightfall, the Division maintained a continuous line from north of the Hulluch Quarries to Fosse 8, with a flank near Madagascar. Despite expecting reinforcements, the I Corps staff were somewhat satisfied, as the 7th and 9th Divisions had broken through enemy lines in several areas.

In the Canal area, the 19th and 6th Brigades of the 2nd Division ceased their advance by 9.45am due to heavy losses and failure to penetrate German positions. The 5th Brigade also retreated to their original trench, leading to a period of consolidation.

The reserve 21st and 24th Divisions experienced a slow, exhausting march into the Loos valley, hindered by unfamiliar terrain, flooded trenches, congested roads, and obstructive wire, while carrying extra supplies. The Guards Division faced similar difficulties, finding their billets already occupied upon arrival at 8.00pm.

By the night of 25th September 1915, earlier opportunities for advancement were lost. Insufficient forces were available to capitalize on the initial breaches in enemy lines. Strong German resistance and heavy rain halted further progress. The First Army HQ, lacking a complete understanding of the frontline situation and unaware of German reinforcements, mistakenly believed their infantry had broken through south of Hulluch. Plans were made to continue the offensive with reserves, despite their exhaustion and the fragmented British defenses. Orders for a renewed attack at 11.00am on 26th September were issued at 11.30pm.

On 26th September 1915, the First Army initiated a renewed attack at 11.00am, despite Sir John French expressing concerns to Sir Douglas Haig about the strategy of pushing reserves through a narrow gap in enemy defenses.

In the Loos area, the 24th Division's Brigadiers met at 1.10am to plan their next steps. Despite earlier reports, Hulluch remained enemy-held. They decided to advance across the Lens – La Bassee road and through the German second line by moonlight, lacking intelligence on German strength or defenses.

At 5.00am, the 15th (Scottish) Division, reinforced by the 21st Division, received orders to recapture Hill 70 at 9.00am. However, artillery support was limited, and fresh ammunition supplies were delayed. Some units mistakenly remained in advanced positions, leading to friendly fire incidents. Many infantry units received late attack orders.

By 5.30am, a German attack against the 7/Royal Scots Fusiliers was repelled. Around 8.00am, the 21st and 24th Divisions, having moved with difficulty overnight, reached positions facing the enemy's second line. They mistakenly believed to have been resting for some time, as ordered by the First Army.

The weakened 45th Brigade advanced on Hill 70 at 9.00am, facing immediate fire and engaging in hand-to-hand combat. Unable to flank the Redoubt, the survivors withdrew, followed by similar fates for the 62nd Brigade. By 10.00am, German counterattacks had retaken the entire Redoubt complex.

At 11.00am, a heavy German bombardment hit the forward positions, leading to many exhausted and leaderless men falling back into Loos village. At noon, the First Army sent the 6th Cavalry Brigade, including the 3rd Dragoon Guards and 1st Royal Dragoons, dismounted, to reinforce the area.

By 3.30pm, a general retirement from Hill 70 occurred due to confused orders.

Simultaneously, small units moved into the Hill 70 positions to reinforce them. The enemy counterattacked the Loos Crassier, now strongly held by the 1/20th Londons.

At 8.00pm, the two cavalry regiments rallied retiring men from the 45th and 46th Brigades, re-entering and clearing Loos village and re-establishing their position on Hill 70's lower slopes.

Finally, at 11.30pm, the remainder of the 3rd Cavalry Division moved to Loos, completing the relief of the 15th Division overnight.

On 26th September 1915 in the Hulluch area, the British forces experienced intense combat with varied success. At midnight, a robust German assault against the 1/South Wales Borderers near the Vermelles–Hulluch road was effectively repulsed, resulting in significant losses for the attackers. However, at 1:00 am, the German 117th Division launched a surprise attack against the forward positions of the 7th and 9th Divisions, causing considerable disruption and ultimately leading to the British loss of the Quarries despite efforts to halt further enemy advancement.

By 7:00 am, a unit dubbed Carter's Force, dispatched from the 2nd Division, arrived with the objective of recapturing the Quarries. They faced delays and reassignments in their operation, complicating their efforts. Around 9:00 am, a German counterattack at Bois Hugo was brought to a halt, but not without inflicting considerable confusion and losses on the British 63rd Brigade. The German forces continued their aggressive stance, capturing Chalet Wood by 10:30 am and forcing the 63rd Brigade into a chaotic retreat.

At 10:50 am, the 21st and 24th Divisions received vague orders to advance without specific objectives. This led to a disorganized and exhausting forward movement, resulting in heavy casualties and minimal territorial gains. By 12:20 pm, the advances of the 63rd and remnants of the 64th Brigades had collapsed, with survivors retreating under pressure.

The afternoon saw a continuation of the retreats, notably with the 21st and 24th Divisions falling back, leaving only isolated groups holding onto advanced positions. Carter's Force launched a delayed attack on the Quarries at 4:00 pm, achieving limited success and halting 200 yards short of their goal after incurring heavy casualties.

In the Auchy area, the 73rd Brigade, severely exhausted from lack of food, water, and rest for 48 hours, maintained their positions east of Fosse 8 under relentless enemy shelling that started at noon and continued through the afternoon and evening.

The day was characterized by fierce battles, significant losses, and minimal advancement for the British forces, reflecting the harsh realities of trench warfare and the challenges of coordinating large-scale attacks under such conditions.

By nightfall on 26th September 1915, the battlefields near Loos and Hulluch witnessed significant shifts. The battered 15th, 21st, and 24th Divisions were being relieved by the 3rd Cavalry and Guards Divisions. While the area was relatively secure from immediate attack, the enemy still controlled key positions like Hill 70 and the Quarries. Concerns grew over the condition of troops at Fosse 8, who were vulnerable to further attacks. Congested roads hindered movement and supply efforts, and hidden enemy soldiers were still being discovered in Loos village. First Army issued consolidation orders at 11.30pm, forming a general reserve from the relieved 9th and 15th Divisions, and XI Corps was tasked with planning to recapture Hill 70.

On 27th September, in the Loos area, the 3rd Guards Brigade faced a heavy artillery barrage on the Vermelles–Loos road, resulting in many casualties. The Welsh Guards' attack on Hill 70 was repelled by machine-gun fire. Meanwhile, the 47th Division successfully captured Chalk Pit Copse.

In Hulluch, the 2nd Guards Brigade advanced under smoke cover to Chalk

Pit Wood and the Chalk Pit, but their further push was halted by machine-gun fire from Bois Hugo. Auchy area witnessed heavy enemy shelling throughout the night, and an attack by the 1/Royal Berkshires against Fosse 8 was stopped 70 yards from the objective. German infantry attacks were successfully repelled by the 2/Wiltshires and 73rd Brigade, though they suffered heavy losses.

By noon, German forces pushed against the 12/Royal Fusiliers, forcing a withdrawal to establish a new defensive line. Major-General Thesiger of the 9th Division was killed while surveying the situation. First Army HQ learned about the loss of Fosse 8 by 2.00pm, leading to the cancellation of a planned Guards Division attack on Hill 70. Major-General Bulfin arrived to command the sector, ordering a counter-attack using the depleted 26th Brigade, which joined the 73rd Brigade at the Redoubt.

The Canal area saw the cancellation of a planned attack by the 2nd Division due to gas lingering in British positions.

By nightfall on 27th September, the British front was thinly held, with exhausted attacking units and scattered reserves. Key positions at Fosse 8, the Quarries, and Hill 70 were lost, and German forces were strengthening as the French Tenth Army failed to occupy their reserves. This signaled a need for the British to regroup and reassess their strategy.

Between 28th September and 3rd October, there was a lull in the fighting. Discussions between British GHQ and French Tenth Army HQ led to a strategic realignment, with the French relieving the 47th Division and the British securing Hill 70. Sir John French promised to supply the 12th and 46th Divisions to replace the 21st and 24th. The French Tenth Army reached Hill 140 on Vimy Ridge, drawing German reserves away from the British front.

From 28th September to 13th October 1915, the Loos area and surrounding regions witnessed continuous and intense fighting. On 28th September, the 85th Brigade of the 28th Division, supported by the 83rd Brigade, faced heavy casualties in fierce trench combat around the Hohenzollern Redoubt. The 2nd Guards Brigade's attack on Puits 14 bis was halted due to severe losses from machine-gun fire.

By 29th September, the struggle in the Hohenzollern Redoubt persisted. Units of the 22nd Brigade were finally relieved, but a night enemy attack led to the loss of parts of Gun Trench. The Loos area saw consolidation of positions, with preparations for the withdrawal of the 21st and 24th Divisions. The 142nd Brigade of the 47th Division took over positions in Loos and on Hill 70, facing heavy German artillery.

The French offensive in Champagne stalled on 30th September. Plans for renewing the Loos offensive were detailed, aiming for a 4th October start, but bad weather and traffic delayed French units in relieving the British.

From 1st to 3rd October, intense close-quarter battles occurred in the Hohenzollern Redoubt, with British forces losing all but Big Willie Trench. The 12th Division, replacing the Guards Brigades, worked on trench preparations amid heavy shelling that claimed the life of Major-General Wing. The offensive's renewal was postponed to 6th October.

On 8th October, a German counter-attack commenced with a bombardment across the front. The Allied right managed to halt the German assault, but British positions at the Quarries and Fosse 8 faced intense enemy bombing. The 2/Coldstream Guards and other units repelled attacks, while the 37th Brigade of the 12th Division briefly captured Gun Trench before withdrawing due to a lack of grenades.

Preparations to renew the offensive continued from 9th to 13th October, with the installation of new gas cylinders and successful captures of enemy positions by the Guards, despite heavy German artillery and mortar fire.

The French Tenth Army's attack on Vimy Ridge on 11th October, alongside a local action at the Double Crassier, resulted in heavy losses and no significant gains. Joffre formally ended the Artois offensive on 15th October due to dwindling ammunition supplies.

On 12th October, Sir John French communicated to Haig that the French Tenth Army would not advance further, leading the First Army to focus on securing key localities and maintaining readiness for future offensives. This period marked a time of relentless fighting, strategic adjustments, and significant casualties, with the front lines experiencing minimal changes despite the efforts.

On 13th October 1915, the British offensive at Loos resumed under favorable weather conditions for gas deployment. XI Corps aimed to recapture the Quarries and Fosse 8, while IV Corps focused on consolidating their line. Despite the 46th Division's lack of familiarity with the terrain and congestion in the trenches, they were instructed to attack aggressively, mimicking the costly tactics of the 9th Division from 25th September.

By noon, a heavy British bombardment targeted enemy trenches, but it proved insufficiently damaging. Concurrently, gas and smoke were discharged across three fronts, signaling an imminent infantry attack. The 1st Division's assault along the Lens–La Bassée road faced intense enemy fire, resulting in 1,200 casualties and a withdrawal after dark. The 12th (Eastern) Division's attack between Gun Trench and the Quarries encountered fierce resistance, with the 7/East Surreys gaining a foothold in Gun Trench, but other units suffering heavy losses due to unexpected enemy trench positions and thin smoke screens.

The 46th (North Midland) Division's assault faced immediate and devastating enemy fire. The 137th Brigade's advance was annihilated, and the 138th Brigade, although initially successful, suffered high casualties from crossfire and halted within ten minutes. The Division lost over 3,500 men without significant gains. The 2nd Division's attack towards Little Willie also faced heavy fire, with minimal success.

By approximately 8.00pm, XI Corps decided to evacuate the Eastern face of the Hohenzollern Redoubt and construct a new trench, which was completed overnight by the 1/Monmouths and reinforced by the 139th Brigade. An enemy bombing attack early on 14th October was repelled by the Sherwood Foresters.

The Loos offensive, marked by continuous minor skirmishes and discussions between French and Haig, effectively ended after this operation. The British army suffered over 61,000 casualties, including 7,766 deaths. The losses were particularly severe among Scottish units and New Army units, who, despite being new to the battlefield, proved their valor. The significant loss of experienced troops and officers represented a serious blow to the army's effectiveness.

Second Battle of Champagne

On the fateful day of 25 September 1915, a significant historical military event unfolded as the Second and Fourth Armies of France's Groupe d'armées du Centre (GAC, Central Army Group) launched a large-scale offensive. This operation, beginning at 9:15 a.m., saw twenty divisions striking with full force, each division spread across a front ranging from 1,500 to 2,000 yards. In a well-coordinated effort, a second wave comprising seven divisions followed closely, supplemented by a strategic reserve of one infantry division and six cavalry divisions.

The German forces, comprising six divisions, were positioned in a robust defensive stance, with their troops spread across a front position and a more rearward Reserve Position (R-Stellung). The French artillery, aided by favorable weather conditions initially, gained an observational advantage. However, the elements soon turned hostile as heavy rain began to pour on the night of 24/25 September, persisting until midday, complicating the battlefield dynamics.

Despite these challenges, the French forces achieved breakthroughs in four critical areas of the German front position. Two of these penetrations advanced deep enough to reach the R-Stellung. Yet, progress was halted due to uncut barbed wire barriers, which proved to be an insurmountable obstacle for the French troops. Complicating matters, in certain sectors, the French artillery barrage inadvertently continued even after capturing the first German line, leading to unintended French casualties.

This battle was marked by significant achievements and losses for the French. They managed to capture 14,000 German prisoners and seize several artillery pieces. However, this victory came at a high cost in terms of French casualties. The Germans, having anticipated the French attack, were able to observe the French preparations from their advantageous positions on higher ground. Consequently, they were well-prepared for the offensive.

The main defensive efforts of the Germans were concentrated at the R-Stellung, where they had strategically relocated the bulk of their field artillery. Additionally, a simultaneous attack by the French Third Army on the Aisne failed to gain any ground. German reserves, under the adept command of General Falkenhayn, swiftly moved to reinforce any breaches in their lines, demonstrating the effectiveness of their defensive strategy.

The strategic decisions and actions of French commander-in-chief Joseph Joffre played a crucial role, particularly in the context of the battles in Champagne. Joffre's tactical acumen was demonstrated when he allocated two reserve divisions to the Central Army Group (GAC) and issued a directive to the Eastern Army Group (GAE) to transfer the majority of their 75 mm field gun ammunition to the Second and Fourth armies, retaining only 500 rounds per gun for themselves. This decision underlined the importance Joffre placed on the operations of these armies.

The narrative of this period is marked by relentless combat and shifting frontlines. On 26 September, under Joffre's orders, the French forces launched another vigorous attack. They managed to advance close to the German R-Stellung (Reserve Position) along a front stretching 7.5 miles and even secured a strategic foothold in one area. This attack resulted in the capture of an additional 2,000 German troops. However, the battles from 27 to 29 September against the R-Stellung were characterized by fierce and fluctuating engagements. Although a breakthrough was achieved on 28 September, the Germans counter-attacked the following day and regained much of the lost ground. This area was predominantly on a reverse slope, which significantly hindered the French artillery's ability to observe and target effectively.

Recognizing the challenges and the need for more ammunition, Joffre made the prudent decision to suspend the offensive temporarily. He instructed that the recently captured territory be fortified and that cavalry units be pulled back. This pause was utilized for consolidation and preparation for further actions. From 30 September to 5 October, smaller-scale French assaults continued against protruding German positions, maintaining pressure on the enemy.

The tide of the battle witnessed a significant shift on 3 October. Joffre, assessing the situation, decided to abandon the pursuit of a breakthrough in the Champagne region. Instead, he instructed local commanders to transition to a strategy of attrition. This marked a change in the nature of the combat, focusing on wearing down the enemy rather than achieving rapid territorial gains. The offensive was formally concluded on 6 November. Despite the advance of the French line by approximately 4 kilometers, the cost was steep: around 100,000 more French and British casualties (including those in Artois) than the Germans.

The scale of the French effort in Champagne was immense, involving 35 divisions against the German equivalent of 16 divisions. During this intense period of warfare, the Fourth, Second, and Third French armies expended a staggering 2,842,400 field artillery and 577,700 heavy shells. This massive use of artillery, coupled with the consumption during the Third Battle of Artois to the north, resulted in the exhaustion of the French stock of ammunition. This campaign stands as a testament to the grueling nature of trench warfare and the immense resources and sacrifices involved in these monumental battles of the First World War.

After the intense engagements of the autumn offensive, the French military entered a period of recalibration and reflection. The offensive had revealed the limitations of French tactics and equipment in the demanding environment of trench warfare. This realization prompted a pause, during which the French focused on rejuvenating their forces, replenishing lost personnel, and amassing additional equipment and ammunition.

A critical challenge faced by the French artillery during the offensive was its inability to neutralize the German artillery effectively. The German guns, often strategically positioned on the reverse slopes of the Champagne hills, remained largely unscathed, undermining the French efforts. Amidst the brutal realities of warfare, some French regiments displayed remarkable esprit de corps, launching attacks with their regimental bands playing and flags unfurled, a vivid testament to their bravery and morale.

On 22 October, Commander-in-Chief Joseph Joffre presented an optimistic perspective of the offensive. He asserted that it had yielded significant tactical victories, inflicted heavy casualties on the Germans, and established moral superiority over the enemy. However, Joffre acknowledged that the shortfall in artillery firepower had been a critical factor in failing to meet the strategic goals of the offensive. Emphasizing the necessity to divert German forces from the Eastern Front, Joffre advocated for continued offensive operations. However, he also advised maintaining minimal troop presence in the front lines during the winter and called for the development of a new strategic approach.

The foundations for the French offensives in 1915 were deeply rooted in military theory, as outlined in "But et conditions d'une action offensive d'ensemble" (Purpose and Conditions of Mass Offensive Action, 16 April 1915) and its subsequent iteration, Note 5779. These documents, derived from frontline reports since 1914, provided detailed guidelines on modern warfare tactics, including infiltration tactics, rolling barrages, and the systematic use of poison gas. They advocated for a new concept of continuous battle, characterized by gradual, step-by-step advances through successive German defensive positions. The approach emphasized methodical, sustained attacks aimed at steadily depleting German infantry reserves. This strategy was designed to gradually wear down the German defenses, eventually facilitating a breakthrough. Importantly, this methodical approach was seen as a way to preserve French infantry while penetrating the deeper German defenses established since 1914. This period marked a significant evolution in French military strategy, reflecting a shift towards more calculated and sustained forms of warfare.

During the autumn battles, the Allies held a significant numerical advantage over the Westheer, the German army in the west, with an excess of 600 infantry battalions. Despite this, they failed to achieve a breakthrough. The pattern was clear: after the initial day of an attack, German reinforcements would arrive, rendering a breakthrough unattainable. Some German divisions, although recently returned from the Eastern Front, were exhausted and contributed little to the defense.

General Erich von Falkenhayn, the German commander-in-chief, had not fully anticipated the scale of the offensive. He spread the Oberste Heeresleitung (OHL, German army high command) reserve across the entire Western Front instead of concentrating it in potentially vulnerable areas. In contrast, French reviews of their offensive highlighted that their reserves were positioned close to the front, poised to capitalize on any breakthrough. However, these reserves ended up congesting the battlefield alongside the leading divisions, complicating logistics and suffering heavy casualties during delays.

The French faced several critical challenges: breakdowns in communication left commanders uninformed of the evolving situation, artillery support was poorly coordinated with infantry movements, and bad weather grounded their artillery-observation aircraft. Many French commanders arrived at a sobering conclusion: achieving a breakthrough in a single attack was unrealistic; it would require multiple, well-planned battles to wear down the German defenses and reopen the possibility of mobile warfare.

The German analysis, as detailed in the report "Experiences of the 3rd Army in the Autumn Battles in the Champagne, 1915," acknowledged weaknesses in their defensive strategy. The French artillery had inflicted severe damage on German field fortifications and breached their barbed wire defenses. However, the German second position remained largely intact. The French initial breakthrough lost momentum due to disorganization among the troops crowding forward, impeding coordinated attacks. The report also noted that French prisoners indicated a lack of systematic reserve deployment to exploit breakthroughs, suggesting that such an achievement was still within reach.

Despite their limited troop numbers, the Germans successfully employed smaller, rapid counter-attacks (Gegenstösse) against the weakened and disorganized French forces. The German report recommended maintaining fewer troops on the front line and emphasized the need for cooperation among all military branches, assistance from neighboring sectors, and the exploitation of flanking maneuvers.

Falkenhayn's reflections in his 1919 memoirs highlighted a critical insight from the autumn battles: quantity alone was insufficient to overcome well-fortified defenses. He dismissed the idea of mass breakthroughs, even with overwhelming force, as unlikely to succeed. These experiences led Falkenhayn to rethink his strategy, culminating in the Battle of Verdun in 1916. There, he aimed to force the French into a similar costly stalemate as experienced in the Second Battle of Champagne, seeking a decisive outcome in Germany's favor. This period of the war underscored the transition from traditional warfare tactics to those defined by entrenched positions and attrition, reshaping military strategies for years to come.

II

Italian Front

Battles of the Isonzo

In April 1915, a clandestine agreement known as the Treaty of London was forged, where Italy was enticed by the Allied powers with the promise of acquiring territories from the Austro-Hungarian Empire, regions predominantly inhabited by ethnic Slovenes and Austrian Germans. This diplomatic maneuver was a critical move in the complex chessboard of World War I.

At the heart of this unfolding drama was Italian commander Luigi Cadorna, a military tactician with a strong belief in frontal assaults. Cadorna, dismissive of the effectiveness of machine guns as evidenced on the Western Front, ambitiously planned to breach the Slovenian plateau, capture the city of Ljubljana, and pose a direct threat to Vienna. This audacious strategy turned the area stretching from the northern Adriatic Sea to the sources of the Isonzo River into a battleground for twelve intense battles, marking a significant chapter in the war.

These operations had a ripple effect, compelling the Austro-Hungarians to redirect a portion of their military might from the Eastern Front to the mountainous terrains around the Isonzo River. This strategic shift was a testament to the Italian assault's impact on the broader war dynamics.

The Soča River, spanning sixty miles and lying entirely within the borders of Austria-Hungary, ran parallel to the Italian frontier. From the Vršič and Predil passes in the Julian Alps to the Adriatic Sea, the river's course encompassed a vital corridor – the "Ljubljana Gate." This narrow passageway, dramatically widening north of Gorizia, offered a strategic link between Northern Italy and Central Europe, traversing the Vipava Valley and skirting the northeastern edge of the Karst Plateau towards Inner Carniola and Ljubljana.

The fierce battles that ensued over this corridor were marked by gradual territorial shifts. By the autumn of 1915, Italian forces had gained a mere mile, and it wasn't until October 1917 that some Austro-Hungarian mountains and several square miles of land had oscillated between the two warring sides. Despite the intense efforts, Italian troops were unable to reach the port city of Trieste, General Cadorna's primary objective, until the Armistice was declared. This protracted struggle along the Isonzo Front not only shaped the course of World War I but also left an indelible mark on the history of the region.In April 1915, a clandestine agreement known as the Treaty of London was forged, where Italy was enticed by the Allied powers with the promise of acquiring territories from the Austro-Hungarian Empire, regions predominantly inhabited by ethnic Slovenes and Austrian Germans. This diplomatic maneuver was a critical move in the complex chessboard of World War I.

At the heart of this unfolding drama was Italian commander Luigi Cadorna, a military tactician with a strong belief in frontal assaults. Cadorna, dismissive of the effectiveness of machine guns as evidenced on the Western Front, ambitiously planned to breach the Slovenian plateau, capture the city of Ljubljana, and pose a direct threat to Vienna. This audacious strategy turned the area stretching from the northern Adriatic Sea to the sources of the Isonzo River into a battleground for twelve intense battles, marking a significant chapter in the war.

These operations had a ripple effect, compelling the Austro-Hungarians to redirect a portion of their military might from the Eastern Front to the mountainous terrains around the Isonzo River. This strategic shift was a testament to the Italian assault's impact on the broader war dynamics.

The Soča River, spanning sixty miles and lying entirely within the borders of Austria-Hungary, ran parallel to the Italian frontier. From the Vršič and Predil passes in the Julian Alps to the Adriatic Sea, the river's course encompassed a vital corridor – the "Ljubljana Gate." This narrow passageway, dramatically widening north of Gorizia, offered a strategic link between Northern Italy and Central Europe, traversing the Vipava Valley and skirting the northeastern edge of the Karst Plateau towards Inner Carniola and Ljubljana.

The fierce battles that ensued over this corridor were marked by gradual territorial shifts. By the autumn of 1915, Italian forces had gained a mere mile, and it wasn't until October 1917 that some Austro-Hungarian mountains and several square miles of land had oscillated between the two warring sides. Despite the intense efforts, Italian troops were unable to reach the port city of Trieste, General Cadorna's primary objective, until the Armistice was declared. This protracted struggle along the Isonzo Front not only shaped the course of World War I but also left an indelible mark on the history of the region.

First Battle of Isonzo

The Italian Army's primary objective during World War I was a bold and ambitious one: to expel the Austrians from their fortified positions along the Isonzo River, known locally as Soča, and its surrounding mountains, with the ultimate goal of capturing the strategically significant port of Trieste. This endeavor, laden with tactical challenges and high stakes, marked a critical phase in the Italian campaign.

Despite enjoying a 2:1 numerical superiority, the Italians faced an uphill battle, both literally and figuratively. Commander Luigi Cadorna, leading the Italian forces, resorted to a strategy of frontal assaults, prefaced by impressive yet brief artillery barrages. However, these tactics proved ineffective against the Austro-Hungarians, who were entrenched in uphill positions fortified with barbed wire, offering them a significant defensive advantage.

The Italian Army did not lack initial successes. They made notable advances, partially capturing Monte Nero (Monte Krn), seizing Monte Colowrat, and securing strategic heights around Plezzo. But these gains fell short of their ultimate goal. The Austro-Hungarian troops, firmly entrenched on the high ground between Tolmino and the Isonzo, formed a robust defensive line that later served as a springboard for the Caporetto Offensive.

The most intense combat occurred around Gorizia, a battleground marked by the formidable natural barriers of rivers and mountains. The Austro-Hungarians, further strengthening their position, constructed bastions at Oslavia and Podgora. Here, the Italian troops, including the Re and Casale Brigades, engaged in grueling urban warfare, navigating street-by-street combat under relentless artillery fire. Although they managed to penetrate the suburbs of Gorizia, further progress was stifled, and they were eventually repelled.

On the Karst Plateau south of Gorizia, the Italians made modest inroads at Sagrado and Redipuglia but were unable to capitalize significantly on these positions.

Meanwhile, on the Austrian-Hungarian side, two commanders emerged as key figures. Major General Géza Lukachich von Somorja, commanding the 5th Mountain Brigade, played a pivotal role in recapturing Redipuglia. Similarly, Major General Novak von Arienti, leading the 1st Mountain Brigade, was instrumental in reclaiming Hill 383, a critical vantage point overlooking Plave.

In early July, the Austro-Hungarian Fifth Army, under General Svetozar Boroević, received a significant boost with two additional divisions. This reinforcement was a turning point, effectively stalling the Italian advance and preventing any breakthrough in the Austro-Hungarian lines.

Ultimately, the Italian gains were modest and came at a great cost. In the northern sector, they managed to capture the heights over Bovec (Mount Kanin), while in the southern sector, they secured the westernmost ridges of the Karst Plateau near Fogliano Redipuglia and Monfalcone. These achievements, while notable, fell short of the strategic objectives, highlighting the challenges and complexities of mountain warfare during World War I.

Second Battle of Isonzo

In the aftermath of the First Battle of the Isonzo, which had ended in disappointment for the Italian forces just two weeks prior, Commander-in-Chief Luigi Cadorna was poised for a renewed offensive against the Austro-Hungarian lines. Unwavering in his military resolve, Cadorna planned a more formidable approach, bolstering his strategy with heavier artillery support, aiming to break the stalemate that had characterized the previous engagement.

Despite the setback in the First Battle of the Isonzo, the overarching strategy of the Italian offensive underwent minimal alterations. One notable adjustment involved General Frugoni's Second Army, which, in this new phase, was relegated to conducting demonstrative attacks across its front. This tactical shift was designed to divert attention and resources, creating an opening for the main thrust of the operation.

The primary responsibility fell upon the Duke of Aosta's Third Army, which was tasked with a critical and ambitious objective: the capture of Mount San

Michele and Mount Cosich. The success of this operation was pivotal, as it would sever the Austro-Hungarian defensive line and pave a path directly to the strategic city of Gorizia. Achieving this would not only signify a significant territorial gain but also serve as a morale booster for the Italian troops.

Cadorna's tactics, though straightforward, were unrelenting in their execution. The plan was to initiate the assault with an intense artillery bombardment, softening the enemy defenses. Following this, the Italian troops were to launch a frontal assault, a daring and direct approach aimed at breaching the Austro-Hungarian lines. They were to navigate through the perilous landscapes laced with barbed-wire fences, and engage in close-quarters combat to secure the trenches.

However, the Italian Army faced significant logistical challenges that undermined their numerical advantage. The dearth of essential war materiel was a critical impediment. Shortages ranged from rifles and artillery shells to basic equipment like shears for cutting barbed wire. This scarcity of resources was a stark reminder of the harsh realities of World War I, where the outcome of battles was often dictated not just by strategy and bravery, but also by the availability of critical supplies and equipment.

In this complex tapestry of war, General Cadorna's resolve to carry out a frontal assault under such constraints underscored the relentless and often brutal nature of trench warfare. As the Italian forces prepared for this formidable undertaking, the shadows of the previous battle loomed large, setting the stage for a confrontation that would test the mettle of the Italian Army and shape the course of the war on the Italian Front.

The Karst Plateau, a rugged and unforgiving terrain, became the backdrop for a grueling and relentless series of close-quarter battles that saw the Italian Second and Third Armies locked in intense combat with the Austro-Hungarian forces. This battlefield was a scene of chaos and brutality, where every conceivable weapon and piece of debris was employed in the savage melee. The fighting here was not just a clash of armies, but a visceral struggle for survival, characterized by the use of bayonets, swords, knives, and even scraps of metal – anything that could be wielded in the frenzied hand-to-hand combat.

The Austro-Hungarian 20th Honvéd Infantry Division, facing the relentless onslaught of the Italian Army and grappling with the treacherous terrain of the Karst Plateau, suffered catastrophic losses. Two-thirds of its effective strength was decimated, leading to a harrowing rout. This breakdown in the Austro-Hungarian ranks was a stark testament to the ferocity of the Italian attacks and the unforgiving nature of the battlefield.

On the pivotal date of 25 July, the Italians achieved a significant strategic victory by capturing the Cappuccio Wood. This location, situated west of Mount San Michele, was not particularly steep but held immense tactical value. It overlooked a vast area, including the critical Austro-Hungarian bridgehead of Gorizia from the south, giving the Italians a vantage point of considerable importance.

Mount San Michele, a key objective in this theater of war, witnessed a brief period of Italian control. However, this success was short-lived. In a desperate and valiant counterattack led by Colonel Richter, commanding a group of elite regiments, the Austro-Hungarians managed to recapture the mount. This intense battle for Mount San Michele underscored the see-saw nature of the conflict on the Karst Plateau.

Further north, in the imposing Julian Alps, the Italians marked another tactical success by overrunning Mount Batognica, located above Kobarid (known historically as Caporetto). The capture of this mountain held substantial strategic importance for future battles, adding a new dimension to the ongoing conflict.

As the battle prolonged, both sides found themselves depleted, not just in manpower but also in essential supplies. The dwindling ammunition reserves eventually led to a wearied cessation of hostilities. The toll of this three-week-long battle was staggering, with total casualties amounting to approximately 91,000 men – 43,000 Italians and 48,000 Austro-Hungarians. This grim tally reflected the sheer intensity and devastation of the battle on the Karst Plateau, marking it as one of the most brutal episodes of the First World War.

Third Battle of Isonzo

The year's third major military offensive on the Italian Front unfolded in the eastern sector of Italy, aptly named the Third Battle of the Isonzo, following the naming convention established by the preceding two battles in the same region. This battle represented another chapter in the ongoing struggle between the Italian and Austro-Hungarian forces, each seeking to gain a decisive advantage in this tumultuous theatre of World War I.

The Italian forces, under the command of Luigi Cadorna, had a brief respite of approximately two and a half months following the grueling and casualty-heavy First and Second Battles of the Isonzo. This period was crucial for recuperation and reorganization. Recognizing the pivotal role of artillery in trench warfare, Cadorna significantly bolstered the Italian artillery capabilities, bringing the total number of artillery pieces to a formidable 1,250. This strategic enhancement was aimed at giving the Italian forces a much-needed edge in the upcoming confrontation.

Alongside the artillery upgrade, the Italian Army was also equipped with the newly issued Adrian Helmets. These helmets, while offering some degree of protection in specific scenarios, were generally regarded as marginally effective. Nevertheless, this represented an attempt to improve the safety and combat effectiveness of the Italian troops.

The primary objectives of the Italian offensive were ambitious and clearly defined. They aimed to seize the Austro-Hungarian bridgeheads at Bovec (known in Italian as Plezzo), Tolmin, and, if feasible, the strategically significant town of Gorizia. These targets were crucial for gaining territorial and tactical advantages in the region.

However, Cadorna's tactic of evenly distributing his forces along the entire length of the Soča (Isonzo) River front did not yield the desired results. This approach, while expansive, proved to be indecisive. The Austro-Hungarians, adept at adapting to the evolving battlefield dynamics, capitalized on this by concentrating their firepower in specific areas, thereby offsetting the Italian spread-out formation.

The focal points of the Italian attack were Mount Sabotino and Mount San Michele, both of which held significant strategic value. The capture of these locations was seen as essential for gaining the upper hand in the battle and for further advancing into enemy territory. As the Third Battle of the Isonzo commenced, the Italian forces, bolstered by their enhanced artillery and new helmets, faced the daunting task of breaking through the well-entrenched Austro-Hungarian defenses, setting the stage for yet another fierce and bloody engagement in the rugged terrain of the Isonzo front.

In the relentless pursuit of breakthroughs on the Isonzo front, the Italian forces, empowered by extensive artillery barrages, embarked on a strategic advance towards several key locations. Their target was the area around Plave (Plava in Italian), located near Kanal ob Soči, which lay beneath the southern expanse of the Banjšice Plateau (Bainsizza), and the critical position of Mount San Michele on the Karst Plateau. This move was part of a calculated effort to outmaneuver the Austro-Hungarian forces defending the city of Gorizia, a linchpin in the region's defensive network.

The plateau near San Michele transformed into a fierce battleground, witnessing relentless assaults and counterattacks. The Italian Third Army, committed to a push forward, engaged in intense combat with the Austro-Hungarian reinforcements. These reinforcements, drawn from the Eastern and Balkan fronts, were under the astute command of Svetozar Boroević, a commander renowned for his tactical acumen. The brutality and intensity of these confrontations led to staggering casualties on both sides, underscoring the high stakes and ferocity of this phase of the war.

Despite the heavy onslaught, the Austro-Hungarians, under Boroević's low-profile yet effective command, managed to maintain their positions. The losses they suffered, though significant, were overshadowed by the even higher toll on the Italian Army. This battle not only highlighted Boroević's tactical prowess but also the constrained nature of the front, where even minor territorial gains were achieved at a great cost.

The respite from this intense combat was fleeting, lasting barely two weeks. The Italian offensive, undeterred by the setbacks and driven by the strategic necessity of breaking the Austro-Hungarian lines, recommenced with renewed vigor.

In this renewed phase of the offensive, the Italians made some headway, momentarily gaining control of Mt. Sabotino. However, this success was short-lived as they faced a robust counter by the Austro-Hungarians. Meanwhile, the Third Army, advancing towards Mt. San Michele, encountered formidable resistance. Their attempts to circumvent the defenses guarding Gorizia were met with relentless machine gun fire, halting their progress.

While the Austro-Hungarians sustained fewer casualties in this stage of the battle compared to the Italians, the losses were proportionally significant for both sides. This parity in losses reflected the intense and evenly matched nature of the conflict, where each side's gains were countered by the other's resilience.

Fourth Battle of Isonzo

The fourth offensive in the series of the Isonzo battles, differing from its predecessors in June, July, and October, was a comparatively brief campaign. This episode is often seen as an extension of the previous offensives, owing to its proximity in time and similarity in tactics and objectives. However, this phase of the Isonzo battles had its distinct characteristics and challenges.

The bulk of the combat was concentrated around the strategic city of Gorizia and the rugged terrain of the Karst Plateau, yet the Italian forces distributed their efforts across the entire Isonzo front. The Italian Second Army, with its eyes firmly set on capturing Gorizia, managed to seize the hilly regions of Oslavia and San Floriano del Collio. These areas, overlooking the Soča (Isonzo) River and the city of Gorizia, were of immense tactical importance.

Meanwhile, the Italian Third Army, responsible for the remainder of the front stretching to the Adriatic Sea, engaged in a series of large-scale attacks. These assaults, marked by their intensity and the high toll of casualties, ultimately resulted in little territorial gain, underscoring the formidable nature of the Austro-Hungarian defenses.

A focal point of these clashes was Mount Sei Busi, a site that had already witnessed severe fighting. The Italian forces launched five separate assaults on this position, each time being repelled with no significant progress, a testament to the stubborn resistance of the Austro-Hungarian defenders and the challenging topography of the battlefield.

As the offensive continued, the intensity of the fighting escalated, reaching its zenith towards the end of November. This period saw the bridgehead of Tolmin (Italian: Tolmino) becoming a hotbed of activity, subjected to heavy bombardment by both sides. The casualty rate soared, marking this phase as one of the most brutal of the entire campaign.

By the first half of December, the nature of the conflict shifted. The massive frontal assaults that had characterized the earlier stages of the battle gave way to smaller, more sporadic skirmishes. This change in the pattern of combat was partly influenced by the onset of severe winter conditions in the mountains of the Karst Plateau, which, along with supply shortages, significantly hindered large-scale operations.

An unofficial truce emerged with the arrival of the harsh winter, bringing a temporary halt to the hostilities. The fighting's intensity and the heavy losses incurred prompted the Austro-Hungarian High Command to seek reinforcements. In a significant turn of events, they requested assistance from the German Empire, which had not yet formally entered the war against Italy. This request set the stage for German intervention on the Italian front, a development that would come to fruition in the subsequent Eleventh Battle of the Isonzo, marking a new and critical phase in the conflict.

III

Eastern Front

Siege of Przemyśl

In the early days of the First World War, a significant and complex military campaign unfolded in Eastern Europe. In August 1914, as Europe was plunged into chaos, the Russian Empire initiated a bold military operation on two critical fronts. On one hand, Russian forces launched an ambitious offensive against German East Prussia, while simultaneously moving against Galicia, a vast and strategically vital province of the Austro-Hungarian Empire, located at the crossroads of modern-day Poland and Ukraine.

The Russian advance into German territory was swiftly countered and repelled, marking an early setback. However, the story was markedly different in the Galician campaign, which witnessed a more favorable outcome for the Russians. The Russian General Nikolai Ivanov, displaying strategic acumen, led a forceful campaign against the Austro-Hungarian forces commanded by Conrad von Hötzendorf. This confrontation, known as the Battle of Galicia, turned into a decisive victory for the Russians. The Austro-Hungarian front, crumbling under the relentless Russian assault, was forced to retreat a staggering 160 kilometers back to the defensive sanctuary of the Carpathian Mountains. Amidst this retreat, the fortress of Przemyśl stood as a solitary beacon of Austro-Hungarian resistance, the only stronghold to resist the Russian onslaught. By the end of September 1914, this fortress found itself completely encircled by Russian forces, becoming an isolated pocket of defiance.

The siege of Przemyśl soon evolved into a microcosm of the wider war, reflecting not only military but also the cultural and ethnic complexities of the Austro-Hungarian Empire. The fortress, its strategic significance magnified, became a focal point of the Eastern Front. In an extraordinary feat of military engineering, the defenders constructed extensive fortifications, digging over 50 kilometers of new trenches and utilizing approximately 1,000 kilometers of barbed wire to create a formidable network of seven defense lines encircling the town. Within these defenses, a sizeable garrison of 127,000 military personnel, bolstered by 18,000 civilians, prepared to withstand the siege laid by six Russian divisions.

The defense of Przemyśl was a vivid illustration of the ethnic diversity of the Austro-Hungarian Empire. The orders issued within the fortress had to be translated into fifteen different languages, catering to a garrison composed of Austrians, Poles, Jews, and Ruthenians (Ukrainians). This melting pot of cultures and languages, however, also brought to the fore underlying ethnic tensions. The besieged town, subjected to relentless artillery bombardment, became a crucible of suffering. As casualties mounted and the specter of starvation loomed, the strains of war exacerbated the mutual distrust and ethnic tensions among the defenders, adding a complex social dimension to the military challenge they faced.

On the 24th of September, the stage was set for a pivotal event in the Eastern Front of World War I. General Radko Dimitriev, at the helm of the Russian Third Army, initiated the siege of a key fortress with six divisions under his command. The opening move of Dimitriev's strategy was marked by a short but intense artillery bombardment, swiftly followed by an order for a comprehensive assault on the fortress defenses.

The fortress, a stronghold of strategic importance, was robustly defended by a formidable force of 120,000 soldiers. These troops were under the leadership of Hermann Kusmanek von Burgneustädten, a commander known for his resilience and tactical acumen. Despite the overwhelming odds and the firepower at their disposal, the Russian offensive encountered stiff resistance. Over the course of three grueling days, the Russian forces launched relentless attacks, but their efforts were met with staunch defense, leading to a costly stalemate. The toll of this intense engagement was heavy, with the Russians incurring approximately 40,000 casualties without making significant headway.

Meanwhile, the dynamics of the Eastern Front were rapidly evolving. During the Battle of the Vistula River, a significant development unfolded as Svetozar Boroevic von Bojna's Third Army, a unit of the Austro-Hungarian forces, commenced its advance towards the besieged fortress, aiming to provide crucial reinforcement. The pressure on the fortress intensified on the 5th of October with continued Russian assaults, this time under the command of General Scherbakov. This phase included a major offensive on the 7th of October, an attempt to break the deadlock.

However, the situation took a turn as the Austro-Hungarian forces drew nearer, compelling the Russians to reassess their strategy. With the advancement of the Austro-Hungarian Third Army, the Russian assault was abruptly called off. In a dramatic turn of events, on the 9th of October, a cavalry unit from the Austro-Hungarian Third Army made a breakthrough, entering the fortress that had been under siege. This development marked a significant shift in the balance of power, and by the 12th of October, the main body of the Third Army had arrived, bolstering the defense and morale of the besieged fortress.

Following their setbacks in the Battle of the Vistula River, the combined forces of the German and Austro-Hungarian armies found themselves in a strategic retreat westward by the end of October. The situation in the besieged fortress of Przemyśl was becoming increasingly dire. On November 4th, in a telling sign of the worsening conditions, an order was issued for civilians to evacuate the fortress, a move underscoring the severity of the siege.

The 10th of November marked the onset of the second siege of Przemyśl. This phase was led by the Russian 11th Army under the command of General Andrei Nikolaevich Selivanov. In contrast to his predecessor Dimitriev's tactics, Selivanov opted for a strategy of attrition. Eschewing direct frontal assaults, he focused on encircling and starving the garrison into submission. By mid-December, the Russian forces intensified their campaign, unleashing relentless artillery bombardment on the fortress, with the aim of forcing a surrender.

The harsh winter of 1914-1915 compounded the misery of the besieged forces. The Habsburg armies, despite their persistent efforts to reach and relieve the fortress, were hampered by brutal weather conditions, leading to significant losses primarily due to frostbite and disease. However, their attempts to break through to Przemyśl were consistently thwarted.

In February 1915, Svetozar Boroevic spearheaded yet another concerted effort to relieve the fortress. Despite these renewed attempts, by the end of the month, all relief operations had been effectively neutralized. Realizing the futility of further rescue efforts, Conrad von Hötzendorf, the Austro-Hungarian Chief of the General Staff, informed Hermann Kusmanek von Burgneustädten that no additional attempts would be made to break the siege. This decision was a critical blow to the morale of the defenders. Meanwhile, Selivanov, now bolstered by sufficient artillery resources, intensified his efforts to subdue the fortress.

On March 13th, the Russian forces achieved a significant breakthrough, overrunning the northern defenses of Przemyśl. In a desperate bid to hold off the Russian advance, Kusmanek organized a makeshift line of defense, buying enough time to destroy any resources within the city that could benefit the enemy upon capture. On March 19th, in a last-ditch effort, Kusmanek ordered a breakout attempt, but these sallies were decisively repulsed, forcing a retreat back into the city.

With the situation becoming untenable and the fortress stripped of any useful resources, Kusmanek was left with no viable option but to capitulate. On March 22nd, a significant chapter in the siege came to a close as the remaining garrison, comprising 117,000 personnel, including nine generals, ninety-three senior staff officers, 2,500 other officers, and the Hungarian war poet Geza Gyoni, surrendered to the Russian forces.

The personal accounts from the besieged city of Przemyśl during World War I offer a raw and unfiltered glimpse into the realities of life under siege. Among these accounts are diaries and notebooks, which have survived the ravages of time and war, providing invaluable insights into the human dimension of this historical episode.

One such diary, belonging to Josef Tomann, an Austrian who was conscripted as a junior doctor, paints a grim picture of the conditions within the hospitals. Tomann's entries reveal troubling aspects of the garrison officers' behavior, noting the recruitment of teenage girls as nurses. Despite their official role, these young recruits, earning 120 crowns a month with free meals, were often subjected to exploitation. Tomann laments their treatment, noting their primary function seemed to cater to the desires of officers and, disturbingly, some doctors. His account further details the rampant spread of venereal diseases among the officers, a testament to the moral decay and desperation within the besieged city.

Another diary, that of Helena Jablonska, a middle-aged, relatively affluent Polish woman, offers a different perspective. Her entries expose the underlying class, antisemitic, and racial tensions that simmered in Przemyśl. Jablonska's observations are candid and often prejudiced, particularly towards Jewish residents. She accuses them of profiteering from the plight of soldiers and hurriedly attempting to conceal their wealth and identities as the city's fall became imminent. Her diary entries from March 18, 1915, are particularly telling, illustrating the heightened sense of panic and distrust among different communities.

The eventual capture of Przemyśl by the Imperial Russian Army in March led to further horrors. Jablonska's notes document a violent pogrom unleashed by Tsarist soldiers against the Jewish population. She describes the Cossacks attacking Jewish individuals as they headed to the synagogue, creating an atmosphere of despair and fear. This tragic episode highlights the additional layer of ethnic violence that compounded the suffering caused by the siege.

In addition to these harrowing personal accounts, the sieges of Przemyśl saw innovative methods of communication. Airmail flights were utilized during both sieges, with postcards and military mail being flown out of the city on twenty-seven occasions. One flight, which ended in a forced landing, resulted in the mail being confiscated by the Russians and sent to Saint Petersburg for postal censorship. Furthermore, balloon mail, including both manned and unmanned paper balloons, was a novel tactic employed to carry messages out of the city. Pigeon mail was also used as a means to send messages, demonstrating the varied and ingenious methods of communication adopted during the sieges.

The capture of Przemyśl marked a turning point on the Eastern Front during World War I, sparking speculations and expectations of a major Russian offensive into Hungary. However, contrary to these anticipations, such an offensive never materialized. Despite this, the fall of Przemyśl dealt a severe blow to the morale of the Austro-Hungarian Empire. The psychological impact was compounded by the fact that the fortress, originally intended to be manned by a garrison of 50,000, ultimately saw over 110,000 Austro-Hungarian troops surrendering. This loss was far more substantial than initially foreseen, highlighting the strategic and symbolic significance of the fortress.

Despite Russian control, the situation in Przemyśl and the broader region of Galicia remained fluid. It wasn't until the summer of 1915 that the Gorlice–Tarnów offensive successfully pushed back the Russian front, returning Przemyśl into Austro-Hungarian hands. This shift in control, however, was temporary. By October 1918, amidst the final throes of the Austro-Hungarian Empire, Eastern Galicia separated and became part of the newly established independent state of Poland.

The Austro-Hungarian army's efforts to relieve the besieged fortress of Przemyśl were marked by a series of disastrous campaigns. These attempts, characterized by insufficient supplies and outnumbered forces, resulted in a series of failed offensives through the treacherous terrain of the Carpathian Mountains. The period from January to April 1915 saw staggering casualties, officially reported at 800,000. Notably, these losses were predominantly due to harsh weather conditions and disease rather than direct combat. While Russian forces also suffered heavy casualties, they were relatively better positioned to replenish their ranks and were somewhat compensated by the capture of 117,000 Austro-Hungarian troops at the end of the siege.

In total, the siege of Przemyśl and the subsequent attempts to relieve it extracted a devastating toll on the Austro-Hungarian army. Over a million casualties were incurred, inflicting irreversible damage on the military capabilities and morale of the Habsburg forces. The empire increasingly found itself reliant on German support, both on the Eastern Front and in the Balkans, a dependency that underscored its weakening position in the war.

Battle of Humin-Bolimów

On the frosty morning of January 16, 1915, amidst the harrowing backdrop of World War I, a significant military engagement unfolded near Borzymów, south of the Eastern Front. The German 4th Infantry Division, known for their disciplined tactics and formidable presence, initiated a series of aggressive attacks against the Russian lines. This particular day marked a grim milestone in warfare: it was the first instance where tear gas shells were employed, adding a new, terrifying dimension to the battlefield. The Germans unleashed a staggering 2,200 tear gas shots after a relentless two-hour artillery barrage, a strategy aimed to disorient and weaken the enemy before the main assault.

The brunt of this assault was borne by the Russian 55th Infantry Division, who, despite their valiant efforts, were overwhelmed and forced out of their trenches by a fierce bayonet attack led by four determined German regiments. In response to this setback, the commander of the Russian 2nd Army, Infantry General V. Smirnov, made a decisive move. He ordered a robust counterattack, marshaling the formidable strength of the VI Army Corps under the leadership of Lieutenant General Vasily Gurko. This counteroffensive brought together a formidable force of 42,895 men, which included the 4th, 16th, 55th Infantry Divisions and a brigade from the 76th Infantry Division, along with 68 machine guns and 130 artillery pieces. The stage was set for a dramatic and intense confrontation.

Despite these efforts, the Russian troops faced a daunting challenge. By nightfall, they were unable to reclaim the lost trenches near the villages of Humin and Dołowatka. The situation was dire, but the Russian infantry, renowned for their resilience and courage, refused to relent. On the night of January 17, in a series of relentless assaults, they managed to encircle the German forces, employing tactical pincer movements that eventually drove the enemy out of the trenches they had captured just a day earlier.

The Germans, undeterred, attempted to renew their offensive, but each time they were met with a wall of unyielding Russian machine-gun and artillery fire. The German troops, despite their tenacity and tactical acumen, could only advance a mere 20 meters over two days of intense and grueling combat. The cost was high: two regiments suffered significant casualties, including the loss of 3 officers and 297 soldiers. Notably, the commander of the 14th infantry regiment was killed in action, rendering their attack unsuccessful. On the Russian side, the toll was equally heavy, with 725 soldiers killed, 101 missing, 3,019 wounded, and numerous others affected by the poison gas.

In preparation for a renewed offensive on Humin and Sucha, Colonel General August von Mackensen, commanding the German 9th Army, strategically amassed a formidable force. This included the reinforced XVII Army Corps and I Reserve Corps, comprising the 4th, 35th, 36th Infantry, and 1st, 36th, and 49th reserve divisions. Additionally, the attack was to receive support from the 26th Infantry Division of the XIII Army Corps on the left flank and the forces of artillery general Friedrich von Scholtz, including the 11th and XX Army Corps, on the right. However, upon discovering the gathering of Russian troops south of Mlawa, Paul von Hindenburg, Supreme Commander of All German Forces in the East, swiftly redirected resources to reinforce this sector. This included the deployment of the XX Army Corps (37th and 41st Infantry Divisions), the 1st Guards Reserve Division, and the 5th Guards Infantry Brigade.

By January 31, 1915, the German forces had amassed a staggering concentration of six divisions, totaling up to 40,000 men, supported by 92 artillery batteries with 596 guns, including 150 heavy artillery pieces and 2 Austrian 30.5-cm mortars. A formidable stockpile of 18,000 shells, some filled with tear gas and chlorine, was also prepared. Meanwhile, the Russian troops received reinforcements, but the Germans had managed to establish an overwhelming advantage in artillery firepower.

It's noteworthy that at this time, defensive combat tactics were not well-developed in any army. Taking a defensive stance was generally seen as a temporary measure to exhaust the enemy and regroup for an offensive. Thus, even with knowledge of an impending enemy offensive, Russian commanders at all levels had little strategy beyond instructing their troops to "hold their positions at all costs." The concept of creating in-depth fortified zones was not yet a common practice.

At 8:30 am on January 31, a heavy bombardment commenced on the Russian positions near Humin and Wola Szydłowska. Subsequently, the Germans launched their attacks, focusing mainly on the 4th and 55th Infantry Divisions. By 4:00 pm, they had successfully driven units from the 4th, 27th, and 55th infantry divisions out of their trenches. During the night, a counterattack was attempted by forces led by Major General Mikhail Sokovin, but it failed to achieve its objective. Additionally, Vasily Gurko was reinforced with the 13th Siberian Rifle Division. The commander of the 2nd Army, V. Smirnov, reported to the commander-in-chief of the armies of the North-Western Front, highlighting the debilitating impact of the enemy's gas shells which led to suffocation and incapacitation of the troops, severely hindering their ability to defend their positions.

On February 1, starting at 5 am, Russian forces initiated a counterattack. Despite the deployment of the 59th Infantry and 13th Siberian Rifle Divisions, this effort proved unsuccessful. By 9 am, the Germans commenced a devastating artillery and mortar bombardment, effectively destroying the forward Russian trenches. At 4 pm, they resumed their offensive, targeting the left flank of the 98th Yuryevsky Infantry Regiment. By nightfall, most of the German assaults were repelled, and the introduction of fresh Russian regiments halted further German advances. The two German corps suffered over 5,200 casualties, captured 6,232 Russian prisoners, 7 machine guns, and, crucially, seized key positions of the first Russian defensive line.

On February 3, the Germans launched an attack on the sector commanded by Major General P. Zakharov. To support Gurko's group (who had fallen ill and returned to his corps only on February 6 under threat of dismissal), the 3rd Siberian Rifle Division was sent. Meanwhile, the 1st Army, led by Cavalry General Alexander Litvinov, initiated a diversionary offensive with the 1st Siberian Corps, reinforced by the 14th Siberian Rifle Division and the 3rd Turkestan Rifle Brigade.

By the night of February 4, the Russian VI Army Corps had partially regained its position and occupied the village of Wola Szydłowska. However, they were unable to recapture the main strongholds from the Germans. In the morning, the Germans renewed their offensive, pushing back the newly arrived 13th Siberian Rifle Division. The 93rd German Reserve Infantry Regiment, reinforcing the brigade of the 4th Infantry Division, delivered a critical blow to the Siberians. The 4th Siberian Rifle Division of the II Siberian Army Corps and Major General N. Karepov's combined division from the IV Army Corps were committed to the battle, managing only to halt the German advance. The 93rd German Reserve Infantry Regiment incurred 36 fatalities, 152 wounded, and 11 missing, and captured 1,556 Russian prisoners.

Meanwhile, from January 21 to February 4, the units of the 1st Army achieved greater success. All corps participated in the offensive, resulting in the Germans being pushed back at Borzymów and Witkowice, and four machine guns were captured (6th Siberian Rifle Regiment). An unexpected assault from the northern flank, which culminated in a severe defeat for the German reserve regiment of Lieutenant Colonel V. Keller, compelled the Germans to cease attacks on the 2nd Army. However, the 14th Siberian Rifle Division, sent to Humin, faced a robust counterattack from German reserves. Unable to cross the Bzura, they suffered significant losses, including the death of the commander of the 21st Turkestan Rifle Regiment. During this counterattack, the 8th German Landwehr Regiment lost seven soldiers, sustained 14 wounded, and captured 325 Russian prisoners.

By late January, intense battles at Dołowatka, Humin, Wola Szydłowska, Bolimov, and Borzymów had engaged nearly all units of the Russian 1st and 2nd Armies. While the front of the 5th Army remained relatively calmer, some of its regiments were also redirected to reinforce the assaults on German-held positions. However, this concentration of forces in a limited area of the front only escalated the casualties without significantly altering the strategic situation. Specifically, in the regions of Humin, Borzymów, and Wola Szydłowska, the Russian troops suffered heavy losses: 7,911 killed, 12,248 missing, and 20,614 wounded. Among them were the commanders of the 18th Siberian Rifle Regiment and the 21st Turkestan Rifle Regiment, Major General S. Moskvin and Colonel A. Selyadtsev, both killed in action. The German army in these areas incurred losses of 57 officers and 2,584 soldiers killed, 4 officers and 1,308 soldiers missing, and 79 officers and 6,811 soldiers wounded.

The Supreme Commander of All German Forces in the East deemed the 9th Army's task as accomplished, with the battle's objective being to engage Russian forces ahead of a decisive offensive in East Prussia. The German troops achieved modest territorial gains, securing key strongholds and tying down significant Russian forces. Over 7,000 Russian prisoners were captured. Emperor Wilhelm II arrived at the front on February 7th to congratulate the troops on their victory and distribute awards.

Yet, there was a palpable sense of disappointment among the military leaders. Lieutenant General C. von Morgen, commander of the 1st reserve corps, expressed frustration, noting that while the 9th Army's attacks east of Rawka achieved excellent tactical success, they failed to make a breakthrough. The use of chemical projectiles, a novel tactic at the time, did not yield the anticipated effect; captured Russians reported symptoms like tearing and headaches but were not rendered incapacitated.

The fighting continued along the entire front, from the mouth of the Bzura to Pilica, until the end of February, albeit with less intensity and ferocity than before. The German troops were unable to penetrate the Russian defenses decisively. However, it became evident that the loss of key defensive positions compelled the Russian command to exert significant efforts to reclaim them, regardless of the high casualties involved.

Carpathian Winter War

In the gripping early days of World War I, the Habsburg Empire found itself reeling under the relentless onslaught of the Russian forces. The year 1914 witnessed a dramatic unfolding in the northeastern regions of Austria-Hungary, where the Habsburgs faced repeated defeats in Galicia and the Carpathian foothills. Amidst this turmoil, the historic Fortress Przemyśl, an impressive yet antiquated stronghold dating back to 1854, became the epicenter of conflict. Situated on the San River, this fortress was a strategic gatekeeper to the Carpathians, and by early November 1914, it fell under siege by the Russians for the second time in mere months.

With a staggering 130,000 troops trapped in the fortress and the looming threat of an invasion into Hungary, the Austro-Hungarian leadership was compelled to take drastic measures. The desperate situation led to a series of bold but haphazard offensives in the winter of 1915: a fierce clash on January 23, followed by a chaotic attack on February 27, culminating in a last-ditch effort to reclaim Fortress Przemyśl in late March.

The formidable Carpathian Mountains themselves played a critical role in this unfolding drama. This natural barrier, stretching 60 to 75 miles wide with peaks averaging 3,600 feet, presented a daunting challenge with its limited passable roads and sparse rail lines. The harsh mountain weather added to the perils, with rainy conditions turning into heavy snowfall by November, and the potential for sudden temperature spikes causing floods in the valleys. This tumultuous landscape set the stage for a military catastrophe, forever altering the course of the war and the fate of empires.

Mountain combat poses significant challenges for any military force, demanding specialized training and equipment for troops to adapt to high altitudes, rugged landscapes, and unpredictable weather. In such environments, maneuvering and sustaining a consistent supply chain becomes a formidable task. Artillery, crucial in warfare, faces its own hurdles in the mountains, where transporting and positioning these heavy weapons on uneven terrain limits their deployment, often relegating them to less advantageous lower grounds, to the detriment of supporting infantry.

This backdrop of mountain warfare intricacies set the stage for the Habsburg military's grave misjudgment. Entrenched in the belief of a 'short war', they failed to prepare for an extended mountain campaign, particularly through the harsh winter months. This oversight was part of a series of miscalculations that would lead to disastrous consequences.

At the center of this ill-fated winter campaign was General Franz Conrad von Hötzendorf, chief of the Austro-Hungarian General Staff. Conrad, driven by the need to counter the threat of invasion and assert the strength of the Central Powers (comprising Germany, Austro-Hungary, Turkey, and Bulgaria), was keenly aware of the geopolitical implications. He feared that any perceived weakness might sway neutral nations like Italy and Romania to join the Triple Entente. The Habsburg military had already suffered a severe blow to its reputation with the failure of its Balkan offensive against Serbia in 1914, culminating in the humiliating cycle of capture and loss of Belgrade at the Battle of Kolubara.

Seeing the Carpathian Mountains as a theatre for redemption, Conrad aimed to recapture the besieged Fortress Przemyśl, believing its fall could spell disaster for both the army and the Dual Monarchy. His ambitious plan, devised in December, involved launching an offensive along a vast 100-mile forested front in the northern Carpathians by the beleaguered Habsburg

Third Army, despite its recent defeats. Concurrently, the newly formed South Army, a mix of German divisions and predominantly Habsburg units, was to flank the Russians. Conrad banked on the capabilities of his troops and the element of surprise, hoping for a stroke of luck to turn the tide of the offensive.

On January 23, 1915, the Habsburg's first offensive in the Carpathian Mountains commenced, spearheaded by the Third Army. This force, comprising 15 infantry and four and a half cavalry divisions, was bolstered by the adjacent South Army's three infantry and two cavalry divisions. Together, this force of 175,000 men embarked on a challenging mission: to seize control of key communication and railway hubs in the towns of Medzilaborce, Lisko, Sanok, and Sambir.

Initial stages of the offensive saw some modest successes for the Habsburg forces, as they managed to penetrate a 24-mile breach in the Russian defenses. However, this early gain was primarily against smaller Russian contingents. By January 26, the Third Army had stretched its front across a 60-mile expanse, securing the crucial Dukla and Uzhok Passes. But the tide of battle was quickly turning. The Russians, mounting powerful counteroffensives, began to reverse the Habsburg's initial gains. Complicating matters, a dramatic and harsh change in weather conditions exacerbated the Habsburg's challenges, leading to significant losses both from the elements and combat. Many divisions were whittled down to the size of mere regiments or brigades.

By early February, the Habsburg's Carpathian offensive was teetering on the brink of failure. The Russians, maintaining control over key mountain passes including the strategic Dukla Pass, were now on the offensive. Utilizing this advantage, Russian forces surged through the pass, posing a direct threat to vital railroad junctions and significantly outnumbering the Austro-Hungarian troops. This shift in balance effectively quashed any hopes the Habsburgs had of lifting the siege on Fortress Przemyśl. By mid-February, the momentum had decisively shifted back to the Russians, who now held the upper hand in the Carpathian battleground.

The brutality of combat exhaustion under harsh winter conditions in the mountains is a harrowing experience beyond the comprehension of those who haven't endured it. Habsburg soldiers, embroiled in World War I's unforgiving battlefields, faced dire shortages of basic necessities. Often, food supplies either failed to reach the frontlines or arrived frozen solid. Soldiers were battered by relentless rain, blizzards, and icy river crossings, leaving their uniforms frozen to their bodies. The lack of adequate winter gear meant that many suffered from lung ailments, frostbite, and some even succumbed to the cold.

The Habsburg Supreme Command's disconnect with these harsh realities was striking. They seemed oblivious to the fundamental challenges of winter mountain warfare. Soldiers were often left exposed in open terrain under subzero conditions for prolonged periods, resulting in widespread frostbite. The struggle to stay awake was a battle against the freezing temperatures. Movement through snow depths of three to six feet was a monumental task, draining both the physical and mental stamina of the troops. They spent hours, sometimes days, shoveling snow for patrols, assaults, and clearing essential roads and trails, further exacerbating their exhaustion.

The psychological toll on the soldiers was devastating. Many, overwhelmed by fatigue and despair, succumbed to apathy, or tragically, chose suicide. This dire situation was not limited to the soldiers; tens of thousands of horses, vital to the supply chain, also perished from overwork and lack of food.

Nighttime brought its own terrors: howling winds, pitch-black darkness, eerie mountain sounds, and temperatures plunging to -25°F. These conditions ensured that many exposed to the elements would not survive the night. Soldiers often endured long, treacherous marches in darkness, haunted by the sounds of wolves preying on the wounded in no man's land.

Compounding these hardships was the lack of reserve forces. The Austro-Hungarian Empire, uniquely among major powers, lacked a reserve army and was late in considering its establishment. Soldiers on the frontlines had no respite; they remained in their positions until death, injury, capture, or disappearance — often indicating they had frozen to death — as no relief or reinforcements were forthcoming.

The first Carpathian Mountain offensive was marred by staggering losses for the Habsburg forces, with casualty rates exceeding 75 percent. These losses were predominantly due to severe frostbite, exposure to extreme weather, and illness, rather than direct combat.

A critical weakness in the Habsburg campaign was the lack of coordination in their attack strategies. Units often engaged the enemy in isolated skirmishes, without synchronizing their efforts with adjacent groups. Even when orders for a coordinated attack were issued, they were frequently disregarded or acted upon too late to make a significant impact. As casualties mounted, the dwindling Habsburg forces found themselves stretched thin, unable to establish secure defensive positions along the increasingly overextended front.

In contrast, the Russian troops demonstrated more effective strategies. They leveraged their closer and more accessible road and rail networks in the lower mountains to regularly refresh their front-line regiments. This logistical advantage diminished as they pushed deeper into the mountains, but it still allowed them to mount substantial attacks across the Carpathian ridgelines well into April 1915.

Russian soldiers, better acclimated to the harsh climate and terrain, also out-matched the Habsburgs in both tactics and leadership. They skillfully timed their counterattacks, often striking during lulls in Habsburg offensives.

Night assaults were a particular forte of Russian commanders, who also excelled in the art of retrograde movement — withdrawing from positions at the last possible moment only to reestablish elsewhere. This tactic forced the Habsburg troops to stay combat-ready in the freezing conditions. Meanwhile, the Russians often held the high ground, a significant tactical advantage in mountain warfare. Coupled with superior artillery and the ability to rapidly reinforce and reposition their troops, the Russians effectively countered the declining Austro-Hungarian forces, exacerbating their challenges and contributing to their eventual defeat in this phase of the war.

During the initial phase of the Carpathian offensive, the Habsburg Third Army faced devastating losses. Only two weeks in, official reports tallied 88,900 casualties. By the end of the offensive, they had lost over 75 percent of their strength, mainly due to severe frostbite, exposure, and illness. The commander of the Third Army, Svetozar Boroević, acknowledged the army's lack of preparedness for a winter campaign in the mountains.

General Conrad, however, had little tolerance for explanations rooted in defeat. Unhappy with the performance of the Third Army, he replaced its leadership by bringing in General Eduard von Böhm-Ermolli from the German front to oversee operations in the Carpathians. The newly formed Second Army, comprising 60,000 to 70,000 fatigued units from the Third Army's right flank, was positioned between the Third and South Armies. Additionally, six and a half infantry divisions were redirected to support this new offensive.

In preparation for the second offensive, Conrad ordered the transfer of the Habsburg VIII Corps from the Balkan front to assist the Third Army in driving the Russians out of the vital Dukla and Uzhok Passes. The rail and communication centers of Lisko, Sanok, and Sambir remained key targets.

As the next offensive's commencement date of February 25 neared, plummeting temperatures and the relentless movement of troops and supplies wreaked havoc on the few roads leading to the front, turning them into impassable mud pits. The lack of adequate manpower and engineering teams compounded the difficulty of maintaining these crucial routes. Concurrently, the spread of disease and worsening hygiene conditions decimated the ranks with frostbite and illness, further depleting the already strained Habsburg forces. Despite these setbacks, the second Carpathian offensive, though slightly delayed, proceeded in late February.

The Second Army initiated its main attack along the strategic roads toward Fortress Przemyśl, focusing on fortified positions similar to those targeted by the Third Army. This offensive, however, was concentrated on a narrower, 12-mile front. A direct assault was deemed necessary due to the increasing military and political pressure to relieve the besieged Fortress Przemyśl and its garrison, which was now in dire straits, facing critical shortages of supplies, including food.

As the offensive unfolded, the Habsburg army, awaiting reinforcements, found its center and left flanks rapidly collapsing under the weight of intense Russian counterattacks. The situation grew so dire that incoming reinforcements were hastily deployed in disjointed segments to plug the rapidly expanding breaches in the front lines. These reinforcements, often undertrained and outnumbered, were essentially sent into battle in a desperate bid to stem the Russian advance.

The chaos and disorientation among the Habsburg troops were acute. Colonel Veith of the Third Army, amidst a blinding snowstorm and dense fog, reported a complete loss of direction, leading to entire regiments wandering aimlessly and suffering catastrophic losses. Similarly, Habsburg Archduke Joseph August, commanding the VII Corps, faced a grim reality with his Hungarian Honvéd Division. In just a span of a few days, the division's numbers dwindled drastically, with losses mounting in the thousands, yet the orders were to continue the assault.

This relentless attrition took its toll on the Second Army, which was essentially drained of its fighting capacity. The second Carpathian offensive, as a result, failed disastrously, leaving the Austro-Hungarian forces stranded far from their objective, the besieged Fortress Przemyśl. This failure was not just a tactical defeat but also a profound blow to the morale and operational strength of the Austro-Hungarian military, deeply impacting their ability to sustain the campaign.

Despite the mounting setbacks, General Conrad remained resolute in his determination. He ordered the V Corps of the Second Army, which was closest to the fortress and had received some reinforcements, to undertake a seemingly impossible mission: to liberate Przemyśl between March 20 and 23. Concurrently, the remaining Habsburg forces in the Carpathians were tasked with fending off continuous Russian attacks. On March 20, the Russians intensified their efforts, launching a barrage of massive assaults aimed at pushing the Habsburg Second and Third Armies back over the mountain ridges.

Meanwhile, the situation for the soldiers at Przemyśl was dire. Having subsisted on horse meat and bread fillers for months, they made a desperate and tragically futile attempt to break out on March 19. This ill-fated endeavor, reportedly aimed at preserving the Austro-Hungarian army's honor and ordered by General Conrad via coded telegram, resulted in a bloody debacle. The garrison, exhausted and overwhelmed, ultimately surrendered. It was later revealed that the Russians had deciphered the Austro-Hungarian code and were thus forewarned of the breakout attempt.

In a striking oversight, neither the command of the Second Army nor the V Corps was informed of the fortress's surrender. As a result, a few days later, V Corps proceeded with its offensive, unaware that it was now a futile exercise. This third attempt, doomed from the start, led to yet another round of severe casualties for the Habsburg forces, further depleting their already strained resources and morale.

The Fortress Przemyśl was more than just a stronghold; it was a symbol of Austro-Hungarian military prowess. General Conrad's fixation on retaining this fortress skewed his strategy on the Eastern Front, ultimately leading to near catastrophic losses for the Habsburg army by the end of the Carpathian Winter War. The campaign's toll was enormous, with hundreds of thousands of lives lost and minimal strategic gains. Conrad's misjudgments also inadvertently paved the way for greater German influence over the Habsburg military command.

Conversely, the Russian strategy to push through the Carpathians and deal a decisive blow to Austria-Hungary was also flawed. This approach compelled them to commit more troops into the difficult mountain terrain, stretching their forces thin and overextending their already limited supply lines. This overreach left them vulnerable when Germany launched the successful Gorlice-Tarnów offensive in eastern Poland in May. This German campaign turned the tide on the Eastern Front, securing a significant victory for the Central Powers and saving the Austro-Hungarian army from potential collapse.

Despite being overlooked in historical narratives of the First World War, the Carpathian Winter War was a pivotal chapter in the Eastern Front's history. It presaged the infamous and bloodier battles of 1916 at Verdun and the Somme, highlighting the sheer brutality of warfare in such harsh conditions. The Carpathian Winter War remains a stark reminder of the unforgiving nature of mountain warfare and its ability to transform landscapes into arenas of unspeakable hardship and suffering.

Second Battle of the Masurian Lakes

In the gripping early months of 1915, a dramatic chess game of military strategy unfolded on the Eastern Front of World War I. The Central Powers, spearheaded by the indomitable German forces under the leadership of the legendary Paul von Hindenburg, were setting the stage for a series of audacious offensives. From the shadowed trenches in western Poland, a land scarred by the fierce Battle of Łódź, Hindenburg's troops prepared to thrust eastward, their eyes set on the strategic Vistula River. Meanwhile, in the icy terrains of East Prussia, near the historic battlegrounds of the Masurian Lakes, another German offensive was brewing.

Not to be outdone, the Austro-Hungarians, led by the formidable General Alexander von Linsingen, were ready to burst forth from the daunting Carpathian Mountains. Their target was Lemberg, a jewel in the Russian defense. In the south, General Borojevic von Bojna led a desperate mission to break the siege at Przemyśl, a fortress groaning under the weight of war.

Amidst this whirlwind of activity, the German high command was a cauldron of debate and decision. Prit Buttar captures the tension: Falkenhayn, with a grudging hand, agreed to dispatch four additional corps to the Eastern Front. His belief in the supremacy of the Western Front was unshaken, yet the elusive victory there forced his hand. He couldn't deny the persuasive arguments of Hindenburg and Ludendorff, who believed that a crushing defeat could be delivered to Russia, potentially ending the eastern conflict.

Ludendorff, with his military acumen, planned a pincer movement against the Russian Tenth Army. The northern offensive, led by Eichhorn's Tenth Army, would launch from Tilsit, slicing through Wladislawow to Kalvarija. The southern strike, helmed by Below's Eighth Army, would surge from Spirding-See near Bialla, aiming for Raigrod and Augustowo. The plan was to pin the Russians with a frontal attack, paving the way for a grand encirclement and potentially leading to assaults on Osowiec and Grodno.

The German forces were meticulously arrayed for this grand strategy. In the north, the Tenth Army, with its formidable corps, was positioned from the Niemen River to Insterburg. The southern thrust, a calculated move by Below, saw the deployment of corps west of Johannisburg and at Ortelsburg. Opposing them, the Russian Tenth Army braced for the onslaught, with their corps strategically positioned across the front.

This was more than a battle; it was a grand orchestration of military might and strategy, a dance of death and glory that would echo through the annals of history.

Erich von Falkenhayn, the mastermind behind the German Great General Staff, was convinced that the key to victory in World War I lay in the Western Front. However, in a strategic maneuver, he diverted four additional army corps to aid Paul von Hindenburg, the esteemed Supreme Commander of All German Forces in the Eastern theater. By February 1915, an astonishing thirty-six percent of Germany's field army was engaged on the Eastern Front.

In a bold move, the German Ninth Army launched an offensive from Silesia into Poland at the end of January. The attack was marked by the use of tear gas, a tactic that backfired disastrously when the gas drifted back onto the German troops, halting their advance. The Russians, seizing the moment, counterattacked fiercely with eleven divisions under a single corps commander. This ferocious engagement resulted in a staggering loss of

40,000 Russian soldiers in just three days.

Meanwhile, in the frostbitten landscapes of East Prussia, the Russian advance was stymied by a network of trenches stretching between the Masurian Lakes. These defenses, manned by the German Eighth Army under General Otto von Below, held firm against the Russian onslaught. The Eighth Army was bolstered by some of the newly arrived corps, while the rest were amalgamated to form the German Tenth Army, commanded by Colonel-General Hermann von Eichhorn. This new force was a critical component of a larger plan: a pincer movement aiming to encircle General Sievers' Russian Tenth Army. Additionally, a new Russian threat was materializing in the form of the Twelfth Army, marshaled by General Pavel Plehve, assembling in Poland.

Despite warnings from Sievers to General Nikolai Ruzsky, commander of the Northwest Front, about the impending German attack, his concerns were dismissed. In a dramatic twist, on February 7, amidst a fierce snowstorm, Below's Eighth Army initiated a surprise offensive. The Russian trenches, hastily constructed and poorly fortified, offered little resistance. The following day, the Tenth Army also surged forward. Despite the challenges posed by deep snow and boggy terrain off the roads, the German forces made significant advances, covering 120 km in a week and inflicting heavy casualties on the Russians, showcasing the relentless might of the German military machine.

Under Sievers' command, Evgeny Radkevich's III Siberian Corps received orders to withdraw to Lyck, where it would establish a new defensive front alongside the XXVI Corps. Meanwhile, Nikolai Epanchin's III Corps, having already suffered significant equipment losses, retreated to Kovno and Olita, effectively removing themselves from the ongoing battle. On the northern flank, Pavel Bulgakov's XX Corps now found itself facing off against the German XXI Corps and XXXIX Reserve Corps.

As described by Buttar, the German advance, while aided by the snow-covered trails left by the retreating Russians, owed much of its progress to the abandoned supplies left behind by the Tenth Army in retreat. Even so, the movements of German supply columns were hampered by the harsh winter weather, which imposed restrictions on everyone involved. The 11th of February brought heavy snowfall and plummeting temperatures, with the mercury dipping to a bone-chilling -15 °C.

By the 12th of February, Otto von Lauenstein's XXXIX Reserve Corps had successfully captured Eydtkuhnen and Wirballen. Two days later, on the 14th of February, the German Tenth Army's XXI Corps, led by Fritz von Below, severed the vital road link between Augustowo and Sejny. Simultaneously, Lyck fell into German hands. With these developments, the Russian XXVI, XX, and III Siberian Corps found themselves perilously close to encirclement.

However, a weather twist on the 15th of February changed the game. Rain and a thaw set in, transforming the once-frozen roads into knee-deep mud. On the 16th of February, the Germans reached Augustowo, while Georg von der Marwitz's XXXVIII Corps captured Suwałki. Eichhorn's Tenth Army now occupied the northern front of Augustowo, while Below's Eighth Army secured the western perimeter. Karl Litzmann's XL Reserve Corps received orders to cross the Augustów Canal on the 17th of February. In the midst of these developments, the III Siberian Corps abandoned their defensive positions, and Bulgakov's XX Corps, now isolated, embarked on a daring eastward retreat.

In the icy grip of winter, the formidable XX Army Corps, led by the strategic mind of Commander P. Bulgakov, faced a dire situation. Outnumbering their standard counterparts with a mighty force of five infantry divisions, their only path to survival lay in a daring breakthrough eastward, cutting through the encirclement towards Grodno.

The vanguard of this immense force, stretching from Suwalki, was the valiant 27th Infantry Division. On the frost-laden morning of February 16, it was this division that ignited the fierce battle at Macharce. In a thunderous charge, 16 Russian battalions clashed head-on with the German 65th Brigade's three battalions, supported by artillery and engineers. Amidst the chaos of battle, the German artillery roared until their shells were spent, facing the relentless advance of Russian infantry and their menacing machine guns.

In a desperate act of defiance, the German soldiers, reduced to a mere 250, sabotaged their artillery to prevent capture, sinking the remnants in a swamp. The Germans, led by the determined Major General E. von Estorff, rallied their forces at Macharce, facing off against the advancing Russian regiments.

The battle raged, with reinforcements pouring in from both sides. The German 31st Division's success in nearby regions only left the 42nd Division to defend Grodno's gates. Despite their valiant efforts, Estorff's brigade, battered and bruised, was forced to retreat.

The Russian onslaught towards Grodno seemed unstoppable. Yet, in a display of remarkable coordination, the German forces, under the swift command of Otto von Lauenstein, responded with decisive action. The 78th Reserve Division hastened to the fray, turning the tide in a grueling battle that lasted until the dawn of February 17.

In a dramatic twist, the encirclement closed around the Russian divisions, trapping them in a steel vice. Simultaneously, German forces captured Augustow, seizing prisoners, artillery, and a symbolic banner. The cost was heavy on both sides, with the Germans enduring significant casualties over two harrowing days at Macharce. But in this brutal clash of titans, it was strategy and cohesion that ultimately tipped the scales.

The German High Command in the East, deeming their operation successful, commenced the elimination of the encircled XX Corps on February 18. The outer defense of the encirclement was entrusted to the R. Kosh group, bolstered by the Königsberg Landwehr, the 1st Cavalry Division, and the 5th Guards Brigade. Meanwhile, K. Litzman's group and the 4th Cavalry Division joined the 10th Army, pushing the offensive towards the Bobr River and aiding in the encirclement of Osowiec. The task of seizing the Narew line fortresses (Osowiec, Łomża, Różan) fell to the 8th Army.

Despite these maneuvers, some Russian forces south of Augustow evaded encirclement. The Siberian Riflemen retreated across the Bobr River, destroying bridges to halt pursuit. The 64th and 84th Infantry Divisions of the XXVI Army Corps, misled by a telegram from the mentally unwell Chief of Staff General Budberg, retreated towards Osowiec, as recounted by Infantry General Aleksandr Gerngross. At Augustow, while suffering significant losses and abandoning artillery and supplies, these divisions managed to escape the tightening noose. Their escape was partly due to the XX Army Corps, which engaged three German divisions en route to Grodno. However, for General Bulgakov's group, the path to salvation was sealed shut, as neighboring corps, led by Thadeus von Sivers, did not launch a counteroffensive.

The German 31st Division took Lipsk on February 18 and Bartniki on February 19 with minimal casualties, capturing many Russian soldiers in the process. Concurrently, the 80th Reserve and 4th Cavalry Divisions engaged in battle on the Bobr River, linking up with other divisions near Lipsk.

On February 20, the German divisions tightened their encirclement. In a daring move on the night of February 21, Bulgakov attempted a new breakthrough amidst a snowstorm. The Russian forces charged the German positions near Lipina and Wołkusze. In the ensuing battle, several German commanders, including Major General E. von Estorff and Lieutenant Colonel R. Kollmann, were killed or wounded.

Despite the ferocity of the Russian assault, the German defenses held firm. After the capture of Kurianka by the 76th Reserve Division, the Russian forces were fragmented into isolated pockets. On February 22, the encircled Russian units, totaling 5,600 men, including a general, surrendered. By February 23-24, the remnants of various regiments, totaling over 10,000 soldiers, managed to reach Grodno, bringing with them a small number of guns and machine guns. The operation ended with a significant Russian loss: 12 generals, 67,500 officers and soldiers, 295 guns, and 170 machine guns captured by the Germans.

The "Winter Battle in Masuria" concluded with the expulsion of the Russian 10th Army from East Prussia, marking a significant victory for the Germans. The operation led to substantial Russian losses, including the capture of elements from four infantry divisions. German strategists highlighted the operation's meticulous planning and execution, which proceeded unhampered by Russian command actions. Although a complete encirclement of the Russian 10th Army was unlikely due to German resource constraints, the Germans nonetheless achieved their primary objective.

On the Russian side, this operation exposed critical shortcomings in leadership at various levels, from the front and army to the corps. These deficiencies included a lack of confidence, internal contradictions, errors in situational assessment, and a rigidity that hindered initiative. These flaws proved costly for the Russian forces.

While the operation didn't radically shift the war's overall trajectory (it wasn't intended to), it solidified German control over East Prussia, effectively clearing it of Russian forces and significantly reducing the threat of another invasion. The Germans captured 40 Russian officers, 1,666 soldiers, 15 machine guns, and 6 artillery pieces.

In contrast, the Russian losses were disproportionately higher. The Russian 10th Army suffered significant casualties, including the death of one general and seven colonels, the capture of 12 generals and 11 colonels, and the wounding of another regiment commander. The 27th, 28th, 29th, 53rd, and 73rd Russian infantry divisions lost 11 banners. In total, the Russians lost 80,500 men, 136 machine guns, 323 guns, and 4 aircraft.

Reports of 100,000 Russian prisoners were circulated in the press but are not corroborated by German headquarters reports or Russian archival documents.

The casualty figures reflect the intense nature of the conflict: the Germans suffered 9,580 casualties (including 205 officers), while Russian casualties might reach 28,743. The high number of Russian prisoners significantly contributed to their disproportionate losses compared to the Germans, nearly fourfold.

First Battle of Przasnysz

In the gripping winter days of February 1915, a remarkable series of military maneuvers unfolded on the Eastern Front of World War I, marking a critical juncture in the conflict. On February 12th, the formidable right flank of General Gallwitz's army group launched a bold offensive, audaciously crossing the icy Skrwa Prawa River. This daring move resulted in the capture of 600 Russian prisoners, showcasing the tactical prowess of the German forces.

The intensity of the battle escalated as the German troops encountered robust resistance from parts of the Russian 4th Siberian and 27th Army Corps near the strategic towns of Różan and Przasnysz. Recognizing the urgency to amplify the assault on key locations like Łomża and Osowiec, the venerable Field Marshal Paul von Hindenburg made a strategic decision. He reallocated the XX Army Corps, bolstered by the formidable 41st Infantry Division, from Gallwitz's command to the 8th Army. This move was aimed at securing a decisive victory in Lomza and Osowiec. In a tactical exchange, Hindenburg dispatched the I Reserve Corps, led by the astute General Lieutenant Curt von Morgen, to Mlava, further intensifying the German offensive presence.

By February 15th, Morgen's corps arrived in Mlawa, setting the stage for an impending confrontation as they advanced towards Ciechanów. This maneuver exerted significant pressure on the left flank of the Russian forces stationed along the Narew River. The following day, General Scholz's group, reinforced by the resilient 11th Landwehr Division, succeeded in dislodging the Russian troops, including the tenacious Caucasian Rifle Brigade, from their positions in Kolno. Meanwhile, Hindenburg urged General Otto von Below to hasten preparations for a decisive offensive aimed at the strategic fortresses lining the rivers Bobr and Narew.

The situation intensified further on February 17th. Scholz's group, comprising the 41st Infantry, 3rd Reserve, 1st and 11th Landwehr Divisions, along with the 5th Infantry Brigade, forced the Russian 10th Army to retreat across the Skroda River. By the evening of February 16th, Russian troops had established a defensive line stretching from Osowiec to Slupno.

The Russian high command, sensing the gravity of the situation, convened a critical meeting on February 17th at the Staff of the Russian Supreme Commander. General Nikolai Ruzsky proposed a bold strategy: concentrating maximum forces in Mlava by deploying both the 1st and 12th Armies, with the 2nd and 5th Armies serving as reserves. This plan included a tactical withdrawal to consolidate the front towards Novogeorgievsk and Warsaw. However, this proposal faced opposition from General of Artillery Nikolai Ivanov and his chief of staff, General of Infantry Mikhail Alekseyev, who warned against the potential exposure of neighboring army flanks amidst the Austro-Hungarian offensive in the Carpathians.

The Supreme Commander, Grand Duke Nikolai Nikolayevich, ultimately decided against a full retreat from the positions along the Bzura, Rawka, and Pilica rivers. Instead, he endorsed an aggressive plan to launch an offensive against Mlava with the combined might of two armies.

On February 17th, in a dynamic episode of World War I, the Russian 76th and 77th Infantry Divisions initiated an aggressive assault on Drobin. Their attacks were characterized by remarkable speed and force, so much so that they succeeded in penetrating through to the position of the German 1st Guards Reserve Field Artillery Regiment. However, this advance was met with a resolute counterattack led by the Guards Reserve Rifle Battalion of the 64th Reserve Infantry Regiment and the formidable Life Hussar Brigade. The German forces, demonstrating tactical finesse and resolve, managed to not only repel the Russian infantry but also to reclaim their initial positions. This counteroffensive resulted in the capture of 6 Russian officers, 2,500 soldiers, 6 machine guns, and 2 artillery pieces. The encounter inflicted significant losses on the German side as well, with 85 fatalities, 5 captured, and 216 wounded.

The following day, February 18th, saw continued hostilities with German troops successfully defending against the onslaught of the 19th Army Corps. The situation was so critical that Erich Ludendorff, the Chief of Staff of the Supreme Commander of All German Forces in the East, urgently inquired General Gallwitz about the engagement of the 1st Reserve Corps. Gallwitz, assessing the situation, decided to redirect these troops towards Ciechanów, intending to circumvent Przasnysz from the south. On February 19th, orders were issued for Morgen's corps and the Wernitz division to execute a pincer movement around Przasnysz, engaging the Russian 1st Turkestan Corps and aiming to encircle them with two reserve divisions.

Concurrently, on February 18th, the Russian Guards Corps was progressively deployed in the Grajewo area, eventually engaging in combat with the German Scholz group. This unfolding scenario led to the Russian commandant Lieutenant General K. Shulman at Osowiec fortress requesting reinforcements. In response, the 3rd Caucasian Army Corps was dispatched, with the first battalions of the 84th Shirvan Infantry Regiment reaching the fortress by evening.

Meanwhile, the XX Army Corps of the German army successfully dislodged the Russian right flank of the 12th Army. Despite efforts, the Russian 4th Siberian Corps' offensive faltered. On February 20th, German artillery commenced a bombardment on Osowiec. Below, anticipating strategic advantage, hoped that Scholz's group would be able to outflank the Russians along the Bobr river, compelling them to abandon Lomza and Osowiec.

However, the Russian 12th Army, under General of the Cavalry Paul von Plehwe, countered by deploying the Guards Corps in the critical area.

For the operations targeting Osowiec, the German 8th Army formed a special group under Infantry General Rudolf von Freudenberg, consisting of the 11th Landwehr Division, the 5th Infantry, and the 6th Reserve Brigades. Additionally, all heavy artillery was allocated to this group. Gustaf von Dickhuth-Harrach's corps successfully withstood further attacks from the Russian 19th and 2nd Siberian Army Corps. By the end of these engagements, German forces had captured a total of 6,800 enemy soldiers. The Wernitz's division made a significant advance against the Turkestan Corps, capturing Kitki. In a rapid response, the Russian 1st Siberian Corps deployed its newly arrived regiments into the fray, intensifying the conflict.

On the 21st of February, in a strategic move, General Paul von Plehwe, commander of the 12th Russian army, directed the 2nd Siberian Corps to relocate to Ostrołęka. From there, starting February 22nd, they were to launch an offensive aimed at striking the flank of the German forces, who had made significant inroads between Przasnysz and the Orzyca River.

The next day, German General von Gallwitz pressed on with his offensive. Plantier's detachment, on the right flank, successfully penetrated through to Slupno. Meanwhile, the remainder of the German formations maintained their positions. They faced opposition from Russian forces, including the 19th and 27th Army Corps, comprised of the 17th, 38th, 76th, and 77th Infantry Divisions, along with a brigade from the 2nd Infantry Division from Novogeorgievsk. Concurrently, the divisions led by Brougel and Wernitz continued to exert pressure on the Russian 1st Turkestan Army Corps. Morgen's corps made modest advancements towards Przasnysz. Gallwitz instructed Morgen not to assault Przasnysz directly, as it was expected to be taken by the approaching 9th Landwehr Brigade. Instead, Morgen was to link up south of the city with the Wernitz division and then target the rear of the 1st Turkestan Army Corps.

On the Russian side, Plehwe ordered the Guards Corps to initiate an offensive from February 23rd. Their objective was to repel the Germans advancing on Łomża, thereby relieving pressure on the Osowiec fortress and securing the Bobr and Narew Rivers. General Savvich was tasked with defending the approaches to Ostrołęka, and the II Siberian Corps was to recapture Przasnysz. This plan required the Russian army to simultaneously advance in divergent directions on both flanks.

At this juncture, the Russian army boasted significant military strength, with 165,633 infantry, 12,685 cavalry, 359 machine guns, 812 guns, and 6 aircraft. In terms of manpower, machine guns, and artillery, these forces outnumbered those of F. von Scholz's group from the German 8th Army. However, two of the Russian corps had not yet fully joined the army.

On February 23rd, Scholz's German group engaged the Russian Guard, but all their attacks were successfully repelled. On the front of the 1st Russian Army, Morgen's corps continued its maneuver around Przasnysz, and the 70th Reserve Brigade occupied Wola Wierzbowska, clashing with units from the Russian 38th Infantry Division. The encirclement of Przasnysz tightened. The 11th Siberian Rifle Division advanced towards the positions of the Wernitz division, but the Germans managed to seize Działyń, just 3 km west of Przasnysz. The progress of the 11th Siberian Division was halted. Elements of the 1st and 2nd Siberian Rifle Divisions advancing from the south reached the areas of Bogdanów, Elżbietów, and Gielniów. The German 1st Reserve Brigade penetrated the southern outskirts of Przasnysz, capturing 2,000 prisoners, 3 machine guns, and 3 artillery pieces. Morgen proposed surrender to the garrison to prevent further casualties, but Colonel A. Barybin, commander of the 250th Baltic Infantry Regiment, declined, stating he had no authority to negotiate a surrender. During the night and morning of February 24th, Przasnysz was stormed by the 1st Reserve Division under Generalleutnant Sigismund von Förster. The Germans took 10,000 prisoners, including 60 officers, a banner, 14 machine guns, 36 guns, and an armored car. The attackers suffered 110 killed, 123 missing, and 474 wounded over five days of combat.

On February 24th, the Russian 11th Siberian Rifle and 38th Infantry Divisions endeavored to penetrate Przasnysz, but their progress was limited. That evening, Cavalry General Litvinov, dissatisfied with the day's achievements, sternly instructed Generals Pleshkov and Scheidemann to renew their attacks at dawn on February 25th, regardless of troop fatigue. He asserted that the Germans were even more exhausted and demanded that by the next day, the 1st Siberian Corps should occupy Przasnysz and the 1st Turkestan Corps should take control of the Chojnowo region. He also requested General Plehve to initiate an offensive with the 2nd Siberian Corps, while other army units were to firmly hold their positions.

During the same day, the German forces managed to bypass Grudusk and Pultusk from the north. The only notable success for the Russians was achieved by the 4th Siberian Rifle Division, which succeeded in crossing the Orzyca River. At 9 PM, General Plehve ordered the commander of the I Siberian Corps, General A. Sychevsky, to strike the enemy with overwhelming force, preventing them from regrouping, and to relentlessly pursue them in case of a retreat.

On February 25th, General von Gallwitz instructed C. von Morgen's group to adopt defensive positions. However, in the morning, communication with Morgen and Wernitz was lost. Following artillery preparation, the 4th and 5th Siberian Rifle Divisions launched an offensive. The 1st and 2nd Siberian Rifle Divisions advanced towards Przasnysz from the south, engaging in intense combat with the Wernitz division.

Infantry General N. Ruzsky, Commander of the North-Western Front, still harbored hopes of encircling the Germans in Przasnysz. He transferred the 1st Siberian and 1st Turkestan Corps under the operational command of the 12th Army's General of the Cavalry P. Plehve. Plehve, encouraged by initial successes on February 26th, ordered Infantry General A. Sychevsky to relentlessly pursue and defeat the enemy, capturing or destroying them if possible, and to demonstrate utmost determination.

C. von Morgen was tasked with advancing against the Russian attacks. However, the Germans in Przasnysz found themselves unable to launch an offensive. On the night of February 26th, the I Siberian Corps began its advance. The German retreat turned chaotic when the 2nd Turkestan Rifle Brigade and the 2nd Brigade of the 38th Infantry Division flanked the German positions, capturing 2 officers, 400 soldiers, and 4 machine guns.

The German forces, under increasing pressure, faced a strong push from the east by the Russian 4th and 5th Siberian Rifle Divisions. In an attempt to counter this advance, the German 6th Infantry Brigade launched a counterattack, but it proved unsuccessful. The 9th Landwehr Brigade, engaged in the thick of the battle, suffered heavy losses, with 396 men killed or missing, and 1,907 wounded. Seizing the opportunity to pursue the retreating Germans, the commander of the 1st Army deployed the 15th Cavalry Division, which successfully captured 4 guns and over 200 prisoners from the 21st Reserve Infantry Regiment and the 2nd Reserve Jaeger Battalion by nightfall.

The offensive led by the corps of the 1st Army continued, albeit at a pace that left the front command unsatisfied. The chief of staff of the army, attempting to reassure Major General Bonch-Bruyevich of the front army's quartermaster general, emphasized that even if certain operations did not unfold as quickly as desired, it did not imply a lack of control over the operation. He assured that the situation, particularly concerning the Turkestan Corps which struggled to break through to Przasnysz from the west, was being closely monitored. Throughout the day, the Turkestan Corps' attacks were consistently repelled by the units of the division of T. von Wernitz.

The 12th Army's attempts to execute a comprehensive encirclement and defeat of the German troops at Przasnysz were unsuccessful. In an effort to intensify the attack on Morgen's group, the II Siberian Corps was reassigned to the 1st Army. Late on February 26th, around 11 pm, two regiments from the 2nd Siberian Rifle Division made a breakthrough into the southern outskirts of Przasnysz, but were subsequently repelled by a nocturnal counterattack. The combat resumed on February 27th, with the Siberian and Turkestan corps pressing the Germans relentlessly.

Faced with this situation, von Gallwitz contemplated a retreat. In a telephone discussion with E. Ludendorff and Colonel Max Hoffmann, the first quartermaster of the Staff of the Supreme Commander of All German Forces in the East, it was concluded that the Russian offensive aimed not only to recapture Przasnysz but also to pave the way for a new invasion of Germany from Mlawa. Consequently, they decided to conserve strength and fortify positions closer to the border. Between February 27th and 28th, Morgen's group was strategically withdrawn.

However, the German retreat from Przasnysz was far from orderly. They found themselves continuously fending off the pursuing Russian forces. On February 27th, regiments from the 1st Siberian Division overpowered the German barricades defending the barracks and triumphantly entered the city amid the ringing of bells. Meanwhile, the 1st Turkestan Corps was stalled at Działyń, and the 38th Infantry Division, repelled by German reserves, failed to break through. By the end of the day, the I and II Siberian Corps had taken control of Jednorożec and the northern outskirts of Przasnysz. The counter-offensive led to the capture of 63 officers and 6,776 German soldiers, along with 12 guns, 29 machine guns, 52 machine gun barrels, and a downed aircraft.

Battle of Łomża

In the early days of March, under the watchful command of General of Infantry A. Dushkevich, the 1st Army Corps, comprising the battle-hardened 22nd and 24th Infantry Divisions, made their dramatic arrival from behind the Vistula to join the 12th Army. As dawn broke on March 2nd, they boldly initiated their offensive, only to be met with a hailstorm of bullets and artillery shells. The 22nd Division alone witnessed staggering losses - 40 officers and 3,500 soldiers - forcing them to halt a mere 200-500 steps away from the German fortifications, with a desperate plan to launch a night assault.

Meanwhile, the formidable 2nd Guards Infantry Division, led by the fearless Lieutenant General Pavel Pototsky, scored a significant victory by capturing the strategically important height 74.4 near Chude village. In a parallel thrust, Lieutenant General S. Savvich's detachment, spearheaded by the 10th Siberian Rifle Division, bravely overran the heavily fortified Kierzek village, overcoming the staunch resistance of four Landsturm battalions and the 75th Infantry Brigade. Their victory was marked by the capture of prisoners, including 10 officers and 260 soldiers, along with 2 machine guns. However, this triumph was shadowed by the death of Colonel B. Dzerozhinsky, the revered commander of the 38th Siberian Rifle Regiment. The V Army Corps, meanwhile, advanced at a painstakingly slow pace, facing increasingly ferocious German resistance.

During this period of intense warfare, the Russian 10th Army, still reeling from the setbacks in the Second Battle of the Masurian Lakes, displayed remarkable resilience. On March 1st, under the new leadership of General of Infantry E. Radkevich, they once again surged forward in an offensive towards Lipsk. The III Siberian and XXVI Army Corps, bolstered by the remnants of the XX Army Corps that had miraculously escaped encirclement, pressed on valiantly.

The Russian 10th Army's advance was notably less contested than its neighboring sectors. By February 26th, Colonel General Hermann von Eichhorn, commander of the German 10th Army, had realized the futility of attacking two formidable Russian fortresses with limited resources. He communicated this to P. von Hindenburg and began a stealthy withdrawal of troops from February 28th, retreating to a more defensible position along the Bóbr River, towards Lipsk and the Augustów Canal.

On March 2nd, E. Radkevich issued a bold attack order. Major General V. Maidel's detachment, consisting of the 1st Cavalry Division and the 1st Separate Infantry Brigade, secured positions along the Neman River and commenced bridge repairs. However, the southern flank of the army suffered a crushing defeat, countered by a potent German offensive led by the 2nd Infantry and 80th Reserve Divisions. The Russians faced heavy losses, with up to 900 soldiers captured, while their own captures from the German 2nd and XXVI army corps were a mere 67 prisoners. By March 5th, the Russian 10th Army's offensive had ground to a halt across most of its sector. The Germans, too, had sustained significant losses, and on the night of March 6th, withdrew the German XXI Army and the XXXIX and XL reserve corps to fortified positions along the Augustow Canal, south of Augustow and Suwalki.

Despite having a considerable advantage in numbers, the 12th Russian Army faced daunting challenges on March 3rd and 4th, failing to achieve their strategic objectives. The Guards, V Army Corps, and Savvich's detachment were embroiled in fierce battles for Błędowo and Lipniki. Even the formidable offensive led by the Guards Corps met with staunch repulsion. This led to a strategic decision to bolster the strike force with an additional brigade from the III Caucasian Corps.

In early March, the German 8th Army, under the leadership of General of the Cavalry Georg von der Marwitz, mobilized the XXXVIII Reserve Corps, including the 75th Reserve and 4th Cavalry Divisions, along with the Königsberg Reserve and the 5th Infantry Brigade. Their mission was clear: to push the Russian forces back beyond the Narew River and secure the crossings near Nowogród. On March 4th, the Marwitz-led force launched a vigorous attack against the Russian Guards Corps, successfully dislodging the 2nd Cavalry Division from Lipnik and consequently causing the retreat of the 5th rifle brigade. However, their further progression was halted by fierce combat on March 5th.

Meanwhile, the 1st Russian Army was demonstrating remarkable activity. On March 3rd, the I and II Siberian Corps engaged in intense combat near Dębsk. The I Turkestan and XXVII Army Corps took position at Stump-Pole, and a brigade from the 79th Infantry Division, dispatched from Novogeorgievsk, joined the fray. Yet, their advance was effectively impeded by the Germans.

In response to the potential breach of the front near Mlava, Artillery General M. von Gallwitz, following consultations with his corps commanders and Lieutenant General E. Ludendorff, chief of staff of the Supreme Commander of All German Forces in the East, opted for a counterattack. This maneuver, aimed at flanking the II Siberian Army Corps, was assigned to the group led by Lieutenant General C. von Morgen. Despite his preference for targeting the presumably less fortified I Cavalry Corps, Morgen's force was bolstered with two regiments from the 76th Reserve Division and the 5th Guards Brigade, with the offensive scheduled to commence post-March 7th.

On March 6th, the Russian offensive, spearheaded by the cavalry unit of Lieutenant General V. Himetz and including the 1st and II Siberian Corps, hit a snag. Their attempts to penetrate the German defenses, fortified with barbed wire and bolstered by the 17th Infantry Division, were unsuccessful. The I Turkestan Army Corps, along with the 38th Infantry Division, once again clashed over the village of Pieńpole, which had been lost overnight. Despite these setbacks, the left flank of the 1st Army made some progress, capturing 10 officers, 727 German soldiers, and 4 machine guns over five days of offensive operations.

However, March 7th saw a replication of the challenges faced by the right flank of the 1st Army. The I Cavalry and II Siberian Army Corps failed to capture Rycice, being repelled by German counterattacks. The 1st and 4th Siberian rifle regiments managed to breach two layers of barbed wire at Grzybowo-Kapuśnik, yet found themselves encircled and barely escaped to their trenches, suffering the capture of 390 soldiers. The Turkestan corps succeeded in capturing Budy Sułkowskie, defended by the 61st Landwehr Infantry Regiment, but were subsequently ousted by a counterattack from the 99th Landwehr Regiment, resulting in the loss of up to 900 prisoners.

On the 8th of March, under the command of Lieutenant General C. von Morgen, the German offensive surged forward with the 1st and 76th Reserve Divisions, along with the 11th Reserve Brigade. This assault was soon reinforced by the 42nd Infantry Regiment and the 5th Guards Brigade. The German forces achieved a significant victory at Grabowo, capturing around 2,000 Russian prisoners. This success, coupled with the failure of a Russian night attack, compelled Generals V. Oranovsky and A. Sychevsky to order a strategic retreat.

The following day, March 9th, Morgen's group continued their aggressive push, driving the Russian forces back towards Przasnysz. Confronted with the looming threat of encirclement, General A. Sychevsky began withdrawing the II Siberian Corps to Przasnysz. In response to the advancing Germans, the commander of the 1st Army instructed a withdrawal to the Przasnysz positions at 21:00, with the cavalry corps tasked to conduct reconnaissance on the right flank and maintain communication with the 12th Army, which was fiercely guarding the crossings on the Orzyc. Under pressure from the Germans, both the Turkestan and XXVII Army Corps also fell back in line with the Siberian Corps.

Concerned about the precarious situation of the 1st Army, N. Ruzsky, the Russian commander, deployed additional support in the form of the XXIII Army Corps and the II Caucasian Corps. By the evening of March 10th, the 4th Don Cossack Division had successfully halted the German advance. However, under continuous German pressure, the Siberian corps retreated once again to Przasnysz. Morgen's troops, having captured 1,200 prisoners in a single day, gained control of Kluczewo and Rzęgnowo.

On March 11th, Morgen's group maintained their momentum, increasing their prisoner count to 1,400. Following air reconnaissance that reported the movement of Russian reinforcements from Ostrołęka to Rusetsk, the Germans dispatched the 3rd Infantry and 9th Landwehr Brigades. The Russian 1st Army, reacting swiftly, fortified new positions near Przasnysz, compelling the Germans to halt and establish defensive positions about 1,500 steps away. Faced with overwhelming Russian forces, consisting of 9 corps and 5 cavalry divisions against his own 6 corps and three cavalry divisions, General M. von Gallwitz ordered his troops to cease their attacks, fortify their positions, and resolutely defend their lines, thwarting any Russian attempts to break out from Przasnysz.

By March 12th, the Russian 1st Army had gained some ground, managing to push back the Germans at Stegna with the 4th and 8th Cavalry Brigades and the 15th Cavalry Division. The Russians also captured Lipa, and under intense artillery fire from the II Siberian Corps, the Germans were forced to abandon Mchowo and Kijowice. This marked the cessation of Gallwitz's second offensive on Przasnysz, demonstrating the resilience and tactical acumen of the Russian forces.

On March 13th, amidst a complex and challenging battlefield scenario, General Ruzsky, facing the southern border of East Prussia, commanded a renewed offensive with the combined might of the 1st and 12th Russian armies. The 1st Army boldly advanced, yet encountered formidable resistance across the entire front. Their progress was limited to capturing positions previously abandoned by the Germans. In a strategic move, Litvinov planned to bolster the Siberian corps' assaults by coordinating with the XIX and XXIII army corps. By the night of March 14th, the I Turkestan Corps had managed to reclaim Grudusk.

Analyzing the day's outcomes, General Gallwitz realized the critical need to push the Russian armies into a defensive stance. He contemplated launching a decisive strike towards Różan and Ostrołęka with two corps at his disposal. On March 16th, Gallwitz tasked Lieutenant General C. von Morgen with recapturing Gmina Jednorożec. The 36th reserve division executed this order with precision, retaking the village, recovering 2 artillery guns, and capturing 2,000 Russian prisoners. The 19th Army Corps of the Russian side also faced setbacks, and the offensive efforts of the 1st Turkestan Corps were successfully repelled.

Meanwhile, at the Russian Headquarters, there was growing anxiety over the unfolding events at Przasnysz. Mid-March saw intense confrontations in the Carpathians. Moreover, the German forces executed strategic, short strikes from Pilica to Nida. These developments prompted the Supreme Commander-in-Chief's staff to reconsider the feasibility of conducting simultaneous offensive operations on different fronts. Compounding these strategic dilemmas was a critical resource crunch. The Russian War Department reported a significant decline in the availability of rifles and artillery ammunition. The demand for shells was at 1.75 million per month, far outstripping supply. The shortage of rifles was particularly acute, with production lagging at about 60,000 per month, notably less than the production rates in Austria-Hungary.

In light of these challenges, on March 13th, the Chief of Staff of the Supreme Commander, General of Infantry N. Yanushkevich, sent an urgent telegram to Ruzsky. He emphasized the severe difficulties in replenishing troop numbers and the scarcity of rifles, stressing the need to conserve ammunition. Yanushkevich urged Ruzsky to consider these constraints in setting immediate objectives for the front-line armies and to restrain army commanders from engaging in isolated offensive actions that did not align with the overall strategic goals. These actions, he cautioned, would only lead to unnecessary losses of personnel and deplete vital firearm supplies.

On March 14th, General of Infantry N. Yanushkevich emphasized to General Ruzsky the importance of consolidating and improving their current military position. Seeking further guidance, Ruzsky consulted with General of Infantry Yuri Danilov, the Quartermaster General of Stavka, on March 15th. Danilov outlined the immediate objectives for the North-Western Front: to secure a foothold on the left bank of the Vistula River, halt the enemy's progression between the Vistula and the Neman, and repel them to establish a stronger defensive line near Bobr and Tsarev. Danilov believed that broader military actions would require a well-equipped army and prudent conservation of firearms.

Despite these strategic advisories, Ruzsky ordered a continuation of the offensive on the night of March 17th. However, the assaults led by the 1st and 12th Army from March 17th to 24th failed to achieve their objectives, resulting in significant troop losses without substantial gains.

A brief pause in hostilities occurred on March 25th. During this lull, General Gallwitz sent a report to P. von Hindenburg, estimating the Russian casualties at around 100,000, including 42,000 prisoners, while the German losses were about 37-38 thousand. Gallwitz acknowledged that although no decisive victory had been secured, the operations effectively thwarted Russian attempts to breach the front.

In the wake of these developments, the operational intensity of the 1st and 12th armies began to wane. This was particularly evident following the dismissal of Ruzsky and his quartermaster general, M. Bonch-Bruyevich, on March 26th, ostensibly due to health reasons. On March 30th, General of Infantry M. Alekseyev, formerly the chief of staff of the armies on the Southwestern Front, was appointed as the new commander-in-chief.

Meanwhile, on March 28th, A. Litvinov established the M. Pleshkov group, comprising the XIX, XXIII, and I Siberian army corps, along with M. Grabbe's detachment. However, reconnaissance reports revealed that the enemy's defenses were formidable, consisting of nearly continuous trenches, sometimes arranged in multiple tiers, and fortified with ditches, palisades, and intricate networks of barbed wire. Given these daunting defenses, the planned attack was deemed unfeasible. Consequently, the troops were instructed by P. Pleve on March 29th to fortify their current positions as robustly as possible and to defend them with utmost determination.

In the first half of March, the Russian 10th Army made concerted efforts to push forward their offensive towards Mariampol, Augustow, and Suwalki. Between March 7th and 8th, the Russian 3rd Army Corps advanced towards Simno. However, the Kovno detachment, facing severe losses, was halted near Mariampol. The remaining forces of the corps found themselves unable to progress, leading to the XV Army Corps being reassigned to the reserve of the commander in chief. In response to intercepted Russian communications detailing the movements of the II Army Corps, the commander of the German 10th Army, X. von Eichhorn, prepared for a swift counterattack by assembling a group under Lieutenant General Otto von Lauenstein, which included the 31st Infantry, 77th and 78th Reserve, and the 1st Cavalry Division.

On March 9th, the Germans attempted an offensive in the latter part of the day, resulting in a halt to the entire Russian 10th Army's advance as the Germans put up a fierce defense. The next day, Lauenstein's group successfully repelled the 73rd Infantry Division. The reinforcements of the Russian 56th Infantry Division were defeated and partially encircled, managing to break free only after considerable struggle and the loss of 3 artillery pieces. By March 12th, N. Kaznakov's cavalry, supported by armored vehicles, attempted a flanking maneuver on the Germans while the Kovno detachment continued its advance towards Mariampol. The III Army Corps, despite attempts to initiate an offensive, was also stopped. The Russian troops suffered significant losses, including 5,400 prisoners and several artillery pieces. In the subsequent days, the intensity of the battles began to diminish.

By March 15th, the German 10th Army shifted back to a defensive posture. Although unable to destroy a significant portion of the Russian 10th Army, the German forces managed to capture 5,400 Russian prisoners. The Russian corps narrowly escaped a devastating blow. The 10th Army headquarters was instructed to transfer control of the 1st army corps of the 2nd infantry and 78th reserve divisions to Gallwitz's army group. Following this, the front's activities transitioned to sporadic offensive attempts by relatively smaller forces. On March 16th, Russian units on the right flank of the 10th Army intensified their efforts. Their objective was to capture Tauragė and Memel, and then move on to attack Tilsit. Apukhtin's detachment, comprising the 1st brigade of the 68th infantry division, 7th and 16th brigades of the state militia, approached Tauragė and engaged in a battle for the city. The Germans resisted fiercely, retreating only on March 20th.

On March 18th, a bold and unexpected move by Potapov's detachment led to the capture of Memel. However, the city soon descended into chaos, with widespread looting and violence reported. The German 10th Army, recognizing the seriousness of this development, dispatched considerable reinforcements to Memel, including the 4th and 6th cavalry divisions and 6 infantry battalions. Confronted with this formidable response, Potapov's vanguard, primarily comprised of Cossacks, quickly retreated upon encountering the enemy. By March 21st, amid intense bombardment and the looming threat of a German landing, Potapov was compelled to withdraw his forces from Memel. However, he was soon ordered by army headquarters to retake the city and to evacuate or destroy all valuable assets only if faced with a superior enemy offensive. During this tumultuous period, hostages were reportedly taken from the local population.

Infantry General E. Radkevich, the commander of the 10th Army, sought to capitalize on the surprise success on the right flank by initiating an offensive across the entire front. The corps on the left flank, including the III Siberian and II Army Corps, were tasked with containing the enemy within the Augustow Forest. On March 22nd, the army's center attempted to drive the enemy from their positions at Mariampol, Suwalki, and Augustow, but made little headway. The deployment of armored vehicles in combat only achieved mixed results; the Germans maintained their positions tenaciously, and one vehicle was lost along with its crew to artillery and machine-gun fire.

By the evening of March 21st, Potapov's unit had to abandon Memel under enemy pressure, incurring losses of 149 men, 4 machine guns, and an artillery piece. Apukhtin's detachment, moving towards Tilsit, faced a severe defeat on March 24th, losing 8 officers and 600 soldiers, including the commander of the 270th Gatchina Infantry Regiment, who was reported missing. Between March 25th and 26th, the 10th Army encountered such strong resistance that even successful assaults could not be sustained. The situation escalated on March 28th and 29th, with the Germans launching counterattacks across the entire 10th Army front, leading to particularly fierce battles. However, by March 30th and 31st, the intensity of combat began to wane.

The 10th Army's offensive ultimately resulted in a modest territorial gain and several partial defeats, particularly on the right flank. From March 18th to 31st, the 10th Army suffered substantial losses, including 2,244 killed, 3,290 missing, and 6,031 wounded. On the other side, they captured 2 officers and 429 German soldiers. The strategic locations of Augustow and Suwalki remained out of Russian control.

Battle of Kalvarija

In the early days of April 1915, a crucial phase of World War I unfolded, marked by intense military operations in the region of Mariampol and Kalvarien. General E. Radkevich, leading the Russian 10th Army, ordered an aggressive operation aimed at capturing Mariampol, a strategic location that had been a thorn in the side of the Russian forces. The Russian army, with its impressive strength of 269,951 men, faced the German forces, numbering 157,525. This significant numerical advantage fueled the Russian hopes of finally crushing the persistent and formidable German resistance.

The Russian artillery was remarkably well-supplied, boasting an allocation of 252 light, 200 mortar, and 209 heavy shells per barrel, a testament to the seriousness with which the Russian command was approaching this operation. However, the battle that ensued on April 5th was anything but straightforward. The Russian forces, particularly the Kovno's detachment near Mariampol, faced an unexpectedly fierce and unyielding opposition. The German troops, despite being outnumbered, delivered a dense barrage of small arms and cannon fire, halting the Russian advance. The 1st Guards Cavalry Division of Russia, caught in the ferocity of the German onslaught, was forced to retreat.

The following day, April 6th, saw a bold and strategic move from the German side. The units of the 31st and 42nd Infantry Divisions, despite their relatively small numbers – with the 31st Division having just 3,000 men – launched a counterattack against the Kovno's detachment. This action led to a significant shift in the battlefield dynamics. The Russian 68th Infantry Division, which had endured days of grueling combat in challenging conditions ("standing for three days in water against the German barriers"), retreated from Mariampol. The 1st Guards Cavalry Division continued its withdrawal, and the 56th Infantry Division could not hold back the German advance. Only the 73rd Infantry Division and a separate infantry brigade managed to make slight progress. Attempts by the Russian 2nd Guards and 3rd Cavalry Divisions to encircle and break into the German rear were unsuccessful. In a specific confrontation, the Germans delivered a crushing blow to the Ust-Dvinsk battalion, inflicting significant casualties and capturing many Russian soldiers. However, this German counterattack was eventually halted by an order from the Supreme Commander of All German Forces in the East.

As the so-called Easter battles raged on, the toll on the Russian 10th Army was heavy: 646 killed, 2,894 wounded, and 958 missing. The German forces, though inflicting significant damage on the Russians, also suffered considerable losses, particularly in the XXI Army Corps, with hundreds killed, wounded, and missing.

The period from April 8th to 11th continued to be marked by fierce and fluctuating combat. The Russian 10th Army's casualties for this period alone were substantial, with over a thousand killed and several thousand wounded or missing. Despite these losses, the Russian forces managed to capture 693 prisoners and 8 machine guns, indicating some measure of success amidst the overall grim scenario of the Easter battles.

Conclusion

The First Battle of Przasnysz and the Łomża operation were pivotal moments, marking a transition in the Russian-German front dynamics between the Vistula and Bobr rivers. From April to mid-July, this region transformed into a fortified defensive stronghold, as both sides diligently constructed new defensive zones and probed for vulnerabilities in their adversary's lines. However, neither side could decisively exploit these efforts.

The German command, still reeling from the aftermath of the Second Battle of the Masurian Lakes, grappled with limitations in personnel and ammunition replenishment. This situation led Lieutenant General E. Ludendorff, the chief of staff of the Supreme Commander of All German Forces in the East, to express despair over the "collapse of hopes." Similarly, the Russian command, extending from the Supreme Command to the North-Western Front's army headquarters, struggled to achieve its strategic objectives. Notably, their ambitions to capture East Prussia and repel the enemy from Russian soil remained unfulfilled, despite maintaining a consistent numerical superiority.

The two-month-long, intense battles along the front line, stretching from Memel to the Narew River's mouth, reflected the Russian army's resilience. Despite halting their offensive due to the Germans' tenacious and adept defense, the Russian troops' actions significantly constrained the Germans from assisting the Austro-Hungarian forces in the Carpathians. This steadfast Russian stance also shattered the Central Powers' main strategic goal for the winter campaign, which had been optimistically outlined in a meeting in Oppeln on December 19, 1914. The envisioned flank attacks, aiming to push Russian forces beyond the Vistula and from the Carpathians, and even further to the middle reaches of the Bug River, failed to materialize. Russia even managed to reserve forces for a potential new offensive in East Prussia, maintaining a strategic threat from both the south and east.

The battles around Przasnysz and Łomża brought heavy casualties to both sides without achieving their primary objectives. These engagements underscored the defenders' advantage, largely due to well-prepared, deep defensive positions, abundant artillery, and, on the German side, effective use of mortars. The German gains during this period were modest compared to the Second Battle of the Masurian Lakes, capturing 67,343 prisoners, a number of guns, machine guns, and regimental banners. Conversely, the Russians endured significant losses, including several aircraft and armored vehicles, which increasingly avoided battle due to enemy artillery fire.

Russian forces also captured a substantial number of officers, soldiers, and military equipment, including machine guns, mortars, guns, and a couple of planes, along with the banner of the German 34th Fusilier Regiment. These outcomes vividly illustrated the grueling nature of trench warfare and the formidable challenge of making breakthroughs in such well-entrenched defensive positions.

Second Battle of the Vistula River

In the midst of the tumultuous First World War, the Russian 2nd and 5th armies, pivotal elements of the Northwestern Front, were thrust into a critical role near Przasnysz. Tasked with fortifying the front along the strategic rivers of Pilica, Rawka, and Bzura, these armies formed a steadfast barrier to the west of the Vistula's middle reaches. Their stronghold, stretching from Novogeorgievsk to Nowe Miasto on the Pilica, was not just a defensive line—it was the linchpin connecting the Northwestern and Southwestern fronts, guarding the vital pathway to Warsaw and shielding the rear formations along the Narew River.

In the wake of intense clashes at Borzymów, Humin, and Wola Szydłowska, reinforcements were urgently dispatched to bolster these critical positions. From the ranks of the 2nd and 5th armies, elite units like the 2nd Siberian, 2nd Caucasian, and a host of Army Corps—1st, 2nd, 5th, and 23rd— were mobilized to reinforce the 1st, 10th, and 12th armies. This strategic movement of forces proved decisive, swinging the outcome of the First Battle of Przasnysz in favor of the Russian troops. Moreover, during the Battle of Łomża, these reinforcements played a crucial role, thwarting the German counterattacks and preventing them from escalating into a full-scale, successful offensive. This period marked a turning point in the war, showcasing the strategic acumen and resilience of Russian military leadership and their troops in the face of overwhelming challenges.

On February 27th, a formidable German cavalry group led by General Rudolf von Frommel was established, incorporating the forces of Major General Karl Dieffenbach's combined division. This unit was composed of regiments from the 11th Army Corps, a joint brigade under Major General Dietrich Karl Hermann Freiherr von Stein from the 17th and 13th army corps, and Major General R. von Zenker's augmented reserve brigade. Additionally, it included the 25th reserve corps with its 49th and 50th reserve divisions and Lieutenant General von Menges' consolidated reserve division, along with the 9th Cavalry Division. Significantly bolstered by heavy artillery, the group featured 12 batteries of 15cm howitzers, 4 batteries of 10cm heavy guns, and a 21cm mortar battery.

On March 5th, the divisions under Dieffenbach and Menges, alongside Stein and Zenker's brigades, successfully breached the Russian defenses along an 8 km front on the Pilica River. This breakthrough set the stage for a northward offensive, effectively isolating Russian forces from Warsaw. The Germans captured a significant number of prisoners and equipment, including 3,400 troops and 20 machine guns. In response, the 5th Army headquarters quickly moved regiments from the 4th Army Corps to the breach, involving the 1st Rifle Brigade, II Brigade of the 2nd Infantry Division, and the 25th Infantry Division. From the left flank, General A. Evert of the 4th Army contributed the 18th Infantry Division of the 14th Army Corps to counter the German advance.

On March 6th, the 5th Army, now reinforced with a group under Lieutenant General N. Korotkevich and Lieutenant General P. Papengut's detachment from the 4th Army, mounted a counteroffensive. They initially pushed back the German forces, but faced renewed challenges due to attacks on the Russian Grenadier Corps by General Remus von Woyrsch's army near Łopuszno and the continued aggression of Frommel's group.

By March 7th, Korotkevich's detachment received further reinforcement from militia brigades, the 59th Infantry Division, and the 6th Siberian Rifle Division. However, the Landwehr Corps ceased their attack due to worsening weather and ammunition shortages, shifting to a defensive stance from March 8th. To maintain momentum in the offensive, General A. von Mackensen decided to transfer the entirety of the 11th, 13th, and 17th army corps to R. von Frommel's command.

The efforts of Generals Korotkevich and Papengut to regain control along the Pilica River proved futile, largely due to the overwhelming presence of German heavy artillery. Between March 8th and 10th, intense battles unfolded around Domanevice, where all Russian advances were effectively repelled by the Germans. On March 1st, General R. von Frommel's group, including G. von Menges's division and the 22nd and 38th infantry along with the 9th cavalry divisions, supported by X. von Stein's brigade, renewed their offensive. However, the Russian 5th Army's defense was notably more robust this time, and despite the Germans capturing a total of 7,150 soldiers, officers, and 16 machine guns during the conflict, they were unable to make significant headway.

The deteriorating situation on the Southwestern Front in the Carpathians, coupled with the failure to launch a successful offensive against von Frommel's group on the Pilica River, prompted the Commander-in-Chief of the Northwestern Front to order Papengut's detachment back to the 4th Army. The German offensive had lost its momentum, partly because their ammunition supplies were depleted. Von Frommel's group suffered heavy losses, totaling 10,000 men, including 2,200 killed and 339 captured.

Up until March 18th, Korotkevich's detachment experienced severe losses, with 36 officers and 3,114 soldiers killed, 7,150 captured, and significant numbers wounded, along with the loss of equipment and arms. The chief of staff of the 5th Army, Major General N. Sievers, reported to the Northwestern Front headquarters that the army was now focused on fortifying its positions without any immediate plans to reclaim lost territory. The 4th Army, including Papengut's detachment and the Grenadier Corps, also incurred substantial casualties, as did the German Landwehr Corps. As a result of the reduced activity on the Pilica River, additional divisions were able to be redeployed to the Carpathians.

By March 21st, R. von Frommel had ceased his attacks.

The March 1915 battles demonstrated the rough parity of forces and the inherent advantage of defensive tactics. Despite incurring significant losses, the German forces failed to achieve their objectives: breaking through the outnumbered Russian lines or preventing Russian troop movements to the Narew River and the Carpathians. This necessitated a shift in focus for the Germans, leading to the reinforcement of Austro-Hungarian forces in the Carpathians and weakening the German 9th Army, as forces were required elsewhere on the Eastern Front.

Attack of the Dead Men

The Osowiec Fortress, a formidable structure erected in the late 19th century, stands as a testament to the strategic military engineering of its era. Located near the Biebrza River in what is now Poland, this fortress was part of the Russian Empire during its construction, situated approximately 50 kilometers from East Prussia. Its strategic importance was underscored by its proximity to a vital railway line running from Bialystok to Königsberg, which, notably, passed directly through the fortress grounds.

During the tumultuous times of the Great War, the Osowiec Fortress emerged as a significant challenge for the German High Command. The fortress's location near the German border and its control over one of the few railway lines through the region's extensive bogs and marshes made it a critical obstacle. For the Germans, the fortress represented a barrier that either had to be captured or neutralized to facilitate any advance into northern Poland.

The German military had previously attempted to seize the fortress in September 1914 and again in February 1915. The second attack inflicted considerable damage on the fortress's defenses through intense bombing. However, the main defensive structures withstood the onslaught, and Russian counterattacks successfully repelled the German forces. By the summer of 1915, the situation on the Eastern Front had shifted dramatically. August von Mackensen's Gorlice-Tarnow offensive had disrupted the Russian defenses, allowing German and Austro-Hungarian forces to advance eastward. Seizing this opportunity, the German High Command, under the direction of Generalfeldmarschall Paul von Hindenburg, planned a frontal assault to capture Poland, with the Osowiec Fortress as a key objective.

The German assault on the fortress was formidable, comprising 12 infantry battalions and up to 30 heavy artillery pieces. On the other side, the Russian defense was led by General Lieutenant Brzhozovsky and primarily consisted of around 500 men from the 226th Infantry Regiment Zemlyansky, bolstered by several hundred militia members. The Russian defenders established multiple lines of defense and redoubts, minimizing the targets for German artillery. Despite the heavy siege artillery causing significant damage to the fortress walls, barracks, and towers, artillery alone was insufficient to capture the fortress. The German forces needed infantry to breach the defenses, a task made exceedingly difficult by the Russian's strategic use of machine guns and defensive works. The ensuing battle would prove to be a grueling and costly endeavor for both sides, marking a significant chapter in the history of the Great War.

The siege of Osowiec Fortress in the early 20th century marked a dark and harrowing chapter in the annals of warfare, primarily due to the introduction of a sinister and deadly weapon by the German forces: chemical gas. This represented a terrifying escalation in the methods of war, bringing a new dimension of horror to the battlefield.

Gas warfare, a relatively recent development at the time, had already shown its gruesome potential. The French had used tear gas in 1914, a mild agent compared to what was to come. The Germans first attempted to use poison gas at Bolimov in early 1915, but the effort was unsuccessful. However, subsequent uses of gas proved catastrophically effective against the Russian soldiers, who were tragically unprepared and unequipped to face this new threat. Many succumbed to the ghastly effects of the gas, suffering indescribable agony and death.

On the fateful morning of August 6, with the winds favoring their diabolical plan, the Germans unleashed their chemical onslaught on Osowiec Fortress. A sinister, dark green smog, comprising a lethal mix of chlorine and bromine, enveloped the Russian defenses. This deadly concoction was a remorseless killer: bromine served as a respiratory irritant, while chlorine, when combined with moisture in the air, transformed into hydrochloric acid. This acid viciously attacked the soft tissues of the lungs, eyes, and nose, causing excruciating pain and internal chemical burns. Russian soldiers, caught in this toxic maelstrom, experienced the horror of choking on their own blood, as their lungs were methodically destroyed from within.

Desperate to survive, some soldiers further from the gas's initial release tried to improvise protective measures, such as binding wet rags or urine-soaked shirts around their faces. Sadly, these makeshift solutions provided minimal relief. The gas's lethal reach extended beyond the immediate battlefield, causing environmental devastation – leaves and grass withered, insects and wildlife perished, and even the brass of guns and ammunition corroded.

The gas attack decimated the Russian defenders, wiping out entire companies in the frontline trenches. Only about a hundred men, though severely injured and burned, managed to survive in the more distant defensive positions. As the gas slowly dissipated, the German infantry, particularly the 7,000-strong 76th Landwehr Division, prepared to advance. Confident that the gas had eliminated most of the resistance, and that any remaining defenders would be easily subdued, the German soldiers moved forward. They were met with a ghastly sight: the first lines of defense littered with the twisted and disfigured bodies of Russian soldiers, whose final moments were marked by unspeakable suffering and death.

As the German troops cautiously advanced over the ravaged terrain, remnants of the previous shelling still visible, they were suddenly met with an onslaught of fierce resistance. The fortress's artillery roared to life, spewing deadly fire upon them, while machine gun volleys mercilessly tore through their ranks. On the flanks, the last reserves of the Russian forces, previously stationed at the rear, surged forth to mount a counterattack against the German infantry. This unexpected maneuver was further bolstered by the approximately 100 surviving soldiers in the trenches. Despite their grievous injuries and the debilitating effects of the gas, they mustered their remaining strength, fixed bayonets, and, like specters rising from their graves, staggered out of their dugouts. They advanced, crawling and limping into the open battlefield, driven by an unwavering determination to defend their land.

The sight that unfolded before the German attackers was one of macabre and haunting intensity. The Russian survivors, their faces marred by chemical burns and partially obscured by blood-soaked rags, moved with a ghostly resolve. They gasped for air through ravaged lungs, their eyes burning with a mixture of pain and vengeance. Blood and lung tissue were expelled with each agonized cough and croak, making them resemble the living dead. This ghastly vision, coupled with the ferocity of the counterattack, sent shockwaves of disbelief and terror through the German ranks. A deep-seated panic ensued, causing the attackers to falter and then hastily retreat in disorder. Chaos reigned as the Germans, gripped by fear, scrambled away, pushing past their comrades, stumbling over barbed wire, and dodging the relentless barrage of Russian artillery shells.

The Russian forces, powered by an almost supernatural tenacity, continued their charge, reclaiming the trenches they had lost just hours earlier. By 11:00 AM, the defensive lines were once again under Russian control, a remarkable turnaround from the dire situation earlier that day. The Germans, demoralized and disoriented, retreated to their original positions.

The details of this battle are wrapped in a shroud of legend and mystery, with casualty numbers and precise records remaining elusive. While it was a tactical triumph for the outnumbered Russian forces, the strategic impact was limited. The Russian hold on Poland remained tenuous, and the severely damaged Osowiec Fortress had to be abandoned weeks later, necessitating a withdrawal of the front lines.

Gorlice–Tarnów Offensive

In the tumultuous early days of the Eastern Front conflict, a remarkable story unfolded. The German Eighth Army, under the astute leadership of Paul von Hindenburg and Erich Ludendorff, orchestrated a series of astonishing maneuvers against their Russian adversaries. They first encircled and decimated the Russian Second Army in the legendary Battle of Tannenberg in late August. Without missing a beat, they pivoted to confront the Russian First Army at the First Battle of the Masurian Lakes. In this fierce encounter, they nearly obliterated their foe, driving them back across the border to the safety of their fortresses.

Meanwhile, the Austro-Hungarian Army was engaged in its own fierce struggle, known as the Battle of Galicia. Initially successful, their fortunes soon reversed into a desperate retreat, halting only at the formidable Carpathian Mountains by late September. In these treacherous terrains, General Franz Conrad von Hötzendorf, the chief of staff of the Austro-Hungarian Army, led a valiant but brutal counterattack against the advancing Russian troops. The ensuing winter battle was a grueling standoff, with horrific losses on both sides, yet the Russians maintained their ground.

By this point, the Austro-Hungarian Army was reeling, with half of its initial forces lost. In a dramatic plea, Conrad sought additional German reinforcements to secure the passes. German Chief of Staff Erich von Falkenhayn initially refused, leading to a tense moment where Conrad threatened a separate peace. The situation was critical, as Prit Buttar describes: the Russian Army, despite recent losses and supply challenges, remained a formidable force. Falkenhayn, recognizing the need for decisive action, proposed a bold plan. He envisaged deploying a massive army of at least eight German divisions, equipped with heavy artillery, to launch an offensive from the west, advancing from Gorlice-Gromnik in the general direction of Sanok. This strategic move was aimed not just at relieving the Austro-Hungarian forces but at delivering a crippling blow to the Russian Army's offensive capabilities.

In April 1914, a pivotal meeting took place in Berlin between Conrad and Falkenhayn, setting the stage for a significant shift in the Eastern Front's dynamics. They agreed on the formation of the Eleventh Army, a formidable force meticulously planned by Falkenhayn. This new army, as detailed by historian Prit Buttar, was a composite of elite units: the Guards Corps augmented by the 119th Division, the XLI Reserve Corps strengthened with the 11th Bavarian Infantry Division, and the X Corps. Additionally, Archduke Joseph Ferdinand's Fourth Army was to be integrated under this new German command. Key modifications were made to optimize this force, including the creation of Korps Kneussl and the inclusion of the Austro-Hungarian VI Corps.

Falkenhayn's strategy also involved reconfiguring existing divisions, drawing inspiration from the resilience of German troops on the Western Front. This reorganization involved reducing the number of regiments and artillery batteries in some divisions, a move aimed at streamlining forces for the formation of the Eleventh Army.

For Conrad, this collaboration meant accepting German leadership in the joint operation. The Austro-German Army Group would operate under a German command, with directives from Falkenhayn channeled through the Austro-Hungarian command structure. The Group included the Austro-Hungarian Fourth Army, commanded by the seasoned Archduke Joseph Ferdinand, alongside a newly formed German Eleventh Army, comprising eight divisions trained in the latest assault tactics.

Leading this formidable Eleventh Army was General August von Mackensen, with Colonel Hans von Seeckt as chief of staff. They faced the Russian Third Army, a sizable force under General D. R. Radko-Dmitriev. Mackensen's army was exceptionally equipped, boasting heavy artillery and mortars, airplanes for artillery direction, and an advanced field telephone service for real-time communication on the battlefield. Each division was further supported by 200 light Austro-Hungarian wagons, enhancing their mobility on challenging terrains.

The Eleventh Army's readiness peaked by 1 May, with strategic deployment across various corps. The XLI Reserve Corps, Austro-Hungarian VI Corps, and Guards Corps were positioned strategically, while the X Corps was held in reserve. The Fourth Army under Joseph Ferdinand was stationed at Gromnik, ready to engage the Russian Third Army, which had its own formidable arrangement of corps under capable commanders.

Falkenhayn, in a strategic move, relocated the German Supreme Headquarters (OHL) to Pless in Silesia, conveniently close to the Austrian headquarters. To ensure secrecy and avoid espionage, the local residents were evacuated from the area surrounding the military buildup. Meanwhile, in the north, the German Ninth and Tenth armies executed diversionary attacks, putting pressure on Riga and creating a distraction.

A significant development occurred on April 22 when the Germans initiated the first large-scale poison gas attack near Ypres. This action revealed a potentially game-changing weapon, but its primary purpose was to divert Allied attention in the west.

General Mackensen, commanding a formidable force, prepared for the upcoming engagement. His army, comprising ten infantry and one cavalry division, totaled 126,000 men, supported by a vast array of artillery, including light guns, heavy pieces, and mortars, spread across a 42 km (26 mi) front. Opposing them were five Russian divisions, significantly outnumbered and under-equipped, particularly in artillery.

The Russian supreme commander, Grand Duke Nicholas Nicholaevitch, was aware of the German movements but did not counteract effectively.

On May 1, Central Powers' artillery commenced preliminary bombardment, adjusting their aim. The next morning, an intense and relentless artillery barrage began, escalating from field guns to heavy howitzers, with mortars joining at 0900. The impact of the massive mortar shells was particularly devastating, causing casualties even at considerable distances from the point of impact. The Russian defenses, described as more ditches than trenches, could not withstand the onslaught.

As the attack progressed, the intensity and coordination of the Central Powers' offensive became evident. Mackensen had meticulously planned the assault, aiming for a uniform and, if possible, simultaneous advance across different sectors. By the end of the first day, the Germans reported capturing 12,000 prisoners. The town of Gorlice, near the frontline, was almost obliterated, its fighting zone reduced to rubble.

Mackensen quickly set his sights on the River Wisłoka, the Russian's third and final line of defense. While Russian reserves in the form of the III Caucasian Corps were dispatched, their delayed and fragmented engagement did little to halt the German advance.

Radko Dimitriev, in a swift response to the Austro-German onslaught, deployed two Russian divisions to counter the breach. However, these units were decimated before they could even report back, effectively vanishing from the Russian military's radar. By May 3, the gravity of the situation prompted Grand Duke Nicholas to dispatch three additional divisions and authorize a tactical retreat. This move signaled the weakening of Russian control over the Carpathians, as evidenced by the withdrawal of the XII Corps near the Dukla Pass and the XXIV Corps near Nowy Żmigród.

The situation escalated when the Korps Emmich, specifically the 20th Infantry Division under Otto von Emmich's command, captured Nowy Żmigród. Capitalizing on an intact bridge over the Wisłoka River, this division swiftly advanced to Wietrzno. By May 5, the Central Powers had breached the three Russian trench lines opposing them, and by May 9, they had achieved all their initial objectives.

Despite the deteriorating front, Grand Duke Nicholas only permitted a limited withdrawal. He dismissed the suggestion of establishing a well-fortified fallback position far behind the frontlines. In response, Russian counterattacks intensified, often involving inexperienced recruits armed with little more than grenades or wooden clubs.

Mackensen, on May 6, observed the widespread retreat of Russian forces along the entire front, from the Vistula to the Carpathians, estimating the capture of 60,000 prisoners. By May 11, Emmich's forces had reached the outskirts of Sanok, and François' had arrived at the San River, marking a rapid 60-mile (97 km) advance in just ten days. Mackensen then focused on securing the San line as a precursor to moving towards Rawa-Ruska.

The Russian military faced devastating losses. According to Buttar, the Russian X and XXIV Corps were virtually annihilated, the IX Corps had lost 80% of its strength, and the III Caucasian Corps had suffered two-thirds casualties. In a candid assessment to Grand Duke Nicholas on May 10, General Vladimir Dragomirov declared the strategic position of the Russian forces as hopeless, particularly highlighting the precarious situation of the Fourth Army in the event of a breakthrough along the lower San.

On May 12, General Mackensen made a strategic move to establish bridge-heads at Jaroslau and Radymno. This effort culminated in the capture of

Jaroslau by May 15, with German forces beginning to cross the San River there on May 17. Radymno fell to them on May 24. In a bid to halt the German advance, Grand Duke Nicholas shifted the XXI and XII Corps of Dimitriev's Third Army under the command of Aleksei Brusilov's Eighth Army. However, this move was not enough, leading to Dimitriev's dismissal and his replacement by Leonid Lesh.

The German offensive continued unabated. On May 28, the German XLI Corps' 81st Infantry Division seized Stubno and Nakło, north of the Przemyśl Fortress. By May 31, the Germans had started capturing the forts around Przemyśl, prompting Brusilov to order the fortress's evacuation. The 11th Bavarian Infantry Division under Kneussl entered unopposed on June 3. In response, Lesh's Third Army retreated towards the Tanew River, while Brusilov's Eighth Army fell back towards Lemberg near Gródek. Additionally, Brusilov was instructed to hand over his V Caucasian and XXII Corps to bolster the Third Army's southern flank, under the command of Vladimir Olukhov, to prevent any further advances by the 'Mackensen phalanx.'

The Central Powers then set their sights on advancing eastward from a bridgehead at Magierów, aiming to recapture Lemberg and cut off Russian communication lines between the Northwest and Southwest Fronts. In this operation, Mackensen led not only his Eleventh Army but also the Austro-Hungarian Fourth Army on the northern flank and the Austro-Hungarian Second Army on the southern flank. The Eleventh Army's formation, stretching from north to south, included multiple corps under various commanders.

The offensive resumed on June 13, and by June 17, the Germans had pushed the front line back by 18 miles near Gródek. After a day of preparation, the German attack intensified on June 19. The Russian forces, overwhelmed by the onslaught, began a full retreat. By June 21, Grand Duke Nicholas had no choice but to order the abandonment of Galicia. On June 22, Mackensen's forces entered Lemberg after advancing 310 km, averaging a rate of 5.8

km per day. This victory was not just territorial; it also had significant strategic implications, as the Galician oil fields, vital for the German navy, were recaptured, yielding 480,000 tons of essential oil supplies.

The Gorlice–Tarnów offensive marked a pivotal moment in the First World War, representing the most significant defeat inflicted upon the Russian Empire by the Central Powers. This 70-day operation stood out in several aspects: the sheer scale of troop involvement (around 4.5 million men, including replacements for combat and non-combat casualties), the staggering number of casualties on both sides (exceeding 1.5 million men), and the volume of captured equipment and supplies, making it one of the largest engagements of the war.

However, this victory for the Central Powers was not without severe costs. The Russian armies, facing heavy losses, were forced to retreat from Galicia in early June 1915. The retreat was so rapid that even prepared fortified positions were left unused. The Russian 8th Army, in particular, faced criticism for its low morale and hasty withdrawal from Lvov on June 22. Despite bringing in 26 infantry divisions over the course of the operation, with two more guard divisions in reserve, the Russian forces struggled to maintain their positions.

For the Central Powers, the toll of the victory was significant. The reserves they brought in, amounting to 6.5 divisions, were fully expended by early July. Despite the Russian troops facing occasional shortages of artillery shells (even though shell consumption was at its highest since the war began), they were well-supplied with rifle cartridges and had a superiority in machine gun numbers. The Russian forces effectively used hand weapon fire, making the frontal assaults of the Central Powers costly in terms of casualties, leading to a gradual narrowing of their breakthrough front.

The data on the captured equipment and prisoners provide a clearer picture of the operation's human cost. The Austria-Hungarian Army High Command

(AOK) and the German Supreme Commander of All German Forces in the East (Ober Ost) reported capturing 3 Russian generals, 1,354 officers, and 445,622 soldiers, along with 350 guns and 983 machine guns between May and early July 1915 in Galicia, Bukovina, and the Kingdom of Poland. Conversely, the Russian side officially reported capturing 100,476 prisoners (including 1,366 officers), 68 guns, 3 mortars, and 218 machine guns from the Central Powers during May and June 1915.

Bug–Narew Offensive

The German military strategists, led by the astute Hans von Seeckt, crafted a bold plan following their triumphant Gorlice–Tarnów offensive. Envisioning a daring push towards Brest-Litovsk, Seeckt suggested that August von Mackensen's Eleventh Army should spearhead this advance. The strategy was masterfully designed, with the Eleventh Army cutting through Poland, flanked by the natural defenses of the Vistula and Bug rivers.

At the heart of this strategy, Mackensen, alongside the influential Erich von Falkenhayn, Chief of the German Great General Staff, aimed to corner the Russian forces in a decisive battle. The plan was a chessboard of military maneuvers: Ober Ost, under the legendary Paul von Hindenberg and Erich Ludendorff, would strike southeastward, while Mackensen veered north. Concurrently, the Austro-Hungarian Second Army would thrust eastward. Adding to this formidable offensive, the Ober Ost Twelfth Army, under Max von Gallwitz, was to advance northeast of Warsaw, complemented by the Ninth Army, led by Prince Leopold of Bavaria, the Woyrsch Corps under Remus von Woyrsch, and the Austro-Hungarian First Army under Paul Puhallo von Brlog, all converging to drive the Russians towards the Vistula.

Meanwhile, the Army of the Bug, commanded by Alexander von Linsingen, and the Austro-Hungarian Second and Seventh Armies, under Eduard von Böhm-Ermolli and Karl von Pflanzer-Baltin, respectively, were tasked with safeguarding Mackensen's eastern flank. The western flank was protected by the Austro-Hungarian Fourth Army, led by Archduke Joseph Ferdinand.

In a pivotal turn of events on 24 June, Russian Tsar Nicholas II, amidst grave concerns, convened with his top commanders in Baranovichi. The decision was monumental: abandoning the Polish salient's defense. The new Russian line was to extend from Riga to Kovno, Grodno, Brest-Litovsk, along the upper Bug, and down to the Dniester into Romania. This strategic shift placed the Third and Fourth Armies under the command of Mikhail Alekseyev's Northwest Front, a formidable array including the Second, First, Twelfth, Tenth, and Fifth Armies. Alekseyev's plan? A calculated, gradual retreat from the salient.

The stage was set: Ober Ost's onslaught would begin on 13 July, followed closely by Mackensen's pivotal advance on 15 July. Capturing the strategic Russian railway center of Włodzimierz Wołyński was a top priority for Mackensen, marking the start of a critical chapter in the Great War's Eastern Front.

Second battle of Przasnysz

On the fateful night of July 13th, under the cover of darkness, the German forces of Gallwitz's army group stealthily advanced to within a mere kilometer of the Russian defenses. Amidst this tense atmosphere, the Supreme Commander of All German Forces in the East, the formidable Field Marshal Paul von Hindenburg, made his presence felt in Willenberg, establishing his command at the heart of Gallwitz's group.

In a display of strategic might, the Germans arrayed the 13th, 17th, and 11th Army corps against a stretch of the front from Grudusk to Stegna. Each division was meticulously organized, with two regiments in the frontline and another in reserve, poised for action. Their formidable opponents? The stalwart units of the Russian 1st, 2nd, and 11th Siberian Rifle Divisions.

Despite facing evenly matched forces along the entire front, Gallwitz ingeniously engineered a double numerical superiority in the crucial sector.

As dawn broke, at precisely 4:45 AM, a barrage of artillery fire shattered the silence, heralding the start of the onslaught. However, a relentless downpour delayed the infantry's advance until between 9 and 10 AM. The German artillery mercilessly pounded deep into the Russian lines, while the advancing infantry was bolstered by groups of sappers cutting through the battlefield.

On the Russian side, the determined 1st Army commander, Cavalry General Alexander Litvinov, swiftly reinforced the heated frontline with the 3rd Turkestan Rifle Brigade and the 14th Cavalry Division. Meanwhile, Mikhail Alekseyev, the Chief of Staff of the North-Western Front, decisively ordered the 21st and 4th Army Corps from the 2nd Army to bolster the 1st Army's defenses.

By midday, the tide had turned significantly. German troops had overrun Grudusk, capturing both the heavily bombarded first Russian line and most of the second. The German 13th Army Corps particularly distinguished itself, compelling the 2nd Siberian Rifle Division to a hasty retreat to rear positions, stretching from Krasnosielc to the village of Szczuki. The Germans carved deep into Russian territory, penetrating between 3 to 10 kilometers.

The day's grim tally for the Russians was staggering: 5,400 soldiers captured, along with 5 artillery pieces and 20 machine guns. On the Russian side, the 1st and 2nd Turkestan rifle brigades of the 1st Turkestan Corps were thrust into the fray.

Come the morning of July 14th, the German 36th Infantry Division boldly marched past Przasnysz. German aerial scouts reported a massive retreat of Russian forces and convoys, signaling a significant shift in the battle's momentum. By noon, the relentless pursuit by the 11th German Army Corps had breached the Russian intermediate positions. On the right flank of Gallwitz's group, the Russians were in full retreat.

As dusk fell, the relentless German offensive finally shattered the 4th Russian defensive line. The 17th Reserve Corps, joining the fray, surged towards Ciechanów and began its advance on Novogeorgievsk. However, the inclement weather proved to be a formidable adversary, hindering the Germans from organizing a swift pursuit and timely deployment of heavy artillery.

At this crucial juncture, the commander of the North-Western Front, M. Alekseyev, arrived at Litvinov's headquarters. Reinforcements were on the move - the 30th and 40th Infantry Divisions, along with the 3rd Turkestan Rifle Brigade, began to reinforce the battle-weary Russian lines.

On July 15th, the German forces pressed on against parts of the 1st Russian Army. Yet, they encountered stiff resistance and couldn't make significant headway across all sectors. The 13th Army Corps launched an ambitious assault against the formidable fortifications of the 1st Siberian Army Corps, now bolstered by the 30th Infantry Division, but to no avail. However, some progress by the neighboring 1st Army Corps compelled M. Alekseyev to authorize a tactical withdrawal of the 4th Siberian Army Corps and the right flank of the 2nd Siberian Rifle Division to avoid being outflanked.

All day, the German 17th Army Corps engaged in fierce combat at the junction of the 30th Infantry and 11th Siberian Rifle Divisions, eventually seizing Hill 124 near Dziki Bór. Despite a robust counterattack by the Russian 14th Cavalry Division, both mounted and on foot, the German advance was momentarily stalled. The 11th German Army Corps, after deploying the fresh 50th Reserve Division, managed to push back two Russian Turkestan rifle brigades. The German Reserve Division, led by T. von Wernitz, captured the redoubts at Długołęka. The renewed offensive from 19:00, bolstered by the entry of the 14th Landwehr Division, forced the Russian 1st Turkestan Army

Corps to retreat. However, the Russians adeptly filled the gaps in their lines with timely reinforcements, preventing a complete breach in the 1st Army's defenses.

As the night of July 16 approached, strategic deliberations were underway at M. von Gallwitz's army group headquarters, focusing on an operation against the Russian fortress of Novogeorgievsk and crossing the Narew River. Yet, the offensive's slowdown on the left flank prompted intervention from E. Ludendorff, the chief of staff for the Supreme Commander of All German Forces in the East. Ludendorff, diverging from the initial plan of establishing a barrier at Ostrołęka, insisted on an assault on the fortress. Gallwitz, however, believed this task should be allocated to the 8th Army and thus redirected his corps' offensive towards Pultusk and Różan.

In a pivotal turn of events on the night of July 16th, A. Litvinov, bolstered by necessary reinforcements, commanded the 1st Siberian and 1st Turkestan corps to launch an offensive, aiming to reclaim lost ground. However, his plans were quickly thwarted. At 4 AM, the Germans unleashed a ferocious artillery barrage, escalating rapidly into a torrential onslaught. By 6 AM, Willem Clifford Cocq von Brougel's division had stormed into Ciechanów. Following a fierce street battle, the city fell into German hands.

The situation escalated as the 17th Reserve Corps neared Nasielsk, posing a dire threat of a breakthrough east of Novogeorgievsk. The German 11th Army Corps advanced towards Gołymin-Ośrodek, and the 50th Reserve Division shattered the defenses of the Russian 30th Infantry Division near Kurowo, driving its remnants back to the village of Łukowo. A desperate counterattack by the 2nd brigade of the 14th cavalry division, mounted and valiant, was devastatingly crushed under the concentrated fire of the German 229th reserve infantry regiment. Amidst this chaos, the commander of the 14th Hussar Mitavsky Regiment, Major General A. Westfalen, was killed, yet the German advance was momentarily stalled.

Meanwhile, the 1st and 2nd Siberian Rifle Divisions bravely fended off the assaults by the 13th Army Corps. However, the 17th Army Corps made a significant breakthrough, capturing the redoubt at Bobowo and taking around 1,000 Russian prisoners. The Germans also breached Gmina Krasnosielc but were repelled by a vigorous counterattack from the 10th Siberian Rifle Division. As the Russian 12th Army's left flank crumbled under the pressure of the 8th German Army and the 1st Army Corps, the German 13th Army Corps seized control of the crossings over the Orzyca. Realizing the gravity of the situation, Litvinov at 13 o'clock ordered a full retreat of the entire 1st Army, but disengaging from the German forces proved impossible.

The Russian withdrawal to new defensive positions was completed by the morning of July 17. The four-day conflict was costly for the Russians: 88 officers and 17,544 soldiers were captured by the Germans, who also seized 13 guns, 40 machine guns, and 7 mortars.

On July 17th, in a strategic move to fortify his forces, A. Litvinov bolstered the right flank of his army with the 21st Army Corps, a reinforcement provided by M. Alekseyev. Additionally, he positioned the 1st Cavalry Corps strategically behind the center. However, the North-Western Front's headquarters decided against deploying the 27th Army Corps to Novogeorgievsk, designating it as a reserve force. Instead, the 63rd Infantry Division from the 3rd Army was dispatched to the fortress. The 1st Rifle Brigade from the 2nd Army was sent to Wyszków. This resulted in a significant strengthening of the defenses in front of the Narew River, but the full assembly of these troops required more time.

Hindenburg's influence on Gallwitz's operational plan prompted a pivotal shift in the offensive's focus, now oriented eastwards towards Ostrołęka. Consequently, the 13th, 17th, and 11th German Army Corps faced off against the bolstered 1st Siberian Army Corps. In the afternoon, a portion of the 4th Army Corps was allocated from Kołaki to Tarnowo. To support this, A. Churin dispatched the 1st Cavalry Brigade to aid the Siberians. Throughout the day, the 2nd Siberian Rifle Division, now reinforced by the 33rd Infantry Division, valiantly defended its position. Meanwhile, the 14th Cavalry Division took advantage of the Germans' slow crossing of the Orzyca River to fortify their trenches. However, both the 30th Infantry and 1st Siberian Rifle Divisions were again driven from their positions, forced into a retreat.

At 13:00, Litvinov ordered a retreat beyond the Narew River but swiftly rescinded this directive 15 minutes later as the 44th Infantry Division and the 1st Cavalry Corps neared the frontline. Nonetheless, by 15:00, the German forces broke through to the rear of the 1st Siberian Division, overpowering both the 14th Cavalry and the 30th Infantry Divisions of the 4th Army Corps, and pressuring the 1st Turkestan Corps. Following an unsuccessful counterattack by the 40th Infantry Division, Litvinov, at 18:30, once again ordered the withdrawal of the 1st Siberian Corps across the Narew River.

Throughout July 18th, Gallwitz's group pursued the retreating Russian 1st Army, reaching the fortifications of Novogeorgievsk with their right wing, and nearing Ostrołęka with their left. In total, during the first phase of the Bug–Narew offensive, the Germans suffered over 20,000 casualties but captured 24,000 Russian prisoners, along with 56 machine guns and 14 artillery pieces. Russian losses were even more severe, exceeding 40,000 men. This marked a significant, though costly, milestone in the offensive.

Narew Offensive

In the thrilling aftermath of their triumph in the Second Battle of Przasnysz, the Germans set their sights on a new strategic objective: seizing control of the Narew River from Różan to Pultusk. This stage of the offensive was no mere skirmish; each fortress along the river had a dedicated corps, and the formidable 17th Army Corps was tasked with crossing the river between these heavily fortified points. The defenses at Różan and Pultusk, bolstered by pre-war forts integrated into a unified defensive system, presented a formidable challenge, impervious to a swift breakthrough. Max von Gallwitz, recognizing the gravity of the situation, called for the reinforcement of the 13th Army Corps against Różan with a colossal 30.5-cm gun and dispatched two mammoth 42-cm mortars to aid the 11th Army Corps against Pultusk.

As July 19 dawned, the Germans were in the throes of preparing for this ambitious offensive. However, they encountered a significant snag: the delay of heavy artillery meant not all corps could initiate their attack simultaneously. Paul von Hindenburg and Erich Ludendorff, ever the strategists, urged for expedited preparations, while also emphasizing the importance of a stringent blockade of the Novogeorgievsk Fortress (now known as Modlin Fortress). Meanwhile, on the left flank, the 8th German Army, stationed at the right bank of the Narew River near the Rozoga River mouth, had a dual option: either to ford the river or to march on Ostrołęka. The withdrawal of the 1st Russian Army beyond the Narew led to the repositioning of the 2nd Army closer to Warsaw. Reinforcements were on the move: the 12th Siberian Rifle and 68th Infantry Divisions from the 5th Army, engaged in fierce combat, were dispatched to Ostrołęka and Białystok, while the 58th Infantry Division from the 8th Army of the Southwestern Front bolstered the Novogeorgievsk garrison.

The night of July 20 marked a pivotal moment. Alexander Litvinov, upon realizing that Max von Gallwitz's army group was advancing with limited forces, issued a bold order for a counteroffensive starting at 10 AM. The plan: the 1st Cavalry Corps would strike at Dzbądz and Gnojno, aiming to outflank the German forces near Różan's fortifications. Concurrently, the 4th Army Corps would target Maków, and the 21st Army Corps would converge on Khrzanowo for a coordinated assault with the cavalry. The Germans, at this point, were perilously close to the Russian trenches, merely 400–800 steps away.

The dawn of the Russian offensive coincided with the 13th German Army Corps' assault on Różan's fortifications, where they managed to seize Hill 132. A fierce and relentless battle ensued in the sectors of the 1st Cavalry,

4th, and 21st Army Corps. In the morning, Russian troops successfully forded the Narew River, pushing back the German barriers and vanguards. However, by midday, the Germans rallied their main forces, repelling the Russians back across the Narew. The village of Gnojno became a fiercely contested battleground, changing hands four times before being ultimately abandoned.

At 21:15, under orders from Mikhail Alekseyev, chief of staff of the North-Western Front, the Russian offensive was halted. The corps retreated to their original positions but maintained vanguards and patrols in the areas still held near Mariew, as ordered by Litvinov. The Germans, seizing the opportunity, pushed back the 2nd brigade of the 33rd infantry division to Paulina. The Russians, facing immense pressure, managed to halt the breakthrough with desperate counterattacks. Misled by a prisoner's false testimony, Litvinov braced for what he believed to be an impending German push to cross the Narew River near Pultusk, involving the entire 25th Reserve Corps.

On July 21st, a momentous day in the unfolding drama of the Eastern Front, General of Infantry Otto von Plüskow was appointed to spearhead a formidable attack on Pultusk within Gallwitz's army group. In a strategic maneuver, the 38th Infantry Division was shifted to the 17th Army Corps, bolstering the operation's defenses. Plüskow's command now comprised an impressive array of forces: the elite 1st Guards, the 50th Reserve, and the 85th Landwehr, along with the 86th and 88th Infantry Divisions, and the Pfeil Brigade.

The night of July 23rd marked the onset of a fierce German offensive. Their artillery unleashed a torrent of fire on the Russian positions. As dawn broke, the German infantry surged forward. The 11th Army Corps, divided into two groups, executed a pincer movement around Pultusk, breaking through the 4th Army Corps' defenses in multiple locations. The 17th Army Corps successfully crossed the Narew River, overpowering the 1st Cavalry Corps.

By noon, the situation had grown dire for the Russians. Litvinov, in a desperate bid to turn the tide, ordered the 1st Siberian Corps to deliver a swift and decisive blow to the enemy's flank. He also directed the 4th Army Corps, cavalry, and the 1st Rifle Brigade to push the Germans back across the Narew and restore control. However, by 18:00, Russian forces were in disarray, suffering multiple breaches in their lines. A perilous 8-km gap emerged between the 1st Turkestan and 4th Army Corps, compelling the commander of the 1st Army to request permission to retreat behind the defensive fortifications of Novogeorgievsk.

By 19:30, a glimmer of hope emerged as the Russian 11th Siberian Rifle Division entered the fray, temporarily stemming the German advance. Litvinov harbored plans for a counteroffensive, contingent on the arrival of the 27th Army Corps. Yet, the overwhelming German artillery superiority resulted in heavy Russian casualties. At 22:00, recognizing the untenable situation, Litvinov ordered a full retreat across the Narew River, instructing his forces to destroy all bridges. By 07:00 on July 24th, the 1st Army had regrouped at a new defensive line. Meanwhile, German forces occupied Różan and Pultusk.

Despite this repositioning, Litvinov was under no illusions about the precariousness of their situation, citing a dire shortage of ammunition and an ill-fortified, defensively weak line. He urgently requested M. Alekseyev to send the 78th Infantry Division to reinforce the 21st Army Corps.

Simultaneously, a new German force emerged on the battlefield on July 24th. An army group led by Infantry General Hans Hartwig von Beseler, detached from Gallwitz's command, was tasked with assaulting the fortress of Novogeorgievsk. This group comprised Lieutenant General Gustaf von Dickhuth-Harrach's corps, the 89th Infantry, 14th and 85th Landwehr divisions, Colonel Pfeil's brigade, the 169th Landwehr brigade, and heavy artillery from all corps west of Pultusk. Gallwitz's new mission: advance to the lower reaches of the Bug River. As the day unfolded, German forces inched closer to the positions of the beleaguered 1st Russian Army. While the 21st Army Corps managed to repel attacks, the 1st Cavalry Corps, followed by the 27th and 4th Army Corps, were forced to retreat. The 1st Siberian Army Corps was deployed in a countermeasure, but the German onslaught continued with relentless success.

In a crucial strategic decision reflecting the intense battles unfolding across multiple fronts, M. Alekseyev, on July 24th, issued a directive for a general withdrawal. This order encompassed the 12th, 1st, 2nd, and 4th armies, retreating to the line Łomża - Węgrów - Siedlce. Concurrently, the 3rd and 13th armies were to continue their defensive efforts at Łęczna - Chełm - Vladimir-Volynsky, with a contingency plan for a further retreat to Kovel if necessary. Notably, the 2nd Army was instructed to secure the right bank of the Vistula River, holding the line of Warsaw's outer forts, while the 1st and 4th armies were to bolster this position from the flanks with "full energy, outstanding firmness and stubbornness." This strategy effectively linked the fate of the 1st Army to the Warsaw bridgehead, amidst the looming threat of a German breakthrough to the middle reaches of the Bug River.

A. Litvinov, in a bold response, commanded his troops to launch an offensive on the morning of July 26th, aiming to drive the Germans back across the Narew River. He also sought the support of A. Churin and the 12th Army, urging his corps commanders to prepare for a fierce initial resistance from the enemy and to respond with skill, speed, decisiveness, and persistence.

The morning of July 26th saw the 1st Army's corps engage the Germans along the entire front, encountering stubborn resistance. The battlefield was chaotic, with settlements changing hands multiple times as attacks were met with intense artillery, machine-gun, and small-arms fire. Despite this, Litvinov remained hopeful of continuing the offensive on July 27th, encouraging his forces with a rallying order at 20:40: "The resistance of the Germans has not yet been broken, but can be broken by our stubborn and persistent efforts."

However, the night of July 27th brought a significant setback as German troops once again penetrated the positions of the 4th Siberian Army Corps, capturing the right flank of the 1st Army. Litvinov was forced to withdraw the 21st Army Corps and fill the gap at Żabin with the 6th Cavalry Division, hastily summoned from the 1st Cavalry Corps at 1:30. By morning, three regiments of the 78th Infantry Division had reinforced the front, but the momentum for an offensive had been lost.

Throughout July 27th, the left flank of the 1st Army continued its unsuccessful assaults on German positions, ranging from Novogeorgievsk's outer forts to Adamowo and Dąbrówka. Litvinov, undeterred, ordered a continuation of the offensive at midnight. Meanwhile, the 12th Army's left flank was retreating under the pressure of the 1st German Army Corps. The 4th Siberian Corps received reinforcements from the 68th Infantry Division, but the Germans, with the 37th Infantry Division, breached the 5th Army Corps' positions. A. Churin, commander of the 12th Army, urgently requested reserves from the front headquarters as a breakthrough to Nowogródek loomed dangerously close. Gallwitz responded by dispatching the 54th Infantry Division, recently arrived from France, to Ostrołęka. However, he deemed it risky to transport the division across the Narew on improvised means, particularly as the 1st Army Corps had already sustained over 3,000 casualties, and the supply of ammunition had nearly ceased following the Russian artillery's destruction of the pontoons.

During July 28th and 29th, the 1st and 12th Russian armies made concerted efforts to repel the German regiments that had crossed the Narew River. These attempts, met with tenacious German resistance, resulted in a grueling stalemate, with only minor territorial gains (about 400 steps in the case of the 4th Army Corps). Observing the Russians depleting their forces in these seemingly futile attacks, E. Ludendorff instructed Gallwitz to focus on advancing towards Ostrow and Małkin, while avoiding direct assaults on the fortresses, and providing cover with the troops of the 8th army. Consequently, on July 30th, Gallwitz directed the group led by infantry general Johannes von Eben (comprising the 2nd, 37th, 54th, and 83rd infantry divisions) to overpower the 4th Siberian Corps and take control of Żabin, while the 13th Army Corps was to attack Strumiany, with the rest of the army group adopting a defensive stance.

In a significant strategic shift on the evening of July 28th, Alekseyev transferred the 21st Army Corps (including the 33rd, 44th, 78th Infantry Divisions) to the 12th Army, along with its combat sector, and deployed additional regiments from the 59th Infantry Division. The 1st Army, from the evening of July 30th, moved the 4th Army Corps (30th and 40th Infantry Divisions) to reserve. In the 12th Army, Chief of Staff N. Sivers initiated the formation of small reserve units within each corps to counter potential German breakthroughs.

July 30th saw a lull in major combat activities for the 1st Army, with Gallwitz's efforts predominantly targeting the Russian 12th Army. By the afternoon, the 4th Guards and 54th Infantry Divisions had breached the 4th Siberian Army Corps' defenses, seizing Goworówek and Żabin by evening. Churin, responding to this development, deployed the 68th Infantry and 6th Cavalry Divisions (from the 1st Army) to the breach, managing to only temporarily halt the German advance.

On July 31st, Gallwitz, upon learning that the 37th Infantry Division's six battalions had been blockaded for five days near Kamionka, reinforced them with heavy artillery and resumed attacks with the 1st and 13th Army Corps. This offensive encountered robust resistance from the Russian 59th Infantry Division, leading to intense fighting over Hill 111 that lasted until evening. Both the 4th Siberian and 21st Army Corps were pushed back but avoided encirclement, retreating to new positions stretching from Brzeźno to Ostrołęka. The German 83rd Infantry Division alone suffered significant losses, with 84 officers and 3,100 soldiers. The Russians, too, faced substantial casualties: since the operation's onset, they had lost 161 officers, 44,926 soldiers, 14 guns, 133 machine guns, and 6 mortars.

Gallwitz then realigned his forces, moving the 50th Reserve Division to the right flank and transferring the 85th Landwehr Division to Beseler's army group for the blockade of Novogeorgievsk Fortress from the northeast. He also positioned the 1st and 13th Army Corps east of the Rozan-Ostrołęka border. In the battles of August 1st and 2nd, despite heavy losses, German troops captured the village of Grabowo and the heights near Borawe, continually fending off counterattacks from the 4th Siberian, 5th, and 21st Army Corps. The German 8th Army forced the 12th Army's 1st Army Corps back at Kupnino and Serwatki. By August 3rd, due to severe losses, both the 1st Army Corps and the 4th Siberian Corps were withdrawn for manpower replenishment and reorganization.

Siege of Novogeorgievsk

The siege of Novogeorgievsk began on August 10th. The German forces, adeptly surrounding the fortress, initiated their bombardment a few days later, focusing their firepower on the northeastern defenses north of the Vistula River. A stroke of fortune aided the Germans when they captured the fort's Chief Inspector, along with detailed plans of the fortifications. This intelligence proved crucial in the ensuing assault.

After three days of relentless bombardment, on August 16th, General X. von Beseler's corps launched a ferocious storming of the forts in the northeastern and eastern parts of the outer belt. Colonel T. von Pfeil's brigade successfully captured forts XV and XVb by 4 p.m., taking 150 prisoners. The 10th and 38th Landwehr Regiments, engaged in a fierce battle, overran Fort XVa by 2 a.m. However, the Russian garrison stoutly repelled attacks on forts XVla and XVIb near Charnovo.

The German onslaught against the Pomekhovsky sector of Novogeorgievsk's northeastern defenses persisted. Attempts by the Russian garrison to recapture the forts of group XV faltered, and Colonel S. Shiryaev of the 455th infantry regiment tragically fell in the counterattacks. The 21st and Pfeil brigades were dispatched to the forts of group XVI, but they too faced staunch resistance from the garrison. Concurrently, the 169th Landwehr Brigade's shelling paved the way for an assault on Group XIV forts. Major General P. Venevitinov, commanding the Pomekhovsky sector, ordered a retreat to the second line of defense and the demolition of the fortifications. However, a lack of pyroxylin and the absence of sappers left the forts intact and ripe for German capture.

The evening of August 17th brought further grim developments for the Russian defenders. Commandant Nikolai Bobyr ordered a retreat across the Wkra River to the redoubts of the fortress's main bypass. The imminent threat to Modlin's airfield prompted the evacuation of aircraft and crews, with the destruction of five faulty ones. In a daring escape, nine planes flew out of the fortress, carrying secret files, the fortress standard, and a stash of St. George Crosses. Tragically, one aircraft went missing during the evacuation.

By August 18th, X. von Beseler's siege artillery advanced to positions closer to Novogeorgievsk's second belt of forts. The Zakrochimsky and Vymyslovsky sectors fell to the Germans. Major General N. Globachev, the fortress's chief of staff, sent a despondent message to the North-Western Front headquarters, conceding that Novogeorgievsk's defense could last no more than a day.

The battle reached a fever pitch on August 19th. By early morning, the Germans had occupied forts X, XI, and XIV. The Russian 249th Infantry Regiment launched a counterattack against Pfeil's Landwehr Brigade at Forts II and III. Despite the German field artillery exhausting its ammunition and nearly being captured, the arrival of heavy batteries turned the tide. By 13:00, forts I, II, and III were in German hands. A final push by the German troops overran the second line of fortifications.

As the evening approached, large contingents of Russian defenders began surrendering. German infantry columns converged on the citadel, while communication with the fortress was lost. The citadel and Zakrochim, on the northern bank of the Vistula, were the last holdouts, with the southern bank forts yet to be stormed. The German heavy artillery now mercilessly shelled the entire citadel area, devastating the remaining fortifications.

In a somber conclusion to this fierce battle, on the night of August 20th, cavalry general N. Bobyr, the fortress commandant, initiated surrender negotiations with X. von Beseler, the commander of the Siege Group. By 4 a.m., the terms of surrender were agreed upon, and an hour later, the German artillery ceased fire.

Russian Retreat

Russian forces, though numerically superior to their German counterparts, faced a critical challenge. Amidst the intense battle, fueled by an ample supply of artillery shells, a strategic twist unfolded. The skilled German and Austro-Hungarian troops under General Remus von Woyrsch achieved a significant breakthrough, crossing the Vistula River near Ivangorod, posing a direct threat to the rear of the Russian-held Ivangorod fortress and the 2nd Army.

On August 2, General M. Alekseyev issued a command for a determined defense of Warsaw's fort line and its suburb, Praga. Yet, as the day turned to evening, a swift change in strategy was ordered: the 2nd Army was to retreat to the Vistula's right bank on the night of August 3. This move, while retaining the fort line, wasn't for a fierce battle but to delay the German advance if possible.

This decision had a domino effect. The 1st and 12th Russian armies were compelled to plan a timely retreat to avoid being encircled by the

Central Powers' forces breaking through from the south. Concurrently, the Novogeorgievsk fortress garrison, now directly under Alekseyev's command, began relocating from their front-line positions to the outer forts on August 3.

The 1st and 12th armies were tasked with a critical mission: cover the withdrawal of the 2nd, 3rd, and 4th armies. The Russian 12th Army witnessed fierce fighting along its entire front on August 3. Despite their valiant efforts, the 4th Siberian Corps was pushed back, with German forces capturing 2,000 Russian soldiers and 14 machine guns.

The situation intensified on August 4. German forces launched a major offensive after 2:00 PM, breaking through the positions of the 1st Siberian Army Corps and forcing back the 12th Army's left flank. The losses were so severe that by midnight on August 5, the 1st Army's commander ordered a strategic withdrawal, repositioning the 4th Army Corps to the army reserve.

As the German onslaught continued throughout the day, Russian troops in the 12th Army sector fought back fiercely, particularly along the Orzyc river. Despite their persistent counterattacks, they were gradually overpowered by the evening. On the night of August 5, as the 2nd Army evacuated Warsaw, they destroyed railway stations and bridges across the Vistula, hindering the enemy's pursuit. By morning, the troops of the 9th German Army, led by Field Marshal Prince Leopold of Bavaria, triumphantly entered Poland's capital.

On August 6, M. von Gallwitz's army group evolved into the formidable 12th Army. To boost their offensive on the left flank, the 11th Army Corps was redeployed. Over three days, Russian forces were driven back across a 25 km front, retreating 4-7 km eastwards. They suffered devastating losses: 85 officers and 14,200 soldiers captured, along with 6 guns, 8 mortars, and 69 machine guns.

On the fateful day of August 7, the 1st Army Corps of Russia's 12th Army faced a daunting attack, leading to their withdrawal from the northern region of Szczepankowo. Concurrently, the right flank of the 1st Army, under relentless pressure from the German 13th and 17th Army Corps, was compelled to commence a strategic retreat. By the dawn of August 8, the entirety of the 1st Army had joined in the retreat.

This retreat had significant consequences. The Novogeorgievsk fortress, a critical stronghold for the Russians, found itself encircled from the south by Lieutenant General Thilo von Westernhagen's division of the German 9th Army. In a strategic move, Ludendorff ordered von Galwitz to initiate a "parallel pursuit" of the retreating Russian forces along the Bug River, aiming to cut off their escape to the east. The formidable task of capturing Novogeorgievsk was assigned to the siege corps led by Hans Hartwig von Beseler. An interesting divergence in strategy emerged: Ludendorff favored an eastern attack from the confluence of the Bug and Vistula Rivers, while Gallwitz argued for a northern approach, devoid of water barriers.

Meanwhile, the German 12th Army, upon realizing the Russian withdrawal, launched into an aggressive pursuit on the morning of August 8. Their continued pressure on the left flank of the Russian 12th Army had devastating effects. The Russian 12th Army, suffering heavy casualties estimated at 80,000 men—30,000 of whom were either killed or captured—was forced into a withdrawal. This decision was made despite objections from the chief of staff of the North-Western Front. The 33rd and 78th divisions were virtually annihilated, and the 44th division's brigade was reduced to a mere 380 men. Ammunition shortages exacerbated the situation, with critically low supplies for various artillery.

The dynamics further intensified with the offensive actions of the 9th German Army, which, after capturing Warsaw, crossed to the right bank of the Vistula River. By the evening of August 10, the Russian 1st and 12th armies had retreated to new positions. The Germans had completely seized the Łomża fortress and secured positions along the Bug River. However, their relentless advance on the Russian armies' junction persisted.

On the night of August 11, the Russian 12th Army withdrew from the Narew River bend. Von Gallwitz was ready to continue his push through the Russian armies' junction, but Ludendorff decisively redirected the attack towards the right flank, along the right bank of the Bug River. The German 17th and 13th army corps successfully pushed back parts of the Russian 1st Siberian and 21st army corps beyond Zuzel and towards Czyżew. The German 11th and 1st Army Corps dealt another blow to the Russian 4th Siberian and 5th Army Corps. Meanwhile, the German 8th and 12th armies were assigned a new objective: advance towards Bielsk Podlaski.

On August 12, the German 8th Army launched a formidable attack on the positions of the 1st Army Corps of Russia's 12th Army. The German 75th reserve division made a significant advance of 20 kilometers. Although the 4th Siberian Army Corps, bolstered by the newly arrived 61st Division, put up a valiant resistance against the 1st German Army Corps, their left flank was eventually pushed back by 7 kilometers. The Russian armies found themselves in an increasingly precarious position.

As the night of August 13 approached, the Russian armies continued their withdrawal, a move that was quickly detected by the Germans. By 3 AM, the Germans had already commenced their pursuit, deploying the 86th Infantry Division. They advanced 18–20 kilometers eastward by evening, while the 1st Army Corps retreated up to 25 kilometers. The Russian 1st and 2nd armies were falling back towards Brest-Litovsk. Within the 1st Russian Army, the 21st Army Corps was unable to hold against the German onslaught, retreating across the Narev River, followed closely by the 27th, 4th, 1st Siberian Army, and 1st Cavalry Corps. Anticipating the untenability of their current positions, A. Litvinov, the commanding officer, ordered a further withdrawal on the night of August 15.

By August 15, the forces of M. von Gallwitz's center and left wing had reached the Myanka River, successfully repelling Russian counterattacks and capturing 2,900 prisoners.

On August 16, German reconnaissance detected the Russian withdrawal towards Białystok. They observed fortifications being erected on the city's outskirts and heavy artillery being positioned. By evening, M. von Gallwitz's troops had reached the Narew River along its entire length. The following day, the Russian 2nd, 1st, and 12th armies initiated an offensive to push the Germans back from Białystok and Velsk, with the heaviest attacks aimed at the junction of the German 9th and 12th armies. The 2nd Austro-Hungarian Cavalry Division was driven back, but the Russian offensive failed to make significant gains in other sectors. However, the Germans were pressed into their trenches. Gallwitz, interpreting intercepted Russian communications, believed that the Russian forces were fortifying defensive positions along the Narew-Bug line for a prolonged resistance.

On August 18, the Russian 1st, 2nd, and 12th armies retreated, leaving rearguards against the German 12th and 8th armies. The Germans pursued, advancing over 13 kilometers by noon. By August 21, they reached east of Brest-Litovsk, capturing Kleszczele. A new objective to reach the Riga-Grodno-Brest line was set by German High Command. From August 23-25, fierce battles occurred as Germans advanced towards Białowieża Forest, confronting Russian rearguards. On August 26, the Germans occupied Białystok and captured Brest-Litovsk, both set ablaze by retreating Russians. This marked the end of the Bug-Narew offensive, a critical point in the Eastern Front of World War I.

Vistula–Bug Offensive

In the gripping summer of 1915, the German Great General Staff and the Austro-Hungarian High Command were intensely focused on the pivotal maneuvers of Field Marshal A. von Mackensen's Army Group. This formidable force was the southern arm of a strategic "scissors" designed to sever the Russian armies from their retreat paths to Brest-Litovsk. On July 11, an urgent directive set in motion von Mackensen's offensive, slated to begin between July 15–16. The initial assault was launched by the Army of the Bug, soon to be joined by the 11th and 4th armies. Their primary target: to overrun Russian defenses along the Wieprz River, aiming to capture strategic positions at the Wolica and Voislavka rivers.

The operation unfolded with a complex coordination of movements. On the right, the Bug Army surged forward towards the Hill, while on the left, the Austro-Hungarian 4th Army pressed towards Lublin. This multifaceted attack was bolstered by Colonel-General Remus von Woyrsch's army on the left flank, challenging Russian strongholds from Pilica to the Vistula, and the Austro-Hungarian 1st Army's daring crossing of the Bug and advance towards Vladimir-Volynsky.

Meanwhile, the Russian Northwestern Front braced for impact. The 4th, 3rd, and 13th armies were tasked with a crucial mission: halt the Central Powers' breakthrough to Brest-Litovsk and safeguard Warsaw's evacuation. The 13th Army, positioned along the Bug River, was reinforced by the 8th Army of the Southwestern Front. Simultaneously, the 4th Army's right flank by the Vistula was buttressed by the 2nd Army, prepared to defend Warsaw's approaches. Despite the Stavka's July 5 directive, which anticipated the South as the main battleground, the July Narew River skirmishes cast doubt on these expectations.

Von Mackensen's forces, although not as abundantly supplied with shells as Max von Gallwitz's army group, were nonetheless equipped to conduct both defensive and offensive operations. By early July, the Russian armies from the Vistula to the Bug had sufficient ammunition for a limited duration of defensive and offensive combat.

On the 13th of July, a pivotal moment unfolded as General of Infantry Alexander von Linsingen, leading the German Bug Army, achieved a significant victory at Starogród, overpowering the Russian 4th Cavalry Corps and driving back the 2nd Caucasian Army Corps. This was soon followed by the German forces inching closer to the Russian lines on July 15, with Linsingen launching a powerful assault with the Beskids, 24th, and 41st reserve corps against the troops of the Russian 13th Army, commanded by Infantry General V. Gorbatovsky. The Germans succeeded in taking a heavily fortified position, but the Russian 2nd Caucasian, 29th, and 31st Army Corps swiftly organized defenses along the main fortified line.

The battle intensified on July 16, with the German 11th Army striking hard against the Russian 3rd Army west of the Wieprz River. Their assault group, comprising the Guards, 10th Army, and XXII Reserve Corps, managed to push back the 9th, 10th, 3rd Caucasian, and parts of the 14th Army Corps. Despite capturing 6,000 Russian prisoners and deploying reserves like the 1st cavalry and 119th infantry divisions, the Germans couldn't penetrate the primary defense zone. Concurrently, the 1st Austro-Hungarian Army launched an offensive targeting the junction between the Russian 13th and 8th armies. On July 14, they seized the western bank of the Bug River near Krystynopol, and on the night of July 16, they crossed the river north of

Sokal. That evening, the Russian 3rd Army was reinforced by the arrival of the 2nd Siberian Army Corps. On July 17, this corps, alongside the 10th Army Corps, mounted counterattacks, managing by day's end to secure a position in the forest near Orchowiec village. Despite this, the German strike group's pressure on the 3rd Caucasus Army Corps led to a breakthrough on the eastern bank of the Wieprz River, posing a threat to the flank and rear of the Russian forces. Consequently, in front of the Austro-Hungarian 4th Army, the Russian troops commenced a retreat. Krasnostav, reinforced by two guards regiments, soon fell to the German Guards Corps. However, the flanking armies of Mackensen's Army Group were stalled.

On July 18, the Austro-Hungarian 1st and 2nd Corps crossed the Bug River, outflanking the Russian 12th Infantry Division in the sector of the 8th Army of the Southwestern Front. This created a gap between the 19th and 60th Infantry Divisions, prompting Aleksei Brusilov to send the 14th Infantry and 11th Cavalry Divisions to the breach. The center and right flank of the army launched an offensive at 7:00 am against the Bug Army, reclaiming some lost trenches. However, developments in the neighboring 3rd Army compelled V. Gorbatovsky to order a strategic withdrawal of the right flank and center of the 13th Army at midnight on July 9.

On the morning of July 18th within the Russian 3rd Army, a sudden shift occurred when the commander of the 2nd Siberian Corps, Radko Dimitriev, under intense German pressure, unexpectedly ordered a retreat. This move triggered a domino effect, leading to the withdrawal of the 9th Army Corps and the 3rd Caucasian Corps. In this turmoil, the 6th Austro-Hungarian Corps broke through the Russian defenses, capturing 3,500 prisoners despite incurring heavy casualties of nearly 7,000 men. In response, the Russian Guards Corps, the last front reserve on the southern flank, was swiftly deployed to confront the Germans. Although they managed to halt the German advance, doubts surfaced about the feasibility of holding this hastily occupied, unfortified line.

In the evening, the Germans resumed their offensive with renewed vigor, penetrating the defenses of the 21st Infantry Division, forcing the 14th Army and Guards Corps into a retreat. The Izmailovsky Life Guards Regiment faced near annihilation. By night, the 9th Army Corps' defense crumbled, compelling M. Alekseyev to authorize a further retreat of the 3rd Army.

The German breakthrough was substantial, spanning 32 km along the front and 12 km in depth. Since the operation's inception, the Germans had captured 16,250 prisoners and 23 machine guns. Capitalizing on their allies' success, the Austro-Hungarian 4th Army pushed back the Russian 4th Army. On July 17, Remus von Woyrsch's army struck the Grenadier Corps of the 4th Army with the Landwehr Corps, achieving a breakthrough of 10 km along the front and 6 km in depth. The following day, a counterattack by the Grenadier Corps failed, resulting in the capture of 2,000 prisoners.

The retreat of the Russian 4th Army was largely unchallenged by the German forces. On the afternoon of July 19, at M. Alekseyev's request, the Supreme Commander, Grand Duke Nikolai Nikolayevich, arrived in Siedlce. After assessing the situation, he granted the North-Western Front's Chief of Staff autonomy to order army withdrawals from the Vistula River line eastward if necessary, including the evacuation of Warsaw. In the evening, the 4th, 3rd, and 13th armies continued their withdrawal, halting combat operations irrespective of their progress. A complaint by the commander of the Guards Corps, General of the Cavalry V. Bezobrazov, regarding the 3rd Army's leader Leonid Lesh's refusal to authorize an offensive, was overlooked by M. Alekseyev.

Meanwhile, von Mackensen's Army Group pursued the retreating Russian forces. Following the arrival of the 13th and 14th infantry divisions, Brusilov ordered an offensive to seize the right bank of the Bug River. On July 20, a fierce battle raged in the 8th Army's sector, with control of many positions and trenches changing hands repeatedly. The 12th and 28th Army Corps succeeded in taking the first line of trenches. However, the

Austro-Hungarians launched a counteroffensive against the 8th Army Corps, expanding their bridgehead across the Bug River and eventually driving back the 12th Infantry Division and its cavalry. By the morning of July 21, the Russian 12th, 13th, and 19th Infantry Divisions had reached the banks of the Bug River near Lake Bely Stok, capturing 27 officers and 1,466 soldiers, and 2 machine guns. Despite these gains, they couldn't retake Sokal and incurred substantial losses. A. Brusilov acknowledged the "extraordinary stubbornness of the enemy."

On July 20th, the dynamics on the Eastern Front saw a significant shift. The Bug Army launched a forceful attack on the left flank of the Russian 13th Army, successfully pushing back the 2nd Caucasian Corps. Despite attempts at counterattacks, the 29th and 31st Army Corps and the 4th Cavalry Corps were driven back. Gorbatovsky, in a state of anxiety, informed Alekseyev that the 13th Army had no prepared defensive positions remaining in its rear. Meanwhile, the 11th German Army held off Russian counterattacks effectively but found its advance halted. Fierce combat ensued north of Krasnostav between the Russian and German guards corps, but the 2nd Siberian Army Corps was forced to retreat, with the 5th Siberian Rifle Division pulling back by the morning of July 21. It was only by noon that counterattacks by the 9th Army Corps and the Guards Rifle Brigade managed to stabilize the situation. By evening, however, the Germans compelled the 9th and 14th Army Corps to retreat.

The Austro-Hungarian 4th Army approached the Russian positions by noon on July 20 and began an artillery barrage. In the afternoon, a tenacious battle resulted in the 9th and 10th Corps breaking through the center of the Russian 4th Army, capturing 6,000 Russian prisoners.

Generals Evert and Lesh blamed each other for the untimely and excessive withdrawal of troops. On July 21, Major General A. Veselovsky led a detachment (three infantry regiments) in an offensive from 5 o'clock, supported by combined brigades of the 6th and 8th infantry divisions.

This push recaptured some ground, taking 400 Austro-Hungarian soldiers prisoner and driving back the 24th Austro-Hungarian division. However, the 37th Honvéd Infantry Division and the 47th reserve division counterattacked, displacing the Russian 15th and 25th army corps from their positions. The situation deteriorated on the left bank of the Vistula, with the 16th Army and Grenadier Corps retreating beyond the river.

On July 22, Alekseyev issued a directive for the gradual withdrawal of the 3rd, 4th, and 13th armies to the Ivangorod-Kovel prepared positions. The 4th Army faced constant German pressure during its retreat. The Austro-Hungarian 8th, 9th, and 10th Corps overran the 15th and routed the 25th Army Corps, capturing 48 officers, 12,400 Russian soldiers, and 23 machine guns over a 23 km front. Evert saw the positions near Lublin as more defensible than the line along the Wieprz River but requested the 3rd Army's support for a robust resistance.

By the morning of July 22, the situation in the Russian 3rd Army's sector had stabilized somewhat. The Guards Corps held its positions and captured 12 officers and 277 soldiers. Considering the Germans to be exhausted, suffering heavy losses, and low on ammunition (as reported by prisoners), L. Lesh ordered a full-scale offensive. The attack began on the night of July 23. Mackensen, anticipating this, decided to adopt a defensive stance until July 29 to wear down the Russian forces and deplete their reserves. Initially, the central corps of the 3rd Army's offensive was successful, capturing 5 guns and 2 machine guns. However, from 5 o'clock, the German Guards and 22nd Reserve Corps counterattacked, recapturing the artillery and forcing the Russian Guard back to their initial positions. At 4 p.m. on July 23, despite L. Lesh considering the situation to be under control, an order was given to withdraw the 3rd Army. Concurrently, a dispute erupted between Lesh and the commander of the Guards Corps, V. Bezobrazov, with the latter accusing the army commander of poor leadership.

The Bug Army, eager to build on its recent achievements, encountered stiffening resistance from the 13th Army under Gorbatovsky. By combining the forces of the 56th and 51st divisions, they successfully reclaimed positions lost by the 2nd Caucasian Corps. In a significant countermove, trenches at Putnowice Wielkie were retaken, capturing 160 prisoners, 6 guns, and a machine gun from the Beskid Corps. However, in the afternoon, the Germans launched a counteroffensive with the 41st and 24th reserve corps. On the night of July 23, the Russian 13th Army began withdrawing to new positions, while intense fighting persisted near Sokal on the front of the 8th Army. The 2nd Austro-Hungarian Army entered the fray along the Bug River, compelling F. Rerberg's corps to abandon their advantageous position on the Bug River bend and revert to previous positions. By the morning of July 23, with vigorous counterattacks and heavy artillery fire, the Austro-Hungarian 1st Army forced the 12th and 28th Army Corps to fall back to their initial positions, leading the 8th Army to assume a defensive posture.

Meanwhile, within the Central Powers' command, a heated debate ensued between Falkenhayn and Hötzendorf regarding the future offensive strategy of R. von Woyrsch's army. Falkenhayn advocated for an attack towards Siedlce and Łuków, proposing to unify this force with the 9th Army under German command. In contrast, the chief of staff of the AOK argued for bolstering the 4th Army's flank and targeting Ivangorod. Lieutenant Colonel Wilhelm Heye, the chief of staff of Woyrsch's army, viewed the proposed crossing at Nowa Aleksandria as futile, anticipating strong Russian resistance. On the night of July 25, despite initial efforts, the planned crossing was abruptly called off by Falkenhayn after pontoons reached the Russian shore under fire.

On the Russian side, the 3rd Army's planned offensive on the night of July 24 did not materialize due to late transmission of orders. The Guards Corps, in particular, was unable to advance without prior preparation. German forces repelled attacks by the 24th Army Corps by 1 a.m., forcing the 9th Army Corps to retreat to their former positions. While combat subsided in the sectors of the 4th and 3rd armies, the 13th Army faced relentless pressure from the German Bug Army, particularly at the junction of the fronts. On July 23–24, Russian attempts to launch offensives with the 2nd Caucasian and 31st Army Corps were thwarted by the enemy's superiority in heavy artillery, leading to the exhaustion of Russian forces. However, on the night of July 25, a counteroffensive saw the Russian divisions forced north by the Beskid Corps and the 24th Reserve, only to partially regain their positions through evening counterattacks. Yet, the 2nd Caucasian Corps was pushed back under the pressure of the Beskid Corps. Following another disagreement with L. Lesh, V. Bezobrazov, the commander of the Guards Corps, was relieved of his command under the pretext of "treatment."

On July 26th, the Russian 13th Army valiantly endeavored to reverse the situation on the western fringes of the Bug near Volodymyr-Volynskyi. Over the next two days, the relentless push from the Central Powers continued, but the Russian forces largely held their ground, except for the 2nd and 5th Caucasian corps which were pushed back. The battlefront of the 3rd Army witnessed significant activity; by the evening of July 26th, the 6th Austro-Hungarian and Beskid German corps had forced the 3rd Caucasian and 14th Army Corps to retreat. Counterattack efforts persisted until the morning of July 27th, achieving an advance of 600 steps towards the enemy, now well-fortified in their newly captured positions. In this two-day skirmish, about 2,000 Russian and 427 German soldiers were captured.

The situation intensified in the sector of the 8th Army of the Southwestern Front. The 2nd Austro-Hungarian Army, led by cavalry general E. von Böhm-Ermolli, launched an offensive on July 25th and successfully crossed the Bug River the following day. A. Brusilov, bolstered by the arrival of the 4th Finnish Rifle Division from reserve, coordinated counterattacks with the 8th, 12th, 17th, and 28th army corps. From July 26th to 28th, these efforts managed to contain the Austro-Hungarian advance. However, the heavy losses incurred during these battles hampered the 8th Army's combat effectiveness, failing to eliminate the enemy bridgeheads on the Bug River.

In a significant development at 1:30 am on July 29th, the Landwehr Corps of R. von Woyrsch's army commenced a Vistula River crossing with four detachments. The targeted section of the Russian 16th Army Corps of the 4th Army was weakened due to the redeployment of two brigades to Ivangorod and the Narew River. By 4:30, all detachments had crossed to the east coast and secured their positions. Russian attempts to repel the Germans back into the Vistula were unsuccessful. By 7:00, a 1160-meter bridge was erected, facilitating the crossing of the last regiment of the 3rd Landwehr Division. Despite Russian artillery damaging the bridge, M. Alekseyev, the chief of staff of the North-Western Front, ordered the 2nd and 4th armies to push the enemy back into the Vistula River. By evening, the Germans, comprising the 3rd and 4th Landwehr divisions, had entrenched themselves on the eastern bank.

Concurrently, on the morning of July 29th, Otto von Emmich's strike group from the 11th German Army penetrated 8 km deep into the positions of the 2nd Siberian Army Corps, severing the Lublin-Kholm railway. Radko Dmitriev, the commander of the 2nd Siberian Corps, reported his inability to hold the new position, prompting L. Lesh, commander of the 3rd Army, to order a last stand and deploy the reserve 10th Army Corps. Despite Lesh's belief in the defensibility of the Wieprz river line, by 18:00, the German guard had crossed the river on pontoons and occupied the prepared Russian trenches before the 10th Army Corps could respond. The sudden appearance of the enemy on the flanks of the Russian Guards and the 5th Siberian Rifle Division led to a disorganized retreat. On the night of July 30th, given the untenable situation, L. Lesh sought permission for a troop withdrawal, which commenced at 3:00.

Amidst the challenging circumstances facing the 3rd Army, the 13th Army demonstrated resilience by successfully fending off the assaults of the Bug Army. This was partly aided by the offensive initiated by the 8th Army of the South-Western Front on the night of July 29, which effectively contained the 1st Austro-Hungarian Army. However, by 5 am on July 30, the enemy detected the withdrawal of the Russian armies to new positions, leading to a pursuit by the 4th Austro-Hungarian and 11th German armies. The 4th Russian Army, striving to counter the Landwehr Corps, which had seized a 25-km stretch of the Vistula's right bank, encountered intense and fierce battles, with only 400–500 meters separating the opposing trenches.

By July 30, the 11th and Bug armies had reached the new positions of the 3rd and 13th armies. On the night of August 1, the 13th Army commenced a retreat, followed by the 3rd Army under L. Lesh, who ordered the withdrawal after learning of V. Gorbatovsky's troops' retreat.

Mackensen, aiming to capitalize on this momentum, formed two strike groups within the 11th German Army. At midnight on August 1, these groups launched an offensive. Although the Russian 3rd Army's main corps managed to repel enemy attacks and maintain their positions, the Bug Army succeeded in crossing the Bug River. By August 2, X. von Köves' corps had captured all the first-line fortifications of the Ivangorod fortress, securing 32 guns. The same day saw the removal of all remaining artillery and ammunition from the fortress, with food supplies being directly transferred to A. Evert's troops. Despite holding their ground, the Russian 4th Army was ordered to retreat on its left flank by M. Alekseyev, the commander-in-chief of the North-Western Front armies, due to a breach in the 3rd Army.

In the afternoon, the 3rd Army faced a concerted attack by the Central Powers on the 10th and 2nd Siberian Army Corps, prompting a hasty retreat. Lesh, responding to this development, deployed the 24th Army Corps and expressed frustration to Alekseyev over the 2nd Siberian Corps' lack of resilience. The 9th Army Corps also found itself in a dire situation, with the 14th Army and Guards Corps being pushed back. Overnight counterattacks by the 3rd Army were repelled by the German 11th Army, leading to a retreat to a new position as directed by Alekseyev by the morning of August 3.

The 13th Army also began a phased withdrawal on the night of August 3 under the pressure of the German Bug Army. In light of the evolving situation on the southern wing of the front, Alekseyev ordered the 2nd Army to retreat to the right bank of the Vistula on the night of August 3. Between August 3 and 4, the Russian forces continued their retreat. Mackensen's army group's regrouping on August 4 allowed the Russian armies to more freely occupy and fortify new defensive lines.

On the night of August 5, Russian forces evacuated both Ivangorod and Warsaw, the capital of the Kingdom of Poland. During this retreat, fortress artillery, a substantial stockpile of shells, railway stations, and bridges in Warsaw were systematically removed or destroyed. The idea of flooding both Warsaw and Novogeorgievsk was contemplated, leading to the summoning of Major General A. von Schwartz, the commandant of Ivangorod, to the headquarters of the North-Western Front armies. By morning, German forces from the 9th Army had entered Warsaw, joining forces with the army of Remus von Woyrsch under the newly formed army group led by Field Marshal Prince Leopold of Bavaria.

During the day on August 5, the 4th Russian Army retreated smoothly to a new line of defense, managing to establish strong positions there. However, in the 3rd Army's sector, the German troops broke through the defenses of the Guards Corps around noon, bringing significant forces into the breach. In other areas, the Central Powers' troops continued to advance steadily. The retreat of the Russian 2nd Army compelled A. Evert to also withdraw the 4th Army on the night of August 7 to the line of the Wieprz River.

On August 7, within the 4th Army, the Russian 15th Army Corps was unable to withstand new attacks by the Austro-Hungarians. Archduke Josef Ferdinand's army, over a 15 km sector, advanced up to 20 km deep, capturing up to 6,000 Russian soldiers. The Russian 6th Infantry Division was reduced to just 2,200 soldiers. At 11 p.m., the 4th Russian Army commenced its withdrawal, which, due to its failure, led to the retreat of the right flank of the 3rd Army. At the new position, Lesh, commander of the 3rd Army, ordered a firm defense, as immediate withdrawal was deemed unfeasible under current conditions.

The situation was further exacerbated by the challenging positions of the 1st and 12th armies on the Narew and Bug rivers. To counter the German advance, led by Gallwitz, divisions were redeployed not only from the armies of the Southwestern Front but also from the 13th Army. On August 6, the 61st and 62nd Infantry Divisions were dispatched to Białystok. This redistribution weakened Gorbatovsky's army, allowing the Bug Army to initiate an offensive on August 8. The 11th German Army drove back the 3rd Army's troops, while the Austro-Hungarian 4th Army and O. von Emmich's German group attacked the 6th Siberian Army Corps of the 4th Russian Army. By the morning of August 9, the 4th Army had been pulled back. On August 10–11, the Central Powers continued their successful offensive in certain sectors, encountering determined resistance from the Russian forces.

To the north, in the sectors of the 12th and 1st armies, the situation grew increasingly dire as German troops reached the lower reaches of the Bug River. The offensive by the army group of Prince Leopold of Bavaria forced a rapid withdrawal of the Russian 2nd Army. Around noon on August 11, Alekseyev issued a directive for a general withdrawal of the southern wing armies, scheduled for the night of August 12.

By 8 o'clock on August 12, all three armies of the Russian southern wing had successfully occupied their new positions without significant interference. A crucial meeting of the Central Powers' commanders-in-chief on the Eastern Front in Lublin concluded with a strategic decision to allocate substantial Austro-Hungarian forces for an upcoming operation in Eastern Galicia and Volhynia, while also advancing Mackensen's army group northeastward. Following orders from Alekseyev, Evert, Lesh, and Gorbatovsky initiated further troop withdrawals towards Brest-Litovsk on the night of August 13.

The German High Command, still hopeful of encircling the Russian troops between the Bug River and Białowieża Forest in a maneuver akin to "little Cannes," assigned Mackensen the task of advancing towards Brest-Litovsk. Concurrently, Prince Leopold of Bavaria's army group near Nemyriv and Kleszczele aimed to cut off the retreat of Russian forces across the Bug River, while M. von Gallwitz's army was to close the encirclement at Belsk.

Early on August 13, the Central Powers detected the Russian withdrawal and promptly began pursuit operations. From August 14 to 20, the Russian army's retreat continued, leading to Brest-Litovsk being semi-encircled as German forces under Prince Leopold of Bavaria and Mackensen reached the Bug River. The Russian 77th Infantry Division and the 24th Home Guard Brigade were urgently sent to reinforce the fortress, joining the already present 22nd, 32nd, 82nd State Militia Brigades, and the 81st Infantry Division. The Germans, arriving at the outer forts of Brest-Litovsk on the morning of August 17, began assault preparations, including deploying heavy mortars.

By August 24, the German forces had amassed a formidable artillery presence around Brest-Litovsk, including heavy howitzers, guns, and mortars. A massive bombardment ensued, with over 24,800 heavy shells fired at the fortress. On August 25, as the city and fortress were engulfed in flames set by the Russian troops, the 6th Austro-Hungarian, Beskidenkorps, and 22nd reserve corps launched their attack. The 119th Infantry Division captured the forts, the 43rd Reserve Division entered the citadel, and by 3 pm on August 26, Arthur Arz von Straußenburg's corps occupied the city, immediately beginning firefighting efforts. Alekseyev, not wishing to see a repeat of Novogeorgievsk's fate at Brest, ordered an immediate evacuation of the fortress. The 4th Army also retreated, even though the enemy had only approached its positions during the day. Starting from the night of August 26, the 2nd, 3rd, and 4th armies were withdrawn in 2-3 stages, employing scorched earth tactics by spoiling roads, blowing up bridges, and obstructing paths.

Radio messages about the withdrawal of the Russian armies to new positions on the night of August 26 were intercepted and decoded at the headquarters of Hindenburg, Mackensen, and Prince Leopold of Bavaria, prompting them to pursue the retreating Russian forces.

The fall of Brest-Litovsk marked the end of the Vistula–Bug offensive, a significant episode in the larger tapestry of World War I. Evert, addressing his troops, invoked the spirit of the 1812 war, urging them to draw lessons and maintain a firm belief in their eventual victory.

Riga–Schaulen Offensive

I n a dramatic twist of military strategy, the legendary generals of Germany, Paul von Hindenburg and Erich Ludendorff, boldly defied the skepticism of Erich von Falkenhayn, Chief of the German Great General Staff. Amidst the lush and challenging landscapes of rivers, forests, and swamps, they launched a daring offensive in 1915. This operation, a masterstroke of strategy, was spearheaded by the Army of the Niemen under Hindenburg's command, in coordination with the formidable forces of M. von Gallwitz on the Narew River and A. von Mackensen between the Vistula and Bug Rivers.

Their target? The formidable Russian Northwestern Front. This offensive wasn't just another battle; it was a continuation of the aggressive push that began near Riga earlier that April. The stakes were high, and the debates intense, leading to a compromise: this offensive would serve as a distraction, yet it was perfectly aligned with the terrain's challenges and the Russian command's focus on Riga and the Western Dvina River.

The ultimate prize for Hindenburg and his forces? The strategic Kovno fortress, a linchpin in the Russian defense near the German border. Their goal was nothing less than to encircle and capture this fortress, a move that would deal a crippling blow to the Russian formations along the Neman River. This bold move, executed with precision and daring, marked a pivotal moment in the Great War's eastern theater.

First Riga Offensive

On the morning of July 14th, the German 41st Infantry Division, after an intense artillery barrage, effortlessly crossed the Venta River. They faced no resistance from the Russian forces under Lieutenant General Gleb Vannovsky, swiftly advancing towards Grivaishen. By 11 AM, bridges for heavy artillery were established, and soon after, German batteries unleashed a barrage from the left bank. Meanwhile, at Papilė, the 6th and 78th reserve divisions successfully crossed the river. The Russian forces, led by Major General Mikhail Grabbe and the 17th Infantry Division, retreated almost without engaging.

Faced with this situation, the 5th Army's commander, Plehve, formulated a plan to flank the advancing Germans. He assembled a force comprising the 17th Infantry Division and the 1st Caucasian Rifle Brigade under Lieutenant General Dmitri A. Dolgov, commander of the 19th Army Corps. Meanwhile, Grabbe's detachment was to hold the rest of the front. However, Grabbe's forces crumbled under the German infantry's onslaught, leading to a two-day delay for reorganization. Eventually, Plehve, heeding Dolgov's more informed perspective on the situation, scrapped the counterattack plan. But the shift in units had already been executed, wasting precious time. To form an army reserve, Plehve had to bring in the 2nd Cavalry Division and 13th Siberian Rifle Division.

Between July 15th and 16th, the German Northern Corps overran the Russian positions near Lielaucė. The 8th Cavalry Division pushed forward, posing a threat to Mitava. The German breach extended 60 km along the front and varied in depth from 6 to 30 km. To counter this, Plehve deployed the 12th and 13th Siberian rifle divisions, reinforcing them with the 4th and 15th cavalry divisions and the Ussuri Cossack brigade, thus forming the 7th Siberian army corps under the temporary leadership of General Lieutenant N. Sulimov. Additionally, a new detachment led by Dolgov was formed using the remnants of Grabbe's forces, the brigade of the 73rd Infantry Division, and the 19th Army Corps, aimed at striking the right flank of the Army of the Niemen.

On July 17th, the corps of Lieutenant General Curt von Morgen initiated an offensive. Following two hours of artillery preparation, the 1st reserve division and Colonel Otto von Homeyer's infantry brigade attacked Russian positions around Schaulen. Despite firing 1,779 heavy shells, the assault was repelled by the 38th Infantry Division. The 6th reserve division also faced defeat; during its offensive, it was encircled by Dolgov's forces and pushed back beyond the Vindava River, with Russian troops capturing 500 prisoners and 7 machine guns. However, the Russians' further advance was halted by the formidable fire from a 15-cm howitzer battery.

While the center of the Army of the Niemen stumbled, its left wing pressed on with vigor. The German 41st Infantry and 78th Reserve Divisions encountered the freshly arrived divisions of the 7th Siberian Army Corps. By 10 AM, a decisive engagement unfolded near Anperhof in dense forests, where the German forces unleashed a barrage of 409 heavy shells. This onslaught proved too much for the Russian soldiers, who subsequently retreated towards Mitava.

Simultaneously, the 6th Cavalry Division skillfully outmaneuvered the Siberian riflemen's positions, and the Life Hussar Brigade cunningly flanked and rear-attacked Dolgov's detachment. The 8th Cavalry Division and the 18th Cavalry Brigade successfully pushed back elements of the Russian 4th and 15th cavalry divisions and the Windau militia detachment. Since the beginning of the operation, the Army of the Niemen had captured a significant 6,000 Russian prisoners and 9 guns. P. Plehve, taken aback by the 7th Siberian Army Corps' unexpectedly poor performance, held N. Sulimov responsible, overlooking the fact that his own indecisive and exhausting orders had contributed to the troops' plight.

O. von Below, despite having a prime opportunity to target the weakly defended Mitava, chose a different strategy. He decided to engage the Russian forces with the 41st Infantry and 8th Cavalry Divisions, while redirecting the rest of the Northern Group's formations to the Russians' rear. On July 18–19, the Niemen Army's cavalry attacked positions held by the Russian 15th Cavalry Division and the Ussuri Cossack Brigade. Although the Russian cavalry initially repelled these assaults, they were forced to retreat under the advancing German infantry. Following several failed attempts, C. von Morgen delegated the primary offensive role to Otto von Homeyer's brigade, concentrating all heavy artillery under his command. Seeking additional strength, P. Plehve requested reinforcements from M. Alekseyev and received the 53rd and 104th infantry divisions.

To address a critical 50 km gap between the 7th Siberian and 19th Army Corps, Plehve formed a new unit under Lieutenant General G. Troubetzkoy, comprising the 2nd and 4th cavalry divisions and 37 guns.

On July 20th, the Southern Group of the Army of the Niemen initiated an offensive with C. von Morgen's corps aiming to capture Schaulen. Due to limited heavy artillery, the preparatory bombardment spanned five hours, yet it effectively pushed back the Russian 3rd and 37th army corps from the left bank of the Dubysa. Plehve, mistakenly confident that the main German assault would target Mitava, underestimated the Southern Group's advance. Consequently, C. von Morgen's corps successfully took Shavli.

Despite Plehve's attempts to reorganize his forces and counterattack near Mitava, the endeavor proved futile. The German forces not only repelled the counterattack but also forced back the right wing of the 5th Army. Although E. von Schmettov's cavalry initially cut off the retreat of D. Dolgov's detachment, Dolgov managed to break through the encirclement the following day.

On July 22, O. von Below strategically redirected the 1st reserve corps under C. von Morgen from Shavli towards the southeast. In response, Plehve swiftly commanded the newly arrived 1st Cavalry and 53rd Infantry Divisions to launch an immediate offensive from Mitava. Concurrently, he ordered D. Dolgov's detachment, along with the 3rd and 37th Army Corps, to withdraw. This move essentially signified the 5th Army's withdrawal from protecting Kovno from the north, shifting its focus to defending the routes to Riga and evading the threat of being encircled.

On July 23, Major General V. Maidel's detachment, comprising the 1st Cavalry and 53rd Infantry Divisions, initiated an offensive from Mitava. They attempted to flank the 41st German Infantry Division but ended up extending their front and engaging with the 8th Cavalry Division. At Lindenfeld, Maidel's forces faced direct confrontation, lacking the resources to capitalize on their initial success. Dolgov's detachment, unable to hold their planned line, retreated while engaged in combat.

During a nocturnal assault, C. von Morgen's corps captured Šeduva. However, the 1st reserve division's delay in the city allowed the Russian 3rd army corps to fortify its position. Under the pressure from the Southern Group of the Army of the Niemen, the 37th Army Corps retreated. In a fierce battle, N. Kaznakov's cavalry detachment (comprising the 1st Guards and 5th Cavalry Divisions) managed to halt the German advance, protecting the army's left flank and maintaining control over the right bank of the Nevėžis River.

Over 10 days, the German Army of the Niemen captured significant spoils: 23 guns, 40 machine guns, and 27,000 prisoners. The Russian 5th Army, though escaping encirclement and forcing the Germans into frontal pursuit, suffered considerable losses and exhausted its reserves. M. Alekseyev, the commander-in-chief of the North-Western Front, deeply concerned about the situation in the Riga and Dvina regions, ordered reinforcements to the Viliya River and Janów areas. Meanwhile, P. von Hindenburg directed the 10th Army to intensify the blockade of Kovno from the west.

On July 24, Plehve, striving to bolster the 5th army's positions, instructed the 3rd and 27th army corps to hold their ground with support from N. Kaznakov's detachment on the left. Detachments under D. Dolgov and G. Troubetzkoy were to counterattack the left flank of the German Southern group. O. von Below, leading the Army of the Niemen, commanded the 5th Cavalry Corps and Otto von Homeyer's brigade to cover a 30-km gap near Mitava and ordered various divisions to execute strategic maneuvers around Panevėžys.

Both armies, wearied by continuous fighting and maneuvering, were in dire need of rest. Thus, on that day, the Germans pursued only lethargically, which Plehve misinterpreted as the end of their offensive.

E. von Falkenhayn, eager for a swift victory, demanded the immediate capture of Mitava. However, the detachment under von Schmettow found itself short on both infantry and heavy artillery for such an ambitious undertaking. Consequently, on July 25, the primary focus of the Army of the Niemen shifted to targeting Russian positions near Panevėžys.

In a significant engagement, the Bavarian cavalry division clashed with the Russian 5th cavalry division, already unsettled from its encounter with the 36th reserve division. Although the Russian forces managed to retreat and regroup under N. Kaznakov, the 36th reserve division successfully pushed back the Russian cavalry from the left flank. This maneuver allowed them to encircle the 37th army corps, which was already engaged against von Beckmann's division. The result was a chaotic 45-km retreat by the Russian forces to the east, effectively severing their escape routes and isolating the 3rd army corps.

Despite the disarray in the Russian ranks, the German forces remained cautious. Their focus was more on safeguarding against potential Russian counterattacks along their extended front, rather than exploiting the disorganization of the 5th Army's left wing and center.

By July 26, the Army of the Niemen had established a formidable presence along a line stretching from the mouth of the Nevėžis River to the Courland coast on the Baltic Sea. The German capture of Panevėžys opened up strategic avenues for offensives in three key directions: north towards Riga, east towards Dvinsk and Vilna, and south around Kovno. With these gains, the Supreme Commander of All German Forces in the East prepared to execute the plan to capture the Kovno fortress. Yet, the mission to seize Mitava remained in play. For this task, the von Schmettow detachment was reinforced with the 8th cavalry, 41st infantry, 6th reserve divisions, and 6 heavy batteries. The 1st and 5th cavalry corps, led by M. von Richthofen and von Schmettow, were directed towards Dvinsk and Vilna. Meanwhile, the 1st and 39th (Northern) reserve corps amassed in Panevėžys, poised to strike the northern front of the Kovno fortress.

In the stretch between the fortresses of Kovno and Osowiec, the Russian and German 10th armies maintained defensive positions, confronting each other with significant force disparities: 332,151 Russian troops against 167,710 Germans. This numerical superiority of the Russian side cast doubts on the potential success of the German operation against Kovno. Consequently, the German 10th Army, commanded by Colonel General Hermann von Eichhorn, initially confined itself to minor strikes, focusing on fortifying positions rather than aggressive advancement.

On July 15th, the German 77th Reserve Division northeast of Suwalki made a significant breakthrough, capturing 300 prisoners. By July 21st, the 79th reserve and 16th landwehr divisions, after expending a massive 3,000 heavy shells, assaulted the Russian positions. Despite initial gains, their momentum was curtailed by the flooding of the Neman River and the robust Russian fortifications on the right bank. The landwehr's march towards Kovno was effectively halted 16 kilometers from the forts.

On July 23rd, the 10th German Army was tasked with tightly encircling the fortress from the west. By July 24th, plans were made to cross the Neman south of Kovno to cut off the garrison's escape route. However, by July 27th, the army had only received an additional infantry brigade and 5 heavy batteries, including one 42-cm mortar. E. Ludendorff informed H. von Eichhorn that no further troop reinforcements were possible.

With no support against Kovno from the south, the commander of the Army of the Niemen, O. von Below, initiated an offensive against Mitava. On July 26th, the Russian cavalry covering the 5th Army's retreat withdrew. By July 28th-29th, reinforcements on both sides were integrated into the battle lines. The 5th Army now comprised 205,477 men, against the Army of the Niemen's 178,564.

M. Alekseyev, still confident in the situation at Riga and Vilno, believed the Germans lacked sufficient strength for a major offensive. However, at a Headquarters meeting on July 28th, General of Infantry Yuri Danilov, the Quartermaster General of the Supreme Commander-in-Chief's staff, emphasized the strategic need to strengthen positions in the Riga–Schaulen region. Following this, Grand Duke Nikolai Nikolayevich ordered the transfer of two infantry and a cavalry division from the Southwestern Front to reinforce the Vilna region and the 5th Army.

From July 29th to 31st, the German offensive on Mitava commenced. The 6th reserve division captured Bauska, advancing 10 kilometers east across the Aa River, with the Homeyer brigade moving north towards Mežotne. The 8th Cavalry Division took control of Gross Eckau, and the 3rd Cavalry Brigade captured Lazhap on the Gulf of Riga shores. In these operations, the Germans took 3,450 prisoners and 6 machine guns. The approach of the Russian 19th and 3rd army corps reinforcements to Panevėžys was countered by an offensive from the corps of von Richthofen, von Schmettov, and von Morgen, stretching from the Lėvuo River to Aleksandrovka, with support from a heavy battery.

By August 1st, Russian forces on the Riga coast and the 7th Siberian

Army Corps began retreating towards Riga. The attacking units of von Schmettow's group occupied Mitava by 4 PM, where wood depots were set ablaze during the withdrawal. By evening, they had already made significant progress towards Riga.

Russian Counteroffensive

On August 2, a pivotal moment occurred when the German 10th Army, under immense pressure, urgently sought reinforcements to capture the key city of Kovno. In a crucial meeting at Lötzen, the army's Chief of Staff, E. Hell, passionately argued the case before Hindenburg, the Supreme Commander of All German Forces in the East. Hindenburg, recognizing the stakes, promised substantial reinforcements: the formidable 6th Landwehr Brigade, additional troops from the 9th Army, and the return of the battle-hardened Beckman division.

The following day, Hindenburg, leveraging his influence, persuaded Falken-hayn of the strategic importance of seizing Kovno swiftly. The Supreme High Command, convinced, allocated a massive amount of artillery shells for the operation, setting the stage for a major assault.

Meanwhile, the Army of the Niemen, under German command, aggressively pursued the retreating Russian 5th Army on August 2–3. They captured over 3,000 prisoners and essential military equipment. However, in a sudden strategic shift, orders came to halt the pursuit. The Army turned its focus towards Vilno, leaving only a token force to defend against a potential Russian counterattack on Riga.

The Russian response was swift and determined. On August 3, General P. Plehve, recognizing the threat to Riga, appointed Lieutenant General N. Lisovsky to fortify the city's defenses and ordered a flanking counterattack against the German Mitava group.

The battlefield dynamics shifted again on August 4. As the Russian 19th Army Corps retreated, Plehve, sensing an opportunity, ordered a counteroffensive on August 5. Despite fierce resistance and minimal territorial gains, the Russians displayed a renewed vigor, causing the German command to reassess their strategy.

By August 7, the Russian troops in the Riga area had established strong defensive positions along the Eckau River. The tense standoff resulted in only 40 German prisoners over two days.

The German Army of the Niemen, eyeing a strategic advantage, aimed to strike at Wilkomir. They gathered three infantry divisions near Panevėžys, though they urgently needed reinforcements and ammunition.

Amidst this, the Russian 5th Army's chief of staff, E. Miller, alerted A. Gulevich, chief of staff of the North-Western Front, about a critical vulnerability. With their front line stretched over 250 versts (approximately 265 kilometers), Miller highlighted a glaring gap: the direct routes to Vilno and Sventiany were dangerously unprotected. He strongly advised against creating intermediate strongholds, which he deemed ineffective under the circumstances. Instead, Miller urged for all available resources to be channeled towards constructing robust defenses near Dvinsk.

As the clock struck midnight on August 8, General Plehve, unsatisfied with the progress in battle, commanded G. Troubetzkoy to spearhead a direct assault. By the night of August 9, this bold move proved to be a resounding success. The Russians captured over 50 prisoners and 3 machine guns, marking a significant shift in the tide of battle.

On August 9, the relentless 5th Army continued to hammer at the center of the German lines, successfully thwarting any German advances near the Riga fortified area. The Russian 19th and 3rd army corps, too, made significant headway in their respective sectors.

By the morning of August 11, the Army of the Niemen maintained its strategic positions along the Aa and Eckau Rivers. German attempts to launch an offensive near the Riga area were effectively repelled, with Russian gunboats playing a pivotal role in the defense.

The momentum continued for the Russians into the afternoon of August 12. In the Riga region, the 13th Siberian Rifle Division launched a vigorous offensive towards the Aa River, successfully dislodging the Germans from the right bank.

As the clock neared midnight on August 13, General Plehve issued decisive orders to Troubetzkoy and M. Grabbe. They were to orchestrate a concentrated attack to breach the German lines. Concurrently, the 3rd and 19th Army Corps were directed to fortify their positions, engage in active reconnaissance, and in the event of a German retreat, to pursue them aggressively.

August 13, 1915, marked another day of intense combat as the Russian 5th Army, led by General Plehve, launched a renewed assault on German lines. The battle was fierce, with the Russians facing determined resistance and counterattacks from the Germans. While the Russian 37th Army Corps and the 4th Cavalry Division made headway and secured Memelhof, their success was contrasted by setbacks for the 1st and 2nd cavalry divisions, which were driven back past the Rovèja River. Additionally, the efforts of Grabbe's detachment did not yield the desired results.

In a strategic response, Plehve ordered the 19th and 3rd army corps to initiate an offensive from 17:00. By dusk, these units had impressively advanced to within 300-600 paces of the German frontlines. However, N. Kaznakov's detachment, under heavy artillery and machine-gun fire from the German positions across the Sventa River, suffered significant losses and was compelled to retreat.

The night of August 14 brought significant leadership changes in the Russian ranks. Plehve replaced Lieutenant General G. Levitsky, the interim commander of the 37th Army Corps, with Major General Januarius Tsikhovich. Furthermore, the detachment under Troubetzkoy was dissolved, leaving him in command of only the 1st and 2nd cavalry divisions.

On August 14, the Russian 5th Army pressed on with its offensive. The army's right wing made slow but steady progress until nightfall. However, Troubetzkoy's cavalry corps and Grabbe's detachment found themselves restrained by the aggressive maneuvers of the 5th German cavalry corps. The offensive by the Russian 19th and 3rd army corps initially showed promise, advancing successfully until noon. However, the situation shifted when the German 1st cavalry corps and the 78th reserve division counterattacked the left flank of the 3rd army corps. This led Plehve to order a strategic withdrawal around 17:00, simultaneously instructing the flanking cavalry to attempt a rear assault on the Germans. Despite these efforts, the maneuver was unsuccessful, and the Russian forces faced continued pressure from the German 1st reserve and 1st cavalry corps, leading to a retreat across the Vadva and Jara-Šetekšna rivers by the morning of August 15.

Although the Russian 5th Army's offensive experienced varying degrees of success and setbacks, their actions effectively secured the Riga-Dvina direction. Importantly, they disrupted the German offensive plans against Vilkomir and delayed the deployment of German divisions earmarked for an assault on Kovno, thereby holding the positions of the Neman army. Consequently, the German 10th Army's planned operation against Kovno was also delayed, underscoring the strategic impact of the Russian 5th Army's efforts despite not achieving a decisive breakthrough.

Siege of Kovno

In a dramatic display of military engineering, the Germans constructed a railroad to transport their mammoth 42-centimeter Gamma-Gerät howitzer. This behemoth artillery piece, hurling 1-ton shells up to 14 kilometers, was a key player in the siege. The German forces began their onslaught on the fortress, targeting its oldest and most venerable structures: the First, Second, and Third Forts. Despite not encircling the fortress completely, the German army's relentless attack disrupted the fortress's defense, which struggled to regroup and resupply.

On August 8, the Germans ramped up their bombardment, but the fortress's garrison, showing remarkable resilience, repelled several incursions. The siege reached its zenith a few days later, inflicting devastating casualty rates of 50-75% on the fortress's defenders. August 14 witnessed over 1,000 defenders falling, yet the fortress's defenses remained unbreached. However, the tide turned when Gamma-Gerät shells obliterated the First Fort, shifting the German focus to the Second Fort and intensifying the battle within the greater fortress complex.

The situation became critical, prompting E. Radkevich, commander of the Russian 10th Army, to seek guidance from Mikhail Alekseyev on August 16. The dilemma was stark: should they let the fortress be completely surrounded, defend the northern forts despite significant losses, or begin evacuating the garrison and military resources? The next morning, Alekseyev authorized the deployment of reserves, including the 4th Finnish Rifle and 65th Infantry Divisions, to fortify Kovno. Radkevich ordered an immediate counterattack by the 3rd Siberian Corps, leading to a fierce nocturnal battle. Although the Germans made inroads into the forts, they were repelled, but Major General N. Yanovsky's detachment suffered a setback in the north.

The climax arrived at 11 a.m. as K. Litzman commenced a ferocious artillery barrage with 208 guns, including heavy and super-heavy howitzers, directed from air and ground. By noon, Kovno's artillery was largely neutralized. The German 40th reserve corps seized the opportunity, penetrating between forts II and III and capturing fort I by 2 p.m. By 6 p.m., the Germans had overtaken all forts in the first division, breaking through the fortress's central defense. The Neman River bridges were seized by Cossack forces, primed for demolition. This pivotal day ended with the Germans capturing 4,000 prisoners and 52 guns, marking a significant shift in the siege's dynamics.

The siege of Kovno took a dire toll on its defenses. Within the First Department of the fortress, staggering losses were incurred: 164 officers and 11,968 soldiers, constituting 75% of the force, were either killed or incapacitated. The fortress's heavy gun batteries lay in ruins, and their anti-assault guns were effectively silenced. A critical issue for the defenders was the dire shortage of ammunition. Armed with Japanese rifles, they faced an acute crisis as there were no compatible cartridges available in Kovno. Appeals for assistance to the 10th Army's command by Grigoriev went unanswered, leading him to lodge a formal complaint to the front headquarters on July 31. His plea for reinforcements was urgent, requesting 12 full battalions to replenish the depleted garrison. However, his complaint was merely redirected back to the 10th Army.

As the night of August 17 approached, the situation grew increasingly desperate. The garrison of the 1st division had completely abandoned the Neman River, and the units of the Second Defense Department vacated their fortifications, fearing encirclement. Commandant V. Grigoriev received orders to salvage whatever possible from the remaining forts. At around 1 a.m., with communication to Grigoriev lost, the 10th Army headquarters transferred command to Infantry General N. Lopushansky of the 124th Infantry Division, defending the 4th department of the fortress. It was discovered that Fort V was still holding out, while Fort IV was left unoccupied. Key bridges over the Neman River were destroyed to hinder the German advance.

At 4 a.m. on August 17, Grigoriev sent a bleak message to the army headquarters: the fortress had been abandoned, and the garrison was in a state of demoralization. Radkevich relayed this to Alekseyev, the Commander-in-Chief of the armies on the North-Western Front, describing the garrison as a disorganized mob incapable of offense or even holding a position. The Germans, under K. Litzman, intensified their attack, bombarding the center of Kovno, the citadel, the station, and the northern forts. By evening, they had captured these forts and crossed the Neman River with multiple divisions, seizing Fort IV. The Russian 10th Army commenced its withdrawal at 6:30 p.m. The Kovno garrison held positions in Rumšiškės and Žiežmariai, while Lieutenant General V. Alftan's forces continued to defend Fort V. Despite the dire situation, Radkevich harbored hopes of reclaiming Kovno and instructed V. Tofimov and N. Lopushansky's corps to push the Germans back across the Neman River and organize an evacuation. Alekseyev also confirmed the task of recapturing the 3rd and 4th defense departments from the Germans and defending them to the last.

However, the situation rapidly deteriorated overnight. The 40th and 54th Don Cossack regiments, along with N. Lopushansky's detachment, were forced to retreat under the German onslaught. By evening, the Germans had captured the last stronghold, Fort V, and completely occupied Kovno. The 40th reserve corps captured up to 20,000 prisoners, 1,300 guns, 100 machine guns, 20,000 rifles, and 810,000 shells, marking a decisive victory for the German forces.

Vilno Offensive

In a strategic chess game of military might, the German High Command in the East, led by Ludendorff, contemplated a daring offensive in the Neman region. Their ambitious goal? To cut off the Russian North-Western Front's retreat from the Kingdom of Poland by piercing through to Vilno and Minsk.

This audacious plan involved breaking through Russian defenses before the 10th Army and the Army of the Niemen, driving them back to the Dvina River. The masterstroke was to unleash cavalry raids against Minsk and Polotsk, aiming to sever the Russian supply lines.

While Ludendorff was the architect of this bold strategy, Falkenhayn, his counterpart, was skeptical. He doubted the feasibility of a winter offensive and deep penetration into Russia. His conservative stance was evident in the August 18 order, which limited operations to a line from Brest-Litovsk to Grodno and called for a redeployment of "surplus" troops. Hindenburg, however, disagreed, finding the front too perilously close to the German border in the Augustow and Suwalki region. He countered with a directive on August 19: the 12th and 8th armies were to press their attacks, with the 10th Army spearheading the charge towards Vilno and the Army of the Niemen providing cover from the north.

The operation unfolded on August 20, as the German 10th Army, reinforced with divisions from the disbanded X. von Beseler group, struck northeast of Kovno. Litzman's group surged across the Neris River, engaging the beleaguered Kovno garrison. The 6th cavalry corps' capture of Yanov posed a direct threat to Vilno. Meanwhile, Radkevich, concerned about the exposed flank at the junction with the 1st Army and the impending fall of Osowiec fortress, contemplated the necessity of evacuating Grodno.

The Russian response was swift. The North-Western Front's headquarters dispatched the 5th Army Corps to reinforce the 10th Army, with orders from Radkevich to halt the German advance between the Neman and Neris rivers. Despite these efforts, the German offensive, driven by the relentless 6th Cavalry and 40th Reserve Corps, forced the Russian 10th Army to retreat. Radkevich, realizing the dire situation, commanded a nocturnal crossing of the Neman River by the 2nd and 26th Army Corps. The Russian right flank, however, was already in disarray, unable to repel the German onslaught.

The fall of the Osowiec fortress necessitated the evacuation of Grodno, a logistical nightmare. Commandant M. Kaigorodov faced the daunting task of transporting artillery, ammunition, and supplies out of the fortress. Despite meticulous planning, the urgency and logistical constraints meant leaving behind a significant cache of military resources.

In the midst of a dire military situation, Major General I. Popov, the chief of staff of the 10th Russian Army, made a desperate plea for assistance on the night of August 23. He reached out to the commander of the 5th Army, Plehve, urging an offensive push to the west with the army's left flank. In a strategic shift, the 20th Army Corps and the fortress of Grodno were reassigned to the 1st Army by the order of Alekseyev, the Commander-in-Chief of the North-Western Front. However, the 5th Army itself was under severe pressure: since August 20, the German Army of the Niemen had been relentlessly driving back the center of the 5th Army, overpowering the 37th Army Corps at Memelhof.

The morning of August 23 saw the German forces intensify their assault, targeting the units led by Tsikhovich, Troubetzkoy, and Mikhail Grabbe, and forcing them into a retreat. This led to the 19th and 3rd Army Corps assuming new defensive positions. The following day, von Schmettov's cavalry, bolstered by additional infantry and artillery, launched a fierce attack on the same detachments, resulting in a significant Russian retreat and the capture of 700 Russian soldiers. Plehve, facing a dire situation, dispatched his last reserve, the 1st Nevsky Infantry Regiment, to support the beleaguered 37th Army Corps. In a drastic measure, Tsikhovich ordered the execution of every hundredth soldier from the 315th Glukhovsky Infantry Regiment, whose two battalions had fled their positions.

Meanwhile, the 10th Army faced a renewed German offensive along the Neman River. After a fierce engagement, the Russian 2nd and 26th Army Corps were compelled to withdraw. The Russian guard divisions and the 5th Army Corps, arriving in Vilno and Lentvaris, were tasked with holding the front at Vilno. On August 24, Radkevich divided his forces into two groups: the Vilno group under Lieutenant General Pyotr Baluyev and the Neman group under General of the Infantry B. Flug. Despite orders to advance, the 10th Army's right wing continued its retreat towards Vilno and the right bank of the Neman River.

The situation escalated on August 26 when the German Army of the Niemen, led by Lieutenant General Shmettov's group, launched a relentless offensive against Friedrichstadt, targeting the 37th Army Corps. By the night of August 27, the Russian positions at the Ponemunok River were overrun. The 37th Army Corps, decimated and disorganized, was forced to withdraw. In an effort to turn the tide, Plehve commanded a counterstrike on the German flanks advancing towards the Western Dvina River. Meanwhile, the chief of staff of the 5th Army, Miller, urgently requested the expedited arrival of the 28th Army Corps from the South-Western Front. The first trains carrying these reinforcements only began to arrive late on the evening of August 27, adding a glimmer of hope to the beleaguered Russian forces.

The Russian 19th and 3rd Army Corps' offensive against the German 1st Reserve Corps faltered, failing to achieve its intended breakthrough. Compounding this setback, the retreat of the 10th Army's right wing necessitated the withdrawal of the Ussuri Cavalry Brigade. By the night of August 28, the Germans had successfully seized the first position at Friedrichstadt, marking a significant advancement in their campaign.

On August 28, in a bid to turn the tide, Plehve issued a decisive command to Trubetskoy: leave a minimal defense and, with the majority of forces, break through into the rear of the German forces advancing towards Friedrichstadt at any cost. However, the German Army of the Niemen had meticulously fortified their defense, leveraging the terrain and villages to their advantage. On August 28-29, although von Schmettov's group was pushed back on the left flank to the Nemenek River, they managed to penetrate the second line of defense near Friedrichstadt. Their artillery obliterated the positions of the

2nd brigade of the 79th Infantry Division in a mere 20 minutes. Despite these gains, the Army of the Niemen was unable to swiftly capture Friedrichstadt or secure the bridges over the Dvina River.

Meanwhile, by August 26, the German 10th Army was closing in on Vilno from the north and northwest, overcoming the mounted barriers of the Russian 10th Army. The Russian 5th Army Corps and the 3rd Siberian Army Corps, facing intense pressure, were compelled to retreat. The divisions of the Russian 2nd and 26th Army Corps also withdrew under the relentless advance of the German 21st Army Corps. On August 27, Radkevich orchestrated a last stand, uniting the 124th Infantry, 2nd Finnish Rifle, and Border Composite Divisions under the command of Lieutenant General Nikolai Istomin of the 5th Caucasian Army Corps, with orders to hold their ground at all costs. The battered divisions of the 34th Army Corps were relegated to reserve status.

By evening, the frontline of the 10th Army's right wing had somewhat stabilized, positioned just a few kilometers north and west of Vilno. However, as night fell, the German forces intensified their push against the regiments of the 2nd and 26th Army Corps.

The strategic deployment of eight Russian divisions north of Vilno ultimately disrupted Hindenburg's plan for a swift capture of the city, crucial for its railway and highway junctions. Moreover, the proactive engagement of the Russian 5th Army thwarted German attempts to quickly overrun Jakobstadt and Friedrichstadt. By this stage, as reported by engineer-general N. Tumanov, chief commander of the Dvina military district, to the staff of the North-Western Front, the construction of fortified positions in Dvina and Vilno was nearing completion. Despite some incomplete dugouts and barriers, these fortifications were ready for troop deployment. This development played a crucial role in facilitating decisions on the defense of the Russian Empire's western provinces and halting the ongoing retreat.

Battle of Dniestr and Zolota Lypa

In a thrilling episode of World War I history, the Austro-Hungarian forces, spearheaded by the dynamic cavalry general Karl von Pflanzer-Baltin, embarked on a daring mission to reclaim eastern Galicia from Russian control. Excluded from A. von Mackensen's army group, these armies were assigned the critical task of immobilizing Russian troops, setting the stage for a dramatic liberation offensive targeting the strategic locations of Buchach and Chortkiv.

The natural barriers of the Dniester River's left tributaries provided a defensive advantage, prompting von Pflanzer-Baltin to make a bold decision: to breach the Dniester between the Strypa and Seret rivers. The main assault was launched by the formidable 3rd Corps, while an impressive cavalry force of up to 9,600 horsemen, led by the intrepid Z. von Benin, planned a covert operation to flank the Russian 9th Army, aiming for Khotyn and Kamenetz-Podolsk. However, the prelude to this maneuver saw the 6th infantry division cross the Dniester, penetrating Russian defenses with fierce determination.

For the Buchach offensive, the 13th Corps was deployed, striking with precision at the Zolota Lipa River's mouth. The German South Army entered the fray two days later, skillfully securing the left flank of the 7th Army with G. Hoffmann's reinforced corps.

The night of July 14 marked a pivotal moment as Austro-Hungarian troops forded the Dniester, confronting the Russian stronghold at Chernelytsia. This maneuver threatened to encircle the Russian 33rd Army Corps near Tluste. A series of relentless counterattacks by Russian forces ensued throughout the day, with sporadic successes. Yet, the morning of July 15 witnessed a renewed Austro-Hungarian offensive, targeting the 2nd Cavalry and 33rd Army Corps, and advancing eastward, even breaching the eastern bank of the Zolota Lypa against the 30th Army Corps.

In these advances, over 2,000 mostly Slovene soldiers from the Carniolan 17th Infantry Regiment met a tragic fate, clashing fiercely with Russian forces. To turn the tide, P. Lechitsky, commanding the 9th Army, orchestrated a vigorous counterattack on July 16, aiming not just at the groups on the Dniester's left bank but also targeting the right flank of the 7th Austro-Hungarian Army with the 32nd Army and 3rd Cavalry Corps.

The intense military operations of July 16–17 transformed into fierce oncoming battles. Karl von Pflanzer-Baltin, making a strategic shift, redirected the 3rd corps' reserves to support Siegmund von Benigni in Müldenberg's group, while bolstering the 13th corps on the Zolota Lypa River with P. Hoffmann's corps and the 48th reserve division of the German Southern Army.

However, the advance of Alois Schönburg-Hartenstein's group along the Seret River's left bank met with stiff Russian resistance and was forced back to Duninov. Reinforced by the 3rd Cavalry Division, they halted further Russian advancements. Despite the Russians capturing over 1,500 prisoners and 3 machine guns, they couldn't completely push the Central Powers' troops back to the Dniester. Meanwhile, an offensive near Dobronoutsy village stalled, and the Austro-Hungarian forces, heavily impacted in the bridgeheads east of the Zolota-Lypa and Dniester rivers, called for a retreat to their original positions.

On the night of July 18, a dramatic twist occurred as P. Hofmann's group launched an assault to support the 13th Corps' left flank on the Zolota Lypa River, coinciding with the Russian 11th Army Corps' attack against the enemy's 1st Cavalry Division. The ensuing battle was fierce and inconclusive.

The Russian bridgehead near Tolstobaby village was eliminated, but Hofmann's and Ignaz von Korda's troops withdrew from the eastern riverbank, shifting to a defensive stance. Intense combat persisted until July 20, ending in a stalemate with both sides entrenched in their respective positions. The planned cavalry breakthrough by Karl von Pflanzer-Baltin was effectively countered by Platon Lechitsky's active military maneuvers.

In this intense engagement, the 7th Army's sole gain was maintaining bridgeheads on the Dniester's eastern bank, which, ironically, demanded more resources than their original right bank positions. Russian forces, by initiating these oncoming battles, thwarted any breakthrough attempts and captured a total of 8 machine guns and 1,827 prisoners throughout the battle.

The temporary lull on the battlefield provided a strategic opportunity for the Russian Supreme Commander to bolster the forces of the Southwestern Front by reallocating troops to extend from Riga to Białystok. On July 25, the 2nd Finnish Rifle and 69th Infantry Divisions were designated for transfer to the Northwestern Front. Following suit, the 1st Kuban Cossack Division departed from the 11th Army on July 29. Despite objections from N. Ivanov, Grand Duke Nikolai Nikolayevich, on July 31, directed that 120 companies from the Southwestern Front divisions be reassigned to reinforce the Northwestern Front. This repositioning continued with the order to deploy the 65th Infantry and 4th Finnish Rifle Divisions on August 8.

Sensing a potential vulnerability due to the reallocation of Russian forces from the Southwestern Front, Karl von Pflanzer-Baltin reignited active military operations, targeting the 9th Army's bridgehead on the right bank of the Dniester River near Chernelytsia, while deliberately sparing the diminished 11th Army. The 22nd Landwehr Infantry Division initiated a feint attack on August 8 against the 33rd Army Corps, leading to an unexpected breakthrough between the 33rd and 30th Army Corps. This allowed the 28th Infantry Division to penetrate the defenses of the Russian 80th Infantry Division.

Counterattacks by the Russian 71st and 80th divisions on the night of August 9 regained some lost ground near Ostra village. However, the Austro-Hungarians renewed their offensive the following morning, forcing the Russian 30th Army Corps to retreat to the left bank and capturing 2,760 Russian soldiers.

In response, N. Ivanov, Commander-in-Chief of the Southwestern Front, ordered the 11th Army to support the 8th Army at Sokal and the 9th Army at Zolota Lypa. However, Dmitry Shcherbachev, commander of the 11th Army, declared his inability to execute the offensive due to the army's exhaustion and the loss of its best divisions. Additionally, heavy rains and the overflowing Zlota-Lipa River hindered active operations. The Austro-Hungarian attacks on the remaining Chernelytsia bridgehead on August 10–11 were successfully repelled, leading to the redeployment of the 3rd Corps to the Italian front on August 12. This shift in focus led both sides to adopt defensive positions.

Further weakening of the Southwestern Front occurred in August with the transfer of the 28th Army Corps to the Northwestern Front, starting from August 20. To compensate, the 30th and 32nd Army Corps from the 9th Army and the 105th Infantry Division from the 11th Army were moved to cover the gaps. Over five weeks, 10 divisions were relocated to the Northwestern Front, significantly easing the situation on the Narew and Neman fronts. This large-scale troop movement was made feasible by the early thwarting of the Austro-Hungarian offensive on the Dniester. The 9th Army not only held its ground but also contributed to the stability of a critical front segment.

Rovno Offensive

In the waning days of summer in 1915, a dramatic military chess game unfolded on the Eastern Front of World War I. The Austro-Hungarian high command, led by the astute Infantry General Franz Conrad von Hötzendorf, hatched a bold strategy to launch a significant offensive on the city of Rovno, spearheaded by the formidable 1st and 4th armies. Their plan was intricately woven with the movements of the 2nd, 7th, and German Southern armies, which aimed to decisively expel Russian forces from Austria-Hungary's borders and, if fortune favored them, seize control of Podolia.

This masterstroke was first conceptualized on August 14th, during a pivotal meeting between General Hötzendorf and his German counterpart, Infantry General Erich von Falkenhayn. Their ambitious goal was to engineer a breakthrough at the critical juncture where the Russian 3rd Army of the NorthWestern Front and the 8th Army of the SouthWestern Front intersected, thereby isolating the 8th Army and paving a path to Rovno.

Meanwhile, the Russian 11th Army faced a fierce frontal assault from the combined might of the 2nd and Southern armies. In a concurrent move, the Austro-Hungarian 7th Army sought to dislodge the Russian 9th Army from the Dniester River, aiming to capture the strategically important city of Kamianets-Podilskyi.

The Central Powers had a trump card up their sleeve: a numerically superior force, particularly against the vulnerable right flank of the Russian 8th Army. Moreover, the entire Austro-Hungarian 4th Army stood ready in reserve, primed to capitalize on any breakthroughs.

However, the Russian Southwestern Front was not to be underestimated. Anticipating the enemy's maneuvers, they shrewdly fortified the 9th Army's position and amassed a formidable reserve of two army corps, ready to thwart any breakthroughs and safeguard the 8th Army. This strategic tension set the stage for a gripping confrontation, with both sides vying for a decisive victory that could alter the course of the war.

In late August 1915, a pivotal moment unfolded in the Eastern Front of World War I. The 1st Austro-Hungarian Army, under the leadership of Archduke Josef Ferdinand, seized control of Kovel on August 25. Following this victory, Ferdinand strategically deployed the 14th Corps to encircle the Russian 8th Army's right flank, while directing the 9th and 10th Corps along the Lutsk highway. Despite their numerical superiority, the Austro-Hungarians faced the challenging terrain of marshes, river cuts, and ravaged roads, with only the Rava-Ruska and Lvov (Lemberg) highway remaining functional.

By August 26-27, the Austro-Hungarian 1st Army had advanced to the Stokhid River. In a concurrent attack, the 5th Corps of the 2nd Army engaged the 6th Army Corps of the Russian 11th Army and successfully crossed the Zolota Lypa River. Reacting to these developments, the commander-in-chief of the Southwestern Front, Nikolai Ivanov, entrusted Aleksei Brusilov with the 39th Army Corps, tasking them to launch a counterstrike northwest of Lutsk. In a strategic decision to consolidate forces, Ivanov ordered the retreat of the 8th and 11th armies on the night of August 8.

The period of August 28-30 saw the Austro-Hungarians intensify their offensive, crossing the Styr River at multiple points. The 14th Corps ingeniously bypassed Lutsk from the east, effectively repelling the counterattacks of the Russian 39th Army Corps. Ivanov, acknowledging the situation, allowed

Brusilov to commence the gradual withdrawal of the 8th Army and sought support from the neighboring 3rd Army to bolster the right flank with cavalry. The 30th Army Corps, initially destined for the Northwestern Front, was redirected to reinforce the 8th Army, with the aid of a rear railway line.

However, on August 31, the Austro-Hungarian 14th Corps launched a decisive attack and captured Lutsk, forcing the 8th Army to retreat across the Styr River. A critical turning point occurred when the 39th Army Corps, equipped with Japanese rifles, ran out of ammunition mid-attack. Meanwhile, on the 11th Army's front, intense fighting erupted at Zolochiv. A robust counterattack by the Russian 22nd and 18th Army Corps recaptured some positions and resulted in the capture of 4,689 prisoners from the retreating Southern Army across the Studzyanka River.

On August 31, Infantry General Franz Conrad von Hötzendorf outlined an ambitious plan for the Austro-Hungarian forces: their mission extended beyond merely clearing Eastern Galicia of Russian troops to delivering a decisive blow. The strategy involved the 2nd Army circumventing protracted battles by bypassing the Ikva River from the south through Kremenets, while the 1st Army aimed to capture Dubno through a flanking maneuver. Simultaneously, the 4th Army was tasked with rapidly seizing Rovno, a key location for Russian reinforcements.

Despite these well-laid plans, when the Austro-Hungarian troops resumed their offensive on September 3-4, they encountered fierce resistance from the Russian 8th and 11th armies. The Russians, particularly the 12th and 39th Army Corps on the right flank of the 8th Army, mounted a successful counteroffensive, capturing 4,453 prisoners and 15 machine guns. However, the Austro-Hungarian forces skillfully flanked and pushed back the attackers.

In a critical maneuver on September 5, the Russian 4th Cavalry Corps, bolstered by the 77th and 83rd Infantry Divisions, encircled and halted the advance of the Austro-Hungarian 7th Cavalry Division. This engagement deep in enemy territory necessitated the deployment of the Austro-Hungarian 1st Cavalry Division and the 1st Brigade of the Polish Legion to secure communications lines. Meanwhile, Austro-Hungarian assaults on Tarnopol's bridgeheads, held by the 11th and 9th Russian armies, were repelled.

By September 6-7, the tide seemed to turn as the Austro-Hungarian 1st Army breached the 8th Army's defenses, capturing 6,000 prisoners and 6 machine guns. In response, Russian General Aleksei Brusilov ordered a strategic withdrawal. Concurrently, the Russian 11th Army repositioned its 6th and 18th Army Corps, while launching an offensive with the 22nd Army Corps to aid the 9th Army. A significant Russian counterattack near Tarnopol on September 7 resulted in the capture of 8,200 prisoners, 21 machine guns, and 14 artillery pieces.

Although an initial Austro-Hungarian counteroffensive captured 3,700 prisoners and 7 machine guns, a shortage of reserves forced them back to their starting positions. The Russian 2nd Cavalry and 11th Army Corps exploited this, driving the enemy across the Seret River and securing 3,355 prisoners, 10 machine guns, and 3 artillery pieces.

The situation further evolved on September 8, when heavy rains hindered the 10th Corps of the 4th Austro-Hungarian Army's attack on Klevan and Tsuman, transforming the Putilovka River floodplain into a swamp and slowing progress. By September 9, the Austro-Hungarian 1st Army had taken Dubno, which the Russians had vacated. Brusilov strategically repositioned the 8th Army to the Stubel River. Meanwhile, the Russian 11th and 9th armies continued their assaults on the junction of the Southern and 7th armies and at Tarnopol.

Despite intense fighting on September 10, the Austro-Hungarians managed to repulse the 6th and 7th Russian army corps and fend off attacks at Khmelivka. However, the Russian 33rd army corps successfully counterattacked, capturing an additional 4,716 prisoners. This forced von Hötzendorf to revise his plans, retaining the 6th Corps, which was initially destined for the Serbian front, as a reserve force.

In a strategic shift, von Hötzendorf bolstered the 2nd Austro-Hungarian Army by reallocating resources from the 1st Army, which, along with the 7th and Southern armies, assumed a defensive posture. He also dedicated the left flank cavalry to combat the Russian 4th cavalry corps near Kovel, and directed the 4th Army to focus solely on the attack on Rovno. However, the arrival of the Russian 30th Army Corps in Rovno on September 11-12 reinforced the 8th Army's right flank, altering the dynamics of the battlefield.

In a significant engagement, the 11th Russian Army's 7th and 6th Army Corps successfully halted the advance of Eduard von Böhm-Ermolli's strike group. Meanwhile, a Russian counterattack at the junction of the Austro-Hungarian 2nd and German Southern armies forced the Austro-Hungarians to retreat across the Strypa River, resulting in significant losses including 91 officers and 4,644 soldiers taken prisoner.

By September 13, the Austro-Hungarian 2nd Army had stabilized its front, but the Southern Army, under pressure from Lechitsky's troops, retreated to the Vosushka River's right bank. The 7th Army also faced challenges, being pushed back to the Strypa River crossings.

The Russian Southwestern Front armies launched a full-scale offensive on September 13. The 9th Army drove the enemy back, the 11th Army's left wing continued to pressure the German Southern Army, and its right wing overpowered the 5th Austro-Hungarian Corps, pushing back the 2nd Army. On September 14, the Russian 11th Army Corps crossed the Strypa River, forcing the Austro-Hungarians to abandon their bridgeheads. However, the retreat of Russian corps in other sectors slowed the momentum of this offensive.

In fierce fighting on September 15-16, the 8th Army's shock group broke through the Austro-Hungarian positions on the Stubel River. By September 17, the front of the Austro-Hungarian 4th Army on the Putilovka River was compromised, leading Archduke Joseph Ferdinand to order a retreat. Despite these setbacks, the Central Powers managed to halt the Russian 11th and 9th armies' offensive. Counterattacks by the 2nd and Southern armies on September 16-17 pushed Russian forces back from the western bank of the Strypa River. By September 18, major combat operations in the Dniester and Strypa regions concluded.

However, on September 18-19, the Russian 8th Army's attack on Lutsk was repelled, and an attempt by the Russian 17th Army Corps to cross the Ikva River failed. Brusilov planned a regrouping to renew the offensive. The situation was further complicated by German advances in neighboring areas and the transfer of the German 24th Reserve Corps to assist the Austro-Hungarians.

On September 23, the Russian 8th Army's 12th, 30th, and 39th Army Corps resumed their attacks on the Styr River, breaking through the Austro-Hungarian lines and partially capturing the 24th Infantry Division. The Russian 4th Rifle Division captured Lutsk the following morning, taking up to 12,000 Austro-Hungarian prisoners, including the commander and banner of the 8th Austrian Infantry Regiment. Despite these successes, the center and left flank of the 8th Army were unable to advance further.

Vilno-Dvinsk Offensive

In the wake of the grueling Sieges of Kovno and Novogeorgievsk, the tides of World War I began to shift dramatically on the Eastern Front. General Erich von Falkenhayn, the mastermind behind Germany's military strategy, faced a critical juncture. With the limited success of Hindenburg's Army Group, he was compelled to rethink his plans. In a decisive move, he chose to scale back operations on the Eastern Front. This strategic pivot was driven by the urgent need to redeploy troops for a fresh offensive against Serbia and to bolster defenses in France and Belgium.

Amidst this strategic overhaul, on August 27–28, 1915, a pivotal directive was issued by Emperor Wilhelm II, under Falkenhayn's urgent recommendation. This directive called for the construction of formidable long-term defensive lines stretching from the Baltic Sea near Mitava to the Narew river and extending to Kovel. This new defensive stance was a significant shift from the previous aggressive campaigns.

Meanwhile, in the Russian camp, significant leadership changes were unfolding. Defying objections, Nikolai Yanushkevich, the chief of staff to the Supreme Commander, ordered a reorganization of the North–Western Front's armies as early as August 17. This led to the creation of the Northern Front under General Nikolai Ruzsky, with Major General M. Bonch–Bruyevich as his chief of staff, comprising the 6th, 5th, and restructured 12th armies. Their crucial mission was to safeguard the routes to Petrograd, especially from the Baltic coast. Concurrently, the Western Front, under Infantry

General Alekseyev and Lieutenant General Arseny Gulevich, was tasked with defending key regions such as Vilno, Grodno-Bialystok, and Brest-Pinsk. Their challenge was intensified by the German forces' proximity to Vilno and their capture of Brest-Litovsk.

On the first day of September, the German 8th and 12th Armies, amassing a formidable force of 335,696 soldiers, initiated a bold offensive towards Grodno and Slonim. The 8th Army, demonstrating remarkable agility, navigated the challenging swampy terrain of the Bobr River within a day, closing in on the fortified positions of Grodno. Concurrently, the 12th Army successfully forded the Svislach River, marking significant progress in their campaign.

Facing this German onslaught were the Russian forces, led by Cavalry General Alexander Litvinov with the 1st Army defending Grodno, and Infantry General V. Smirnov with the 2nd Army holding the line in the Lida region. The battle escalated rapidly, with the Grodno garrison unleashing heavy artillery fire by the afternoon of September 1. Despite their limited heavy artillery, the German 8th Army focused its firepower on select forts, though initial attacks were stoutly repelled by the defending forces.

However, the tide turned on the following day. The German forces managed to seize the intermediate trenches between the forts and crossed the Neman River. Simultaneously, from the north, elements of the German 10th Army's 3rd reserve corps, advancing from Druskininkai, effectively cut off all routes to Vilno, compelling the garrison to abandon the forts under the looming threat of encirclement. By September 3, the Germans had penetrated the fortress, leading to a retreat of the 20th Army Corps and the garrison. This German victory resulted in the capture of 3,600 prisoners and 6 heavy artillery pieces.

This shift in the battlefront, marked by the Central Powers' offensive, the fall of Grodno, and the German advance to the Western Dvina and

Lutsk, prompted a significant decision from Emperor Nicholas II. On September 5, he resolved to take supreme command himself. Infantry General Alekseyev was appointed as the new Chief of Staff of the Supreme Commander, and Lieutenant General Mikhail Pustovoitenko assumed the role of Quartermaster General of the Headquarters.

Meanwhile, Hindenburg orchestrated a major strategic maneuver, directing the primary assault towards Dvinsk and Vilno. This involved the redeployment of the Army of the Niemen and the 10th Army, concentrating nearly all available cavalry at the junction of these forces, totaling 502,357 men. In the Riga sector, the Russian 12th Army of the Northern Front, under General V. Gorbatovsky, held their ground, while the Russian 5th Army, commanded by General Paul von Plehwe, defended the Dvina direction. The Vilno-Minsk axis, a crucial and challenging front, was under the command of General E. Radkevich's 10th Army, comprising 300,147 soldiers.

The Russian forces, despite their numerical superiority, faced a strategic challenge against the Germans, similar to the situation in the Gorlice–Tarnów offensive. The Germans, adept in their military tactics, launched an attack on the strongest Russian army. The German 10th Army's strike zone was strategically chosen to confront mainly Russian cavalry units. The area stretching from Ukmergė to Wuqiang became a key battleground, with the German 1st and 21st army corps being deployed there.

On September 9, the Russian defenses at Širvintos were breached, allowing the Germans to penetrate 20 km deep. The Russian cavalry, led by Lieutenant General N. Kaznakov, was forced to withdraw by the order of Plehve, the commander of the 5th Army, leaving the 10th Army's flank exposed. By September 10, Kaznakov's detachment was pushed back in a battle with the German cavalry and Beckman's division, retreating behind Utena. Another Russian unit, under Lieutenant General Mikael Thylin, was driven back 10 km from the Širvinta River.

This retreat led to a significant gap of 60 km between the Russian 5th and 10th Armies, which the German divisions swiftly exploited. On September 12, German cavalry took control of Novo-Sventiany, while their infantry advanced towards Maišiagala and Pabradė. The Russian 3rd Siberian Corps and the 2nd Finnish Rifle Division were hurriedly shifted to the 10th Army's right flank for reinforcement. Meanwhile, the 2nd and 26th Army Corps were repositioned to Leipalingis to cover the left flank of the 10th Army.

By September 11, Alekseyev had already issued a directive for the 2nd Army to join the Sventiany Offensive, incorporating reserve corps from the 1st, 4th, and 3rd armies. However, the troop mobilization was hindered by poor road conditions due to rain and German disruptions to communications. General Aleksei Evert, commanding the Western Front, ordered the 10th Army to form a strong group on the right flank, launch an offensive northwest of Vilno, and bridge the gap with the Northern Front's cavalry corps led by General Vladimir Oranovsky.

The situation intensified as the right flank of the Army of the Niemen broke through to Utena, posing a threat to Dvinsk. By September 14, the German 1st and 39th reserve corps had pushed back the Russian 5th Army's left wing to Dvinsk, capturing a 60-km bridgehead from Lake Salava to Ilūkste. The German 10th Army's strike group advanced to Vileyka and Molodechno. Despite capturing Sventiany and Naroch, the German advance was halted at the outskirts of Vilno by the combined strength of the Russian Guards, 3rd Siberian, and 5th Caucasian Corps.

It wasn't until September 15 that General Oranovsky's cavalry corps intervened, confronting the German cavalry near Sola and Smarhon'. However, the very next day, Russian forces had to abandon Vilno to avoid encirclement. By this date, the German 12th, 8th, and 9th armies had successfully crossed the Neman River and secured control over the western bank of the Shchara River. Meanwhile, Army Group Mackensen, comprising the 11th and Bug armies, broke through the defenses of the Russian 3rd Army.

The situation escalated on September 16 when Johannes von Eben's German forces pushed back Oranovsky's cavalry. Despite this setback, the Russian 2nd Army Corps arrived in time to halt the German advance. Along the Ashmyanka River, German cavalry divisions were stopped by regiments from the Russian 5th Army Corps. Garnier and Richthofen's cavalry divisions occupied Zhuprany, Baruny, Vileyka, and Smarhon', forming a defensive line to the west and southeast, and even attempted to sabotage the Minsk-Smolensk railway on September 20.

On September 17, the 3rd German cavalry division advanced towards Molodechno but was halted a few kilometers from the city by the Russian 27th Army Corps. The German 1st and 4th cavalry divisions encountered resistance from the regiments of the 36th army corps in Ashmyany.

That same day, Supreme Commander Nicholas II, effectively guided by Alekseyev, issued a directive for the Western Front armies to withdraw to a new defensive line starting the night of September 18. The 2nd Army was tasked to capture Sventiany and Mikhalishki, reestablish contact with the 5th Army of the Northern Front, and push the Germans back from Vileyka and Smarhon' to Lida and Vilno. To counter the German cavalry and penetrate the enemy's right flank, Oranovsky's forces were reinforced with detachments led by Generals Kaznakov, Prince K. Toumanov, and Prince S. Belosselsky-Belozersky. The 1st Army, redeploying northwards, assembled near Polotsk under this protective cover.

The Russian maneuvers were aided by the German High Command's decision to withdraw troops for deployment against the French offensive in Champagne and Artois, and in Serbia. Considering the operation against Russia effectively completed, the German command withdrew 23 divisions from Russia by the end of September, including units from the army groups of August von Mackensen and Hindenburg. The remaining German forces ceased their offensive after September 20 and retreated to newly established fortified lines.

Between September 19-20, the Russian 2nd Army and a group led by Infantry General Vasily Flug launched an offensive to reclaim territory along the Ashmyanka and Neris rivers. The Russian 27th, 36th, and 4th Siberian army corps successfully drove Garnier's cavalry from Smarhon'. However, Flug's corps faced a counterattack from the Eben group, targeting the 3rd Siberian and 2nd army corps. German 1st and 21st army corps were positioned behind their second echelon cavalry.

The Russian 10th Army, facing increasing pressure, was compelled to fall back to Molodechno. On September 23, Russian Headquarters issued orders for a strategic counterattack: the cavalry of the Russian 2nd Army was to strike at the rear of the Germans from the town of Narach, while the Russian 5th Army was tasked with securing the approaches to Polotsk. In response, the German commander, X. von Eichhorn, directed a pursuit of Radkevich's withdrawing forces.

On the left flank of the Russian 5th Army, General Kaznakov's cavalry corps launched an offensive between September 17-19, successfully pushing back the German cavalry. However, the arrival of the German 2nd cavalry division forced Kaznakov to retreat back towards Polotsk. By September 26, the gap between the Neman River and the German 10th Army was sealed by the 8th cavalry and 3rd infantry divisions.

Between September 24-26, the German 10th Army, bolstering its right wing, advanced to the Berezina River near Smarhon'. After establishing fortified positions, the 10th Army switched to a defensive stance, effectively completing its encircling offensive. Despite these maneuvers, the Russian armies managed to avoid encirclement and posed a potential threat to the German lines.

On September 27, Hindenburg declared the offensive operation complete, instructing his armies to settle into long-term "winter" positions stretching from the mouth of the Berezina River to Lake Narach, and between Dinaburg and Mitava. However, the Russian command, led by Alekseyev, was not ready to concede. Planning a counteroffensive, Alekseyev aimed to push the Germans back to their original positions. Consequently, on September 28, Oranovsky's cavalry group was assigned the mission of breaking through to the German rear near Sventiany and driving the enemy back beyond Panevėžys and Wiłkomierz.

On the evening of September 27, the left wing of the German 10th Army began retreating to fortified positions, with the cavalry units of Garnier and Richthofen covering their withdrawal. Oranovsky's cavalry group's transition to offensive operations was delayed until the evening of September 28, by which time the German cavalry had already begun their movement. Oranovsky's attempts to attack Dunilovichi with two divisions proved unsuccessful. Subsequent cavalry attacks on September 30 were also repelled. However, the situation changed with the arrival of the Russian 1st Siberian and 1st Army Corps. Renewed attacks on Pastavy eventually succeeded, resulting in the liberation of the city.

In a determined bid to halt the German advance towards Polotsk, Aleksei Evert proposed a strategic move to the Russian Supreme Commander: the transfer of reserve corps from the Russian Western Front and the leadership of the 1st Army to bolster this critical front. On September 25, Alekseyev issued the pivotal directive, and the first corps entered the battlefield towards the end of September. By October 2, the headquarters of the 1st Army had established itself in Seslavino, laying the groundwork for a fresh offensive aimed at Tverečius and Komai. This offensive was to be carried out by three formidable corps: the 1st Siberian, 1st, and 4th armies.

However, by this juncture, a formidable German army group under the command of artillery general F. von Scholz, originating from Richthofen's cavalry corps, along with three infantry divisions, had taken positions to the north of Lake Narach, along the Dvinsk-Jakobstadt road. The Russian 1st Army launched a series of assaults on October 4-6, but they were met with staunch resistance from these German forces and were ultimately repulsed. Recognizing the futility of further attacks, A. Evert ordered a halt to these costly offensives on October 7. Subsequently, from October 10 onwards, both the 10th and 2nd armies adopted defensive postures, and the German 10th Army ceased its attacks on Smorgon'.

Meanwhile, the 1st Russian Army assumed a defensive stance between Myadzyel and Lake Drūkšiai. Their primary mission was to provide support to the neighboring 5th Army, specifically in the defense of Dvinsk. Throughout the month of September, the German Army of the Niemen had been steadily advancing towards Dvinsk and Jakobstadt, albeit at a measured pace. On September 28, the Army of the Niemen underwent a reorganization, resulting in the formation of the 8th Army. Portions of its right flank became the foundation for the army group led by Scholz. Between October 6-10, the positions of the 5th Army near Sivishki were breached. On October 11, the Russian 1st Army, bolstered by the cavalry group of Oranovsky and the 6th Siberian Army Corps, initiated an assault on the German flank near the lakes Drūkšiai and Demmern. This assault yielded some gains as Russian forces managed to capture a portion of the enemy trenches. However, further advances were effectively stymied, and repeated assaults until October 19 proved fruitless, including the attempt to seize Ilūkste, which was also repelled by the 5th Army.

The German offensive against Dvinsk resumed on October 23, featuring extensive aerial reconnaissance and artillery adjustments by pilots. The intense artillery fire demoralized the defenders, leading to the German occupation of Ilūkste by evening. However, attacks on October 26-27 saw limited success, as Russian troops effectively defended and counterattacked. It wasn't until November 2-3 that Germans dislodged Russians from the Dvina bridgehead, but they failed to capture Dvinsk, missing their primary objective in the Western Dvina River offensive.

IV

Gallipoli Campaign

Landing at Cape Helles

In the early 1900s, the once-mighty Ottoman Empire, dubbed the "sick man of Europe," was reeling from political chaos, military setbacks, and internal conflicts. It was a time of dramatic transformation, marked by the rise of the Young Turks, a group of audacious officers who overthrew the existing power structure and placed Mehmed V as a symbolic Sultan. This new regime embarked on ambitious reforms to modernize the empire and redefine its identity.

Germany, sensing an opportunity, stepped in with substantial investments and diplomatic muscle, gradually overshadowing Britain, the region's former dominant force. German officers lent their expertise in revamping the Ottoman army. Despite this bolstering, the empire's finances were strained by the First and Second Balkan Wars, prompting financial aid offers from France, Britain, and Germany alike.

The empire was torn between factions: one favoring closer ties with Britain and another, led by the influential Enver Pasha, advocating for a stronger alliance with Germany. In December 1913, Germany intensified its involvement by sending a military mission led by General Otto Liman von Sanders to Constantinople. The strategic location of the Ottoman Empire made its position crucial in the brewing storm of European conflict, drawing keen interest from Russia, France, and Britain.

The July Crisis of 1914 saw Germany propose an anti-Russian alliance to the

Ottomans, offering territorial gains in return. With the British ambassador absent, the pro-British faction in the Ottoman cabinet found itself isolated. Unbeknownst to them, Britain's entry into a European war could drastically alter their plans. On the cusp of World War I, the Ottoman leaders secretly forged an alliance with Germany, a pact that did not initially commit them to military action.

The tension escalated when Britain seized two Ottoman battleships under construction in its shipyards, a move that alienated pro-British supporters in Constantinople. In response, Germany cunningly offered two of its cruisers to the Ottoman navy. The pursuit of these ships by Allied forces culminated in a dramatic escape to Constantinople, facilitated by the Ottomans' controversial decision to open the Dardanelles.

As war loomed closer, the British naval mission, led by Admiral Arthur Limpus since 1912, was withdrawn, and command of the Ottoman navy passed to Rear Admiral Wilhelm Souchon of the Imperial German Navy. The closure of the Dardanelles by the German commander further signaled the Ottomans' leaning towards Germany.

The success of German forces in Europe bolstered the pro-German faction in the Ottoman government, leading to a declaration of war against Russia. The renamed German cruisers, now part of the Ottoman navy, launched an offensive in the Black Sea, targeting Russian ships and ports. Despite Allied demands to expel German missions, the Ottomans formally sided with the Central Powers, prompting Russia, Britain, and France to declare war.

This entry into the war ignited multiple fronts: the Ottomans launched a jihad, sparking the Caucasus Campaign against Russia, and operations began in Mesopotamia with a British landing aimed at securing oil facilities in the Persian Gulf. Plans were also underway for an Ottoman assault on Egypt in early 1915, targeting the strategic Suez Canal, a vital link to British India and the Far East.

By the end of 1914, the dynamic and mobile warfare on the Western Front had given way to the establishment of extensive trench networks stretching from the Swiss border to the English Channel. This shift marked the end of the open, maneuver-based warfare and the beginning of a grueling and static trench warfare.

The Central Powers, comprising the German Empire and Austria-Hungary, effectively sealed the overland trade routes between Britain and France in the west, and Russia in the east. The naval situation was equally challenging: the White Sea to the north and the Sea of Okhotsk in the Far East were largely inaccessible due to ice in winter and their considerable distance from the Eastern Front. Moreover, the Baltic Sea was under the tight blockade of the Kaiserliche Marine, the Imperial German Navy, while the crucial Black Sea passage through the Dardanelles was under the control of the Ottoman Empire. Although the Ottomans were initially neutral, they soon began laying mines in the straits, halting trade with Russia even before officially entering the war.

During this period, Aristide Briand put forward a proposal to strike against the Ottoman Empire, which was ultimately dismissed. The British also made a failed attempt to bribe the Ottomans into joining the Allies. In a significant strategic move, Winston Churchill, the First Lord of the Admiralty, proposed a naval assault on the Dardanelles. Misinformed about the Ottoman troop strength, Churchill suggested using older battleships, ineffective against the German High Seas Fleet, for an operation on the Dardanelles, complemented by a small land force. The aim was not just to weaken the Ottomans but also to encourage Bulgaria and Greece, former Ottoman territories, to join the Allies.

In early January 1915, Grand Duke Nicholas of Russia requested British assistance against an Ottoman offensive in the Caucasus. This plea sparked the initiation of plans for a naval demonstration in the Dardanelles, intended to force the Ottomans to divert troops from the Caucasian front.

The Dardanelles naval campaign reached its climax on March 18th with a dramatic but unsuccessful attempt to force a naval passage through the straits. This bold effort resulted in the sinking of three battleships and severe damage to four others, largely due to mines laid along the Asiatic shore. In the wake of this setback, plans shifted towards a land assault to neutralize the coastal defenses protecting the straits. However, these preparations in Egypt were poorly concealed, even being openly discussed in a newspaper interview by the French commander.

On March 24th, the Ottoman war effort saw a significant reorganization. Enver Pasha, the Ottoman Minister of War, appointed Marshal Otto Liman von Sanders to unify and command the military forces around the Dardanelles. Liman's arrival at Gallipoli sparked a strategic redeployment of troops. He concentrated the garrisons on the peninsula and repositioned the 5th and 7th divisions to Bulair, with the 9th Division stretching from Suvla Bay to Sedd el Bahr, and the 11th Division guarding the Asiatic shore. Additionally, the 19th Division was stationed near Boghali as a reserve force, ready to move where needed.

Liman advocated for a mobile defense strategy, moving away from the previous approach of guarding the coast with continuous defenses. This redeployment was carried out under the cover of night to avoid detection by Allied reconnaissance. The 9th Division, under Colonel Halil Sami Bey, was split into northern and southern zones, with the 27th Regiment and some mountain artillery in the north, and the 26th Regiment in the south. Reserve forces were strategically placed to support either zone.

In the northern zone, Lieutenant-Colonel Ali Chefik Bey positioned the 2nd Battalion along the coast, supported by heavy artillery. In the southern zone, Lieutenant-Colonel Kadri Bey organized his forces into battalion areas, with companies supported by field artillery and reserves positioned strategically. The central "Krithia sector" and the southern "Sedd el Bahr sector" were similarly structured, with companies guarding key positions and reserves ready to respond to any landings.

On the Asiatic shore, the 3rd Division was deployed near Troy, with units extending to Yeni Shehr, while the 11th Division remained in reserve near Ezine. These careful preparations and strategic placements by the Ottoman forces reflected a nuanced understanding of defense, aiming to counter the impending Allied landings with a flexible and responsive military strategy.

The primary goal of this military operation was to support the fleet in breaching the Straits by capturing the Ottoman forts along the European side of the Narrows from behind. This would provide a strategic vantage point to control the forts on the Asiatic side. The key target was the Kilitbahir plateau, which overlooked the Ottoman forts in the Narrows and spanned most of the peninsula's width between Maidos and Soghanli Dere. This plateau, extending about 4 miles westward from Kilitbahir and up to 2 miles in breadth, with heights reaching 600–800 feet, was heavily fortified by the Ottomans with trenches and barbed wire, stretching south to Kakma Dagh ridge and north to Gaba Tepe.

General Sir Ian Hamilton, leading the Mediterranean Expeditionary Force (MEF), planned a dual-pronged assault with additional diversionary attacks. The Anzac Corps was to land unexpectedly between Gaba Tepe and Fisherman's Hut, seizing the area just before dawn without prior bombardment. Their mission was to secure the left flank and then push eastward towards Maidos, cutting off Ottoman communication lines to the south. Concurrently, on the Gallipoli peninsula around Cape Helles, supported by naval forces, a covering force would secure the beaches, followed by the main force aiming for the village of Krithia and the Achi Baba hill. Five beaches, labeled S, V, W, X, and Y, were chosen for the landings, with V and W being the primary sites at the peninsula's tip.

To the north, near Bulair, the Royal Naval Division (minus two battalions) would conduct a feint at the peninsula's narrowest point, aiming to keep

Ottoman forces occupied during the main landings. This diversion would include all-day naval bombardments and visible transport ships to enhance the illusion. In contrast, to the south near Cape Helles, a French regiment from the Corps expéditionnaire d'Orient would execute a temporary landing on the Asiatic shore at Kum Kale. This move was designed to distract Ottoman artillery, confuse command structures, and delay Ottoman reinforcements from Asia to Gallipoli.

Despite assurances from a 1905 Admiralty report about abundant valley water, extensive preparations were made to ensure adequate water supply for the troops. This included the arrival of the Indian 9th Mule Corps from France, equipped with thousands of mules and carts. Additionally, a Zion Mule Corps, composed of Jewish Russian émigrés from Palestine, was formed in Egypt. The critical need for water transportation was so pressing that a mid-April request was sent to Egypt, urging the immediate deployment of the Zion Mule Corps, regardless of its incomplete equipment.

The Royal Naval Air Service (RNAS), operating from HMS Ark Royal, played a crucial role in supporting the Anzac landing at Gallipoli. This support included both seaplanes and a kite balloon. Additionally, Number 3 Aeroplane Squadron RNAS, equipped with 18 aircraft, provided vital air support for the Helles operation. The pilots maintained continuous patrols over Helles and the Asiatic coast in ideal flying conditions, with each pilot conducting three sorties from dawn throughout the day. These aircraft played a key role in the operation, with observers using wireless technology to direct naval gunfire onto Ottoman positions. Despite the overwhelming number of Ottoman targets, the aircraft observers managed to guide naval gunfire effectively. Once the troops were securely ashore, ships began responding to signals from the aircrews, who used flare guns to communicate with ships not equipped for wireless reception.

The pilots embarked on missions to bomb Ottoman artillery, camps, and troop positions, as well as conducting photographic reconnaissance missions. They kept a vigilant watch over the entire peninsula, extending up to Bulair and along the Asiatic coast. The airborne observers, launched at 5:21 a.m., provided crucial information on troop movements and reported the presence of the battleship Turgut Reis in the Narrows, leading to its pursuit by HMS Triumph. Despite challenges posed by the terrain, the air patrols continued throughout the day.

V Beach, the site of one of the landings, was a narrow strip of land, approximately 300 yards long and 10 yards wide, flanked by Cape Helles, Fort Etrugrul, and the old Sedd el Bahr castle. The beach, fortified with wire and defended by about a company of Ottoman soldiers from the 3rd Battalion of the 26th Regiment, was a formidable obstacle. The first troops to land were the 1st Battalion, Royal Dublin Fusiliers, arriving in boats towed or rowed ashore. They were followed by troops disembarking from the SS River Clyde, a converted collier equipped with machine guns and modified to allow rapid deployment of soldiers.

The landing operation faced significant challenges. The Dubliners' boats were delayed, and upon their late arrival at 6:30 a.m., they were met with intense Ottoman gunfire. Many soldiers were killed or wounded in the boats or as they waded ashore, and the survivors sought shelter under the beach's bank. The River Clyde's attempt to establish a bridge to the shore using the steam hopper Argyll failed, leading Commander Edward Unwin to lead an effort to position transport boats for disembarkation. Despite heavy gunfire, some troops managed to reach the shore, but many were hit or drowned due to the weight of their equipment. A subsequent disembarkation attempt resulted in such heavy casualties that further efforts were postponed until darkness.

General Hunter-Weston, observing the landings at W Beach from HMS Euryalus, initially received optimistic reports at 7:30 and 7:50 a.m., suggesting the landings were progressing well. Based on this information, he ordered the main force to commence landing at 8:30 a.m. However, by 9:00 a.m., the reality on the ground remained unknown to him, and the return of the boats from the shore was hindered, delaying the arrival of the second wave. Despite this, wounded soldiers were evacuated, and Brigadier-General Henry Napier led several platoons towards the beach.

Unaware of the dire situation that had befallen the first wave, Hunter-Weston at 9:00 a.m. directed the troops on the River Clyde to advance towards the left flank and W Beach. At 9:30 a.m., an attempt by a company of the 2nd Hampshire to disembark resulted in heavy casualties, leading to the suspension of the effort. Napier, arriving on a vessel near River Clyde, tragically mistook a group of deceased soldiers for live men and was killed shortly after disembarking.

By 10:21 a.m., General Hamilton, who had been monitoring the landings from HMS Queen Elizabeth, instructed Hunter-Weston to halt the landing at V Beach and redirect the remaining forces to W Beach. Throughout the afternoon, battleships including Queen Elizabeth, HMS Albion, and HMS Cornwallis bombarded the Ottoman defenses at V Beach, but with little impact on the intensity of Ottoman fire. A later attempt to land troops from River Clyde around 4:00 p.m., after bridge repairs, saw only a few soldiers reaching safety beyond the beach.

In the evening, the battleships intensified their bombardment, but an Ottoman machine-gun crew successfully repelled a British assault at 7:00 p.m., forcing survivors to retreat. After nightfall, the dead and wounded were cleared from River Clyde's gangways, a grim task that lasted until 3:00 a.m. A surgeon aboard treated an astonishing number of 750 men despite his own injury.

Around midnight, Hunter-Weston planned an attack on Hill 141, but it was deemed impractical for a night operation. Troops were reorganized for a morning assault following a bombardment by HMS Albion.

Meanwhile, the Ottoman defenders, despite their prepared positions and the absence of surprise or effective covering fire from the ships, faced communication challenges and artillery range issues. Major Mahmut, commanding the 3rd Battalion, 26th Regiment, struggled to locate the landing site amid the chaos. Requests for reinforcements were delayed until the early hours of April 26. Despite repelling an assault in the afternoon, the Ottoman battalion suffered significant losses, leading to a morale collapse the next day when outflanked by troops on S Beach. The Ottomans retreated rapidly, leaving behind many wounded. Efforts to regroup failed, and the survivors fell back to a line 1.5 kilometers from Krithia by late afternoon. By April 27, the beach defenders had incurred 575 casualties, highlighting the intense and costly nature of the combat during the Gallipoli Campaign.

W Beach, situated northwest of Cape Helles near Tekke Burnu, featured a small gully and was approximately 350 yards long, varying in width from fifteen to forty yards. Steep cliffs flanked the beach, while a more accessible approach lay over central sand dunes leading to a ridge with sea views. The Ottoman defenders, an infantry company from the 3rd Battalion of the 26th Regiment, had heavily fortified this beach. They laid mines and extensive barbed wire, including a shoreline barrier and underwater trip wires. Trenches on the high ground offered commanding views, and two machine guns concealed in the cliffs provided enfilading fire.

Beyond the beach center, a ridge was overlooked by higher ground entrenchments. About 600 yards away, near Hill 138, lay two redoubts, heavily wired and lacking any cover. Another barbed wire line extended from the southern redoubt to cliffs near a lighthouse, effectively blocking an advance from W Beach towards V Beach.

The 1st Battalion of the Lancashire Fusiliers, embarked on the cruiser Euryalus and battleship HMS Implacable, prepared for the assault. Transferring to cutters, they approached the beach around 5:00 a.m. As they neared the shore, Ottoman gunfire erupted, causing significant casualties. The preliminary bombardment had not sufficiently cleared the wire obstacles, and the Fusiliers faced intense fire as they struggled ashore.

Small groups of Fusiliers managed to breach the wire, capturing trenches behind the dunes. Some tows, deviating north, landed unopposed and secured a trench atop a cliff, repelling an Ottoman counter-attack. The main landing's intensity lessened after offshore heavy shells hit an Ottoman trench. The Fusiliers advanced, cutting through more wire and assaulting the southern cliff end.

By 7:15 a.m., the British had penetrated far enough inland to obscure the Ottomans' view of the area. Brigadier-General Hare's group, which had outflanked the Ottoman defenses to the north, advanced towards X Beach but encountered resistance from Hill 114, where Hare was wounded. The second wave landed around 7:30 a.m., facing minimal losses and preparing to assault Hill 138. However, navigation was hampered by inaccurate maps and damaged equipment, causing delays and confusion. Attacks on the redoubts were repelled, while troops fought towards Hill 114 from both the beach and X Beach. Captured Ottoman soldiers near W Beach indicated that only one division was positioned south of Krithia.

At 8:30 a.m., Hunter-Weston, assessing the situation, ordered the main force to commence landing and redirected some troops initially destined for V Beach to W Beach as reinforcements. These reinforcements began arriving at 9:00 a.m., and by 10:21 a.m., General Hamilton had ordered all troops intended for V Beach to be diverted to W Beach instead. The first reinforcements faced significant long-range rifle fire as they neared the beach, but the cliffs provided cover, allowing them to land and join the Lancashire Fusiliers on the flanks.

By 11:30 a.m., the Fusiliers on the left flank had established contact with troops from X Beach and successfully captured Hill 114. Meanwhile, on the right flank, troops landing to assault Hill 138 found themselves pinned down halfway to the crest. However, a subsequent attack, supported by bombardment from HMS Swiftsure and Euryalus, allowed for the capture of the first redoubt at 3:00 p.m.

After overcoming barbed wire obstacles, the troops took the second redoubt with minimal opposition and few casualties, as the Ottoman garrison had retreated. The capture of these redoubts enabled the British forces near the lighthouse to advance toward V Beach, though they were halted by more barbed wire. Efforts to cut through the wire were visible and met with intense fire. Observers from Queen Elizabeth and Albion, stationed a mile offshore, could only watch, unable to provide support due to a lack of clear information about the situation on land.

It wasn't until 5:00 p.m. that the full extent of the disaster at V Beach was communicated to Colonel Wolley-Dod at W Beach. He ordered troops from the captured redoubts to seize the cliff above V Beach, but the Ottoman defenders quickly halted this advance, and the British troops were forced to dig in, marking the end of efforts to relieve V Beach.

On the northern flank, Hill 114 was secured, but further advances towards the second objective from W Beach did not materialize. Despite a numerical superiority of 6:1 over the Ottoman forces, the British awaited new orders, which were not issued due to the loss of the landing force commander and communication difficulties with the headquarters staff still at sea. The plan for a coordinated advance collapsed in the absence of leadership on the ground, leaving the twelve battalions between Hill 114 and Hill 138 in a stalemate against a modest Ottoman defense.

S Beach was located within the Straits, nestled in a small break in the cliffs at the northern end of Morto Bay, about two miles from V Beach. Above the cliffs lay de Tott's Battery, an abandoned fortification. This area was relatively undefended, with only one Ottoman platoon stationed on the beach and another positioned half a mile inland. The landing operation involved four trawlers, each towing six lifeboats, navigating against the currents of the Dardanelles and avoiding mines. Although Ottoman artillery on the Asiatic shore was active, it targeted other areas, allowing the trawlers to approach the shore without being attacked.

As the trawlers reached shallow waters, the lifeboats were released. The landing party, consisting of three companies from the 2nd Battalion of the South Wales Borderers and supported by the battleship Cornwallis, made their landing under fire from the Ottoman platoon positioned in a trench halfway up the cliff. Two companies landed directly on the beach, while another scaled the cliffs at Eski Hissarlik Point to seize de Tott's Battery.

In an unsanctioned move, Captain Davidson of the Cornwallis landed with a group of sailors and marines to reinforce the landing party, resulting in a total of 63 casualties across the Borderers, sailors, and marines. Upon capturing de Tott's Battery, the British forces overlooked the Ottoman platoon, taking fifteen prisoners. By 8:00 a.m., the landing was complete. From their vantage point on the cliffs, the British could observe the unfolding disaster at V Beach, but their orders were to wait for an advance from the south.

Following claims from a prisoner about the presence of an additional 2,000 Ottoman troops nearby, the British commander at S Beach decided to focus on consolidating their position rather than attacking the Ottoman rear at Sedd el Bahr. It was later discovered that the only nearby Ottoman forces consisted of a company, minus the platoon already engaged, and another company that had been redirected from Krithia to Sedd el Bahr before the landing.

The impromptu landing by Captain Davidson and his group caused a delay in the Cornwallis reaching V Beach, where it was scheduled to oversee and regulate the landing operations. This decision inadvertently impacted the timing and coordination of the broader landing efforts in the area.

X Beach, a 200-yard stretch of coastline under a low, eroding cliff on the Aegean shore, was situated roughly a mile above Tekke Burnu and around the corner from W Beach. Remarkably, the Ottomans had not established any substantial defenses at this location, and only a small contingent of twelve soldiers was present to guard the beach. This minimal defense was quickly overwhelmed by the bombardment from HMS Implacable, which commenced once the troops headed for W Beach had disembarked. The landing party at X Beach, sailing parallel to the battleship until about 500 yards from the shore, managed to reach the beach and climb atop the cliff without incurring any casualties by 6:30 a.m. By 7:30 a.m., the rest of the battalion and their equipment had arrived.

As the British forces advanced inland from X Beach, they neared a location where two Ottoman reserve companies were encamped. One of these companies, already dispatched towards W Beach, encountered the advancing British troops. Lieutenant-Colonel H. E. B. Newenham, the British commander at X Beach, organized a three-pronged attack: one group was to form a defensive flank to the northeast, two platoons were to advance directly and establish a position 500 yards from the beach, and the remaining forces were tasked with capturing Hill 114 to the right, aiming to connect with the troops at W Beach.

The northeastern attack commenced around 8:00 a.m. but was halted after 800 yards by Ottoman small-arms fire. However, the right flank successfully reached the top of Hill 114 by 11:00 a.m., to the applause of sailors aboard the Implacable. The British line along the beach was lengthy and punctuated with gaps, particularly on the left flank, where they engaged Ottoman defenders.

The lack of reconnaissance prior to landing and reliance on a single inaccurate map meant the strategic importance of the cliffs above X Beach wasn't fully recognized beforehand. The slopes of hills 138 and 141, clearly visible from X Beach, were within striking distance and could have potentially isolated the Ottoman forces defending W Beach. Additionally, S Beach in Morto Bay, located 2 miles away, was visible from X Beach. However, the forces at X Beach focused primarily on their immediate landing operation. Communication between the officers at X Beach and those at S Beach was limited, with little to no information exchanged between these groups throughout the day.

The main force began its landing at X Beach around 9:00 a.m., encountering minimal resistance from the Ottoman forces, aside from distant gunfire on the left flank. Two battalions from the main force had been redirected to reinforce the landings at Y and S Beaches, leaving the 1st Border and 1st Inniskilling battalions as the divisional reserve, to be deployed in emergencies. Initially, the landing party at X Beach was not under the command of Brigadier-General W. R. Marshall, and the main force lacked clear directives for advancing to their second-phase objective, a line stretching from Y Beach to Sedd el Bahr. With no updates from the other landing sites, the relatively unchallenged landing at X Beach led Marshall to anticipate a swift link-up with the forces from W and V Beaches.

Upon ascending the cliff, Marshall, while briefing his officers, received a request for assistance from the left flank and promptly dispatched the reserve company. He then ordered the Borderers to the cliff top and sent another company to aid the troops on Hill 114. Shortly afterward, British forces were seen retreating on the left, chased by Ottoman infantry. Marshall was preparing a counter-charge when he was wounded, and Major C. D. Vaughan was killed.

The Ottoman infantry, advancing to within a few hundred yards of the shore, were driven back by a bayonet charge from the British. Rather than pursuing the retreating Ottomans, the British focused on reestablishing their position. By 1:00 p.m., some information had trickled in, but there was still no word from W Beach or divisional headquarters. Observations revealed that the troops on W and V Beaches were delayed, as Ottoman forces still occupied hills 141 and 138, though their exact strength was unknown. Despite the uncertainty, Marshall was resolute about his orders concerning the reserve battalions and instructed them to establish a defensive perimeter of 600–800 yards.

The outnumbered Ottoman forces managed to stifle the momentum of the invading British, buying time to organize their defenses and gather reinforcements. At 6:00 p.m., Marshall reached out to Hunter-Weston, proposing an advance to Y Beach, but was instructed to hold position until morning and complete the original plan. Subsequently, an order from W Beach, issued by Colonel Wolley-Dod, instructed an advance of the right flank towards X Beach to establish contact. However, this maneuver became unfeasible as the Ottomans launched a counter-attack on Y Beach, further complicating the situation for the British forces.

Y Beach, significantly northward along the Aegean coast near Krithia, was positioned behind the main Ottoman defenses at Cape Helles. The deep coastal waters allowed boats to approach within mere yards of the steep, 150-foot high cliffs, which had two gullies offering easy access to the top. Remarkably, the area was undefended, with the nearest Ottoman troops comprising two platoons a mile south near Gully Ravine, a platoon of the 2nd Battalion, 26th Regiment at Sari Tepe, and the 25th Regiment stationed 5 miles away at Serafim Farm. The 1st Battalion, 26th Regiment, positioned between Semerly Tepe and Sari Tepe, was held in reserve for two days in anticipation of another landing.

The landing operation at Y Beach involved the cruisers HMS Amethyst and HMS Sapphire, the transport N2, eight trawlers, and was supported by the battleship HMS Goliath and the cruiser HMS Dublin. Around 2:30 a.m., troops transferred to trawlers, which, escorted by Goliath and the cruisers, moved towards the shore. At 4:15 a.m., the trawlers reached shallow waters, and the troops disembarked in boats under the cover of a bombardment targeting Cape Helles.

The Plymouth Battalion of the Royal Naval Division (RND), led by Lieutenant-Colonel Godfrey Matthews, the 1st Battalion of the King's Own Scottish Borderers under Lieutenant-Colonel Archibald Koe, and a company of the 2nd Battalion, South Wales Borderers, landed at Y Beach between 5:15 and 5:45 a.m. Initial scouting efforts led to an encounter with four Ottoman soldiers, resulting in two being killed and two captured. Two companies advanced towards Gully Ravine, and marines moved southeast across the ravine to search for a suspected Ottoman artillery position.

By mid-afternoon, the landing force at Y Beach awaited the anticipated advance from Cape Helles in surprisingly calm conditions. A marine search party ventured southeast but found no Ottoman artillery and retreated unchallenged by 11:00 a.m. Despite attempts to communicate with X Beach, no updates were received, and distant gunfire from X Beach offered the only indication of ongoing combat.

With no instructions from the 29th Division Headquarters, Matthews ordered his forces to fortify their position. By 3:00 p.m., still without signs of an advance from Cape Helles, the troops withdrew from the ravine to establish a new defensive perimeter along the cliff top. The challenging terrain and lack of proper digging tools meant the new trenches were shallow, offering limited protection. From the ships, this repositioning was not visible, and the efforts to establish an effective defensive line were hampered by the terrain and equipment limitations.

At Serafim Farm, Sami Bey, the commander of the Ottoman 9th Division, was promptly informed of the Allied landing at Y Beach. In response, by 1:00 p.m., he dispatched an infantry battalion, an artillery battery, and a machine-gun section to the landing site. Around 4:00 p.m., Ottoman artillery began shelling the area, intensifying their assault with infantry around 5:40 p.m. The initial Ottoman infantry attack, conducted by a company, was disrupted by naval gunfire from the Allied ships. However, as night fell and the naval bombardment ceased, the Ottoman forces launched a more determined attack.

By 11:00 p.m., Ottoman reinforcements had bolstered their numbers to one and a half battalions. Facing increasing casualties, the British commander, Matthews, signaled for reinforcements but received no response. The dawn of April 26 saw the Ottoman forces withdraw after suffering about 50% casualties, having inflicted significant losses of 697 men on the British, including the mortal wounding of Lieutenant-Colonel Koe and the death of his adjutant. The situation was further complicated by ammunition shortages, exacerbated by the need to supply different types of rifle ammunition.

Throughout the night, morale among the British troops waned, particularly after a misdirected salvo from a ship landed among the beachhead. At 6:30 a.m., the ships received a distress call from an isolated party onshore that had run out of ammunition. This was the first indication to the naval forces that the situation on land was deteriorating. As boats arrived to evacuate this group and its wounded, other troops on the beach mistakenly believed a general withdrawal was underway, leading some to board the boats.

Unbeknownst to Matthews and those still repelling Ottoman attacks on the heights, the evacuation had already commenced. Shortly thereafter, Matthews requested naval fire support for an impending Ottoman attack, which breached the British lines at 7:00 a.m. With no reserves, the British troops rallied and managed to repel the attackers with a bayonet charge, securing the beachhead once again.

After the attack, Matthews discovered that the right flank positions were abandoned. Realizing that troops closer to the beach were already re-embarking, he decided to continue the evacuation, focusing on protecting the gully until the wounded were removed. By 11:00 a.m., all troops had left the beach, and the rearguard quickly followed, encountering no Ottoman gunfire during their departure. That afternoon, a naval officer led a search for survivors on the beach, finding no opposition from Ottoman forces, indicating a temporary lull in the conflict at Y Beach.

Before dawn, a fleet consisting of eleven troopships, along with HMS Canopus, HMS Dartmouth, HMS Doris, two destroyers, and several trawlers, gathered off Bulair. The warships commenced a day-long bombardment just after first light, with a destroyer making a close pass near the shore. Later, the troopships deployed their boats, and lines of eight cutters towed by trawlers simulated a landing. In the late afternoon, troops began boarding the boats, which moved towards the shore just before dusk and returned after nightfall. During the night, Lieutenant-Commander B. C. Freyberg undertook a daring solo mission, swimming ashore to light flares on the beach and scout inland. He discovered that the Ottoman defenses were merely decoys and returned safely to his ship. Following this reconnaissance, the decoy force sailed south to join the main landings.

At 5:15 a.m., the French battleships Jauréguiberry and Henri IV, accompanied by the cruisers Jeanne d'Arc and Latouche-Tréville, and supported by the British battleship HMS Prince George and the Russian cruiser Askold, began bombarding Kumkale. This was in preparation for the landing of the 6th Régiment mixte Coloniale near the fort on a small, undefended beach. However, the strong current from the Dardanelles delayed the landing force, which only managed to reach the beach by 10:00 a.m. Despite the lack of surprise, the prolonged bombardment had severely rattled the Ottoman defenders, who had mostly retreated across the river by the time of the landing. The fort and village of Kum Kale were quickly captured with minimal casualties.

The remainder of the disembarkation also faced delays due to the strong current, but by 5:30 p.m., the French forces began advancing towards Yeni Shehr and the Orkanie Mound. However, this advance was halted by determined Ottoman defenders. Reconnaissance aircraft reported incoming Ottoman reinforcements, leading to the abandonment of the attempt. Throughout the night, the French used searchlights to illuminate the area and Jauréguiberry continued with a slow bombardment. At 8:30 p.m., Ottoman counter-attacks commenced and lasted until dawn, but these efforts resulted in heavy losses and were ultimately unsuccessful.

On April 26th, a complex and confusing encounter unfolded near the Kum Kale cemetery. Ottoman troops initially captured the cemetery, and shortly afterward, a group of 50-60 Ottoman soldiers approached the French lines carrying white flags and seemingly surrendering by dropping their weapons. As French and Ottoman troops intermingled and officers began negotiations, a sudden turn of events occurred when Capitaine Roeckel was abducted by the Ottoman troops. This abrupt action reignited hostilities. The situation became chaotic as the two sides were still entangled; some Ottoman soldiers managed to slip through, seizing control of several houses and capturing two French machine guns. Although the French recaptured the houses, their attempt to retrieve the machine guns led to significant losses. The French suspected that the initial surrender had been a genuine act, but it was subsequently exploited by other Ottoman troops as a ruse. In retaliation, the French executed nine Ottoman prisoners.

Throughout the day, the Ottoman commander called for reinforcements. By the end of this diversionary action, the French had suffered 778 casualties, while the Ottoman defenders incurred 1,730 casualties, including 500 reported as missing. By April 27th, the French forces had successfully landed on the right flank of the British forces at Helles. The Ottoman commander, General Weber Pasha, faced criticism for his lack of preparedness, poor tactics, communication failures, and inadequate leadership. However, the flat terrain in this area had facilitated more accurate bombardment from the offshore Allied forces.

During the departure of Allied forces, an Ottoman artillery battery at Tepe inflicted severe casualties. In response, the French ship Savoie moved closer to shore to bombard the Ottoman positions.

In a separate operation on the night of April 25-26, six French troop transports, accompanied by two destroyers and a torpedo boat, appeared off Besika Bay (now Beşik Bay). The warships started a bombardment, and boats were lowered from the transports to simulate a landing. The cruiser Jeanne d'Arc joined the bombardment at 8:30 a.m. before the force withdrew to Tenedos at 10:00 a.m. This demonstration kept the Ottoman garrison occupied in the area until April 27th. The Turkish Official Account later noted that the landings at Kum Kale and the feint at Besika Bay were recognized as diversions. The transfer of Ottoman troops from the Asiatic shore to the Helles front was delayed not by concerns about Allied landings on the Asiatic side but due to a shortage of boats and the threat of Allied submarines. It was only by April 29th that troops from this area started to appear on the Helles front.

Landing at Anzac Cove

In the dramatic shadows of World War I, the Ottoman Turkish Empire aligned with the Central Powers on October 31, 1914, setting the stage for a pivotal conflict. The Western Front had become a grueling deadlock, compelling the British Imperial War Cabinet to seek victory by opening a new front against Turkey. This strategic shift led to naval operations in February 1915 aimed at breaching the Dardanelles. However, the challenges of the sea campaign soon made it clear that a land offensive was essential. Thus, the Mediterranean Expeditionary Force was born, commanded by General Ian Hamilton, with a bold plan to seize the Gallipoli Peninsula through a series of daring amphibious landings. The goal was ambitious: to capture Constantinople, the Turkish capital, hoping to pressure Turkey into seeking an armistice.

Lieutenant-General William Birdwood spearheaded this mission with the ANZAC, an inexperienced yet determined corps made up of Australian and New Zealand soldiers. Despite lacking their mounted brigades and failing to secure a brigade of Gurkhas, the ANZACs, numbering over 30,000, were a formidable force. Their target was a strategic beachhead between Gaba Tepe and Fisherman's Hut. The plan was intricate: land at dawn under the cover of naval bombardment, swiftly secure key hills, and disrupt Turkish reinforcements, synchronizing with the British 29th Division's separate assault.

Birdwood's strategy involved a stealthy approach to the peninsula, rejecting a more conspicuous landing method in favor of smaller, nimbler vessels. The Australian Division, led by Major-General William Bridges, was to lead the charge, with the goal of seizing strategic ridges and hills. Following them, the New Zealand and Australian Division, under Major-General Alexander Godley, would continue the push. The planners, perhaps overconfident, underestimated Turkish defenses, setting the stage for a fierce and historic battle.

The Ottoman Turkish Army, inspired by the German Imperial Army's structure, relied heavily on conscription. Infantrymen served for two years and artillerymen for three, followed by a lengthy twenty-three-year reserve duty. The pre-war force boasted 208,000 soldiers across thirty-six divisions, organized into corps and field armies. Each division, comprising three infantry and one artillery regiment, numbered around ten thousand men— about half the size of their British counterparts. This army was no novice force; from the highest commanders to company leaders, these soldiers were seasoned by their experiences in the Italo-Turkish and Balkan Wars, presenting a stark contrast to the less experienced ANZACs.

The British were unable to keep their preparations for an impending assault a secret. By March 1915, the Turks had intelligence of a sizable force amassing at Lemnos, comprising fifty thousand British and thirty thousand French troops. They predicted only a handful of likely landing sites: Cape Helles, Gaba Tepe, Bulair, or the Dardanelles' eastern Asiatic coast.

In anticipation, the Turks formed the formidable Fifth Army on March 24. Commanded by German General Otto Liman von Sanders, this force, exceeding 100,000 men, was structured into two corps with six divisions and a cavalry brigade. The Fifth Army's deployment strategy was strategic: the III Corps stationed at Gallipoli, the XV Corps on the Asiatic coast, and additional divisions positioned for rapid support. The 9th, 19th, and 7th Divisions were allocated critical defensive roles along the coast, from Cape Helles to Bulair, with the 19th Division held in reserve at Maidos. Crucially, the ANZAC landing zone at Gaba Tepe was under the watchful guard of the 2nd battalion of the 27th Infantry Regiment, setting the stage for a significant military confrontation.

The ANZACs, braced for a crucial operation, ceased their training on April 19th. The preparation for the planned landing on April 23rd involved stocking ships and boats with coal and supplies. However, due to unfavorable weather, their departure from Lemnos was postponed until the dawn of April 24th. Leading this maritime procession were the Royal Navy battleships Queen, Triumph, Prince of Wales, London, and Majestic, accompanied by the cruiser Bacchante, seven destroyers, and four transport ships, all carrying the 3rd Brigade. This formidable fleet was followed by the remainder of the force, each embarked on their designated transport ships.

In the early hours of April 25th, at 01:00, the British flotilla halted at sea. Thirty-six rowboats, each towed by steamers, embarked the first wave of troops from the 9th, 10th, and 11th Battalions. By 02:00, a Turkish sentry spotted these movements, and by 02:30, the sighting was reported to the 9th Division's headquarters. At 02:53, the fleet advanced toward the peninsula, halting at 03:30 as they neared their destination. The final approach, a mere 50 yards from shore, was completed silently with oars.

Around 04:30, Turkish sentries opened fire, but by then the first ANZAC troops had already landed at Beach Z, known as Ari Burnu at the time and later renamed Anzac Cove in 1985. The landing spot, one mile north of their intended target, presented unexpected challenges: instead of an open beach, the ANZACs faced steep cliffs and ridges rising up to 300 feet. Ironically, this navigational error proved advantageous, as the intended landing site at Gaba Tepe to the south housed a formidable Turkish strong-point with artillery batteries and infantry ready for a counter-attack. The unique topography of Anzac Cove offered some protection from direct Turkish artillery fire. Within fifteen minutes of landing, the Royal Navy commenced bombardment of Turkish positions in the hills, marking the beginning of a fierce battle.

As the ANZACs approached the Gallipoli shores in rowing boats, chaos ensued. The 11th Battalion landed north of Ari Burnu point, while the 9th and most of the 10th Battalion reached the point or slightly south. Their mission to swiftly assault the first ridge line was immediately complicated by an unexpected hill descending nearly to the water's edge. Amidst small arms fire from the Turkish 8th Company, 2nd Battalion, 27th Infantry Regiment, the officers scrambled to orient themselves. The Turkish troops, with a presence at Anzac Cove and around Fisherman's Hut, were also guarding the Gaba Tepe strong-point with outdated Nordenfelt machine-guns and other minor positions to the south.

Despite the disarray, men from the 9th and 10th Battalions began ascending the slope of Ari Burnu, using gorse branches and bayonets for leverage. Upon reaching the peak, they found an abandoned Turkish trench. The Australians quickly advanced to Plugge's Plateau, encountering a defended trench, but the Turks had already retreated to a higher summit, firing upon the Australians as they emerged onto the plateau. Major Edmund Brockman of the 11th Battalion swiftly organized the troops, positioning the 9th Battalion on the right flank, the 11th on the left, and keeping the 10th in the center.

Meanwhile, the second wave of six companies landed in the darkness, under hostile fire. The 12th Battalion extended the beachhead to the north of Ari Burnu and southwards. Some troops were killed during the landing, but those who reached the shore pressed inland. In the south, the 9th and 12th Battalions approached 400 Plateau, while in the north, the 11th and 12th Battalions faced fire as they ascended Walker's Ridge. Turkish artillery bombarded the beachhead, damaging several boats. The Australians managed to advance to Russell's Top and The Nek, a strategically important high ground, but could only progress about a thousand yards inland before coming under fire again.

This initial push and subsequent hesitation to advance played into the

Turkish defensive strategy, which aimed to buy time for their reserves to organize a counter-attack. Colonel Ewen Sinclair-Maclagan, leading the 3rd Brigade, altered the corps plan amidst concerns of a southern counter-attack, deciding to hold the Second Ridge instead of advancing to the Third or Gun Ridge.

At the break of dawn, 05:45, a crucial moment unfolded as Lieutenant-Colonel Mehmet Sefik of the Turkish 27th Infantry Regiment received orders to dispatch his 1st and 3rd Battalions westward, bolstering the 2nd Battalion near Gaba Tepe. These battalions, already alert and gathered in Eceabat from a night of military exercises, faced a delay as Ari Burnu wasn't marked on their maps. Concurrently, Colonel Halil Sami, in charge of the 9th Division, commanded the division's machine-gun company and an artillery battery to reinforce the 27th Infantry Regiment. This move was quickly followed by the addition of a 77 mm artillery battery.

In a decisive move at 08:00, Lieutenant-Colonel Mustafa Kemal, leading the 19th Division, received orders to dispatch a battalion for support. However, Kemal took the initiative to personally lead the 57th Infantry Regiment and an artillery battery towards Chunuk Bair, recognizing its strategic importance — control of these heights meant domination over the battlefield. Fortuitously, the 57th Infantry, scheduled for an exercise near Hill 971, had been ready since 05:30, awaiting commands.

By 09:00, Sefik and his battalions neared Kavak Tepe, making contact with his 2nd Battalion which had been tactically retreating. An hour and a half later, the regiment was strategically deployed to halt further ANZAC advancement. Around 10:00, Kemal reached Scrubby Knoll, where he rallied retreating troops, reorganizing them into a defensive formation. As the 57th Infantry Regiment received their counter-attack orders, Scrubby Knoll, referred to by the Turks as Kemalyeri (Kemal's Place), was established as the Turkish headquarters for the remainder of the campaign.

Baby 700, a notable hill in the Sari Bair range adjacent to Battleship Hill or Big 700, was misnamed for its presumed elevation above sea level; in reality, it stands at a height of only 590 feet.

In a strategic move, Maclagen dispatched the 11th Battalion, Captain Joseph Lalor's company from the 12th Battalion, and Major James Robertson's company from the 9th Battalion towards Baby 700. Brockman, leading his own company, split his forces, sending half up each fork of Rest Gully, while he and a reserve platoon ascended Monash Valley. However, their progress was hindered as Turkish artillery targeted them with air-burst shrapnel shells, scattering the companies. Additionally, redirection of troops by senior officers to different areas diluted the forces heading to Baby 700, resulting in only fragments of the units reaching their destination.

Upon reaching Baby 700, Captain Eric Tulloch of the 11th Battalion, with just sixty men remaining, decided to advance towards Battleship Hill, leaving Lalor's company to fortify The Nek. Tulloch's group skirted to the right before heading for the summit. They crossed the first rise without opposition but encountered Turkish fire at the second rise from about four hundred yards away. After a brief exchange of fire and a pause in Turkish aggression, the remaining Australians pushed forward, reaching the abandoned Turkish position. Advancing under continuous fire, they were eventually forced to retreat due to increasing casualties and Turkish fire intensity. No other ANZAC unit would reach as far inland that day.

At 08:30, Robertson and Lalor led their companies up Baby 700, choosing a direct ascent over Tulloch's right-flanking route. They crossed the summit, advancing onto the northern slope and taking cover. A nearby spur leading to Suvla Bay was fortified with Turkish trenches. Around 09:15, Turkish forces began descending from Battleship Hill, engaging in an hour-long firefight with the Australians. A group from the 9th, 11th, and 12th Battalions attempted to charge a Turkish trench, but were repelled by machine-gun fire and forced into a general retreat. The Turks, having secured Battleship

Hill, now began pushing the Australians off Baby 700. From his vantage point in Monash Valley, Maclagen observed the Turkish assault and began directing all available forces towards Baby 700 in a desperate attempt to hold the position.

The 2nd Brigade's arrival at Gallipoli, between 05:30 and 07:00, followed by the 1st Brigade between 09:00 and 12:00, marked a deviation from the original timetable.

Initially destined for Baby 700 on the left, the 2nd Brigade was redirected to the right to counter an escalating Turkish assault. By 07:20, Bridges and his staff, lacking a briefing from any senior officers on the beach, ventured to find the 3rd Brigade headquarters.

The 1st Brigade, positioned on the opposite flank from the 3rd Brigade and already engaged in combat, received a call for reinforcements from Colonel Maclagen. Responding, Colonel Percy Owen of the 1st Brigade dispatched two companies from the 3rd Battalion and one from the 1st Battalion to aid the 3rd Brigade.

Meanwhile, Lalor's company was pushed back to The Nek, and the Turks threatened to retake Russell's Top. At 10:15, Maclagen expressed to Bridges his concerns about their ability to maintain their position. In response, Bridges sent two companies from the 2nd Battalion as reinforcements.

By 11:00, Swannell's company reached Baby 700, joining the seventy remaining men from Robertson's and Lalor's companies. They launched an immediate counter-charge, pushing the Turks back over Baby 700's summit and then digging in for defense. The two companies from the 2nd Battalion arrived to support, but all units suffered casualties, including the deaths of Swannell and Robertson.

At this stage, the 3rd Brigade was severely depleted, with most men either killed or wounded. The defense line was now held by five weakened companies from the 1st Brigade. On the left flank, Gordon's company from the 2nd Battalion, along with survivors from the 11th and 12th Battalions, made five attempts to capture Baby 700's summit but were repelled by Turkish counterattacks, resulting in Gordon's injury. Facing this dire situation, Maclagen again requested reinforcements for Baby 700. Bridges' remaining reserves consisted of two companies from the 2nd Battalion and the 4th Battalion. With the 1st New Zealand Brigade beginning to disembark at 10:45, it was decided that they would be deployed to reinforce the position at Baby 700.

The commander of the New Zealand Brigade fell ill, prompting Birdwood to appoint Brigadier-General Harold Walker, a staff officer already onshore, as the acting commander. By noon, the Auckland Battalion had landed and was directed north along the beach towards Walker's Ridge, en route to Russell's Top. Confronted with the challenge of navigating the ridge in single file along a narrow goat track, Walker instructed them to take a route over Plugge's Plateau. Subsequently, as each New Zealand unit disembarked, they were similarly directed towards Baby 700. However, the threat of Turkish fire led to their dispersal in Monash Valley and Rest Gully. It wasn't until after midday that two Auckland companies reached Baby 700.

By 12:30, two Canterbury Battalion companies had landed and were dispatched to support the Aucklanders, who had been reassigned to Plugge's Plateau, positioning themselves to the left of the 3rd Brigade. The Canterbury companies awaited the arrival of the rest of their brigade, forming a line on the Aucklanders' left. However, from 12:30 to 16:00, no further infantry or artillery landed. The ships carrying the New Zealanders remained in the bay, as the available steamers and rowboats were occupied transporting the wounded to the hospital ship. The 4th Australian Brigade, still at sea, was not scheduled to land until the evening.

The landing operations resumed around 16:30 with the arrival of the

Wellington Battalion, followed by the Otago Battalion around 17:00, who joined the Aucklanders in the line. The remaining Canterbury companies landed next, extending the corps' left flank at Walker's Ridge. The unfolding situation ashore necessitated changes in the disembarkation schedule, leading to a 17:50 order for the 4th Australian Brigade to begin landing to reinforce the defense. However, it would take until the next day for the entire brigade to come ashore. Turkish artillery fire had forced the transports carrying the divisions' artillery batteries further out to sea, delaying their landing.

MacLaurin's Hill, a 1,000-yard-long section of the Second Ridge connecting Baby 700 to 400 Plateau, presented a steep slope down to Monash Valley on the ANZAC side. In the coming days, Quinn's, Steel's, and Courtney's Posts would be established here. The first ANZAC troops to reach the hill, from the 11th Battalion, discovered the Turkish defenders had already retreated. As the Australians crested the hill, they faced fire from Baby 700, but the terrain ahead sloped gently into Mule Valley. Upon arrival, Major James Denton's company from the 11th Battalion began fortifying their position, receiving orders from Maclagen to hold the hill at all costs. By 10:00, Turkish forces advancing from Scrubby Knoll engaged the Australians on the hill from about 300 yards away. The 11th Battalion, spread between Courtney's Post, Steele's Post, and Wire Gully, soon received reinforcement from the 3rd Battalion.

The 400 Plateau, named for its elevation, was a large, flat area on the second ridge line, roughly 550 by 550 meters in size, and about 910 meters from Gun Ridge. The northern part of the plateau was known as Johnston's Jolly, and the southern part as Lone Pine, with Owen's Gully separating them.

Under the original landing plan, the 11th Battalion was to cross this plateau heading north. The 10th Battalion, positioned south of the plateau, aimed to seize a Turkish trench and artillery battery behind Gun Ridge. The 9th Battalion, located even further south, was tasked with targeting the artillery battery at Gaba Tepe. The 12th Battalion was in reserve, and the 26th Jacob's Mountain Battery was to set up their guns on the plateau. Unbeknownst to the ANZACs, the Turks had positioned an artillery battery on 400 Plateau.

After landing, members of the 9th and 10th Battalions made their way to 400 Plateau. Lieutenant Noel Loutit's platoon from the 10th Battalion, along with Brigade-Major Charles Brand, was the first to arrive. They encountered a Turkish battery in the Lone Pine sector preparing to move. As the Australians fired, the battery retreated down Owen's Gully. Brand stayed on the plateau, instructing Loutit to pursue the Turkish battery. However, the guns were hidden at the head of the gully, and Loutit's platoon passed them. Around the same time, Lieutenant Eric Smith with 10th Battalion scouts and Lieutenant G. Thomas with a platoon from the 9th Battalion arrived, searching for the guns. They came under Turkish machine-gun fire from the Lone Pine area. Thomas's section located the battery in the gully, charged the gun crews, and captured the guns. Although the Turks removed the breech blocks, rendering the guns inoperable, the Australians further damaged them to ensure they couldn't be used.

By this time, most of the 9th and 10th Battalions, along with brigade commander Maclagen, had reached the plateau. Maclagen ordered them to dig in on the plateau, instead of advancing to Gun Ridge. Unfortunately, some units had already moved past that area, following orders to keep advancing at all costs.

Lieutenant Loutit, Lieutenant J. Haig of the 10th, and thirty-two men from the 9th, 10th, and 11th Battalions crossed Legge Valley and ascended a spur of Gun Ridge, just south of Scrubby Knoll. Reaching the top, they found Gun Ridge, around 370 meters inland, heavily defended by Turkish troops. After a reconnaissance of Scrubby Knoll, where one man was wounded, they returned to their group, which was under Turkish fire. By 08:00, Loutit requested reinforcements, and Captain J. Ryder of the 9th Battalion, with half a company, advanced to form a line on Loutit's right. Soon, they faced fire from Scrubby Knoll and risked being encircled. Ryder requested more reinforcements, and Captain John Peck of the 11th Battalion led a group to their aid. By 09:30, the men on the spur, outflanked by the Turks, began retreating. At 10:00, the Turks set up a machine-gun on the spur, firing at the retreating Australians. Only eleven survivors, including Loutit and Haig, managed to reach Johnston's Jolly for cover. Further back, two companies from the 9th and 10th Battalions began digging a trench line.

The 2nd Brigade began their landing at 05:30. Their original orders were for the 5th, 6th, and 8th Battalions to move across 400 Plateau towards Hill 971, while the 7th Battalion was to ascend Plugge's Plateau before heading to the same destination. Tragically, one company of the 7th Battalion, led by Jackson, suffered heavy losses near Fisherman's Hut, with only forty men surviving.

At 06:00, Major Ivie Blezard's company from the 7th Battalion, reinforced by parts of another company, was deployed onto 400 Plateau on orders from Maclagen to bolster the defense. The situation was chaotic, and when Lieutenant-Colonel Harold Elliott, commander of the 7th Battalion, landed, he quickly realized the plan was unraveling. He rushed to the 3rd Brigade headquarters for clarity. Maclagen redirected him to regroup his battalion at the southern end of the beachhead, effectively shifting the 2nd Brigade to form the division's right flank instead of the left.

Colonel James McCay, the 2nd Brigade commander, upon arriving, was persuaded by Maclagen to reposition his brigade to the south, swapping roles with the 3rd Brigade. McCay established his headquarters on the seaward slope of 400 Plateau, now dubbed McCay's Hill. Recognizing the strategic importance of Bolton's Ridge to their right, McCay instructed Brigade-Major Walter Cass to secure it. Cass directed the 8th Battalion, under Colonel William Bolton, to take position on Bolton's Ridge, making them the only ANZAC battalion that stayed intact throughout the day.

By 07:00, the rest of the brigade had arrived, with companies and battalions being hurriedly sent to the front line without specific orders beyond supporting the 3rd Brigade. At 10:30, the 26th Jacobs Mountain Battery positioned their guns on either side of White's Valley and commenced firing on Turkish positions on Gun Ridge by noon.

Within two hours, half of the Australian Division was engaged in the battle for 400 Plateau. Many officers misunderstood their orders, believing they were to take Gun Ridge rather than hold their current positions. They attempted to advance, causing a gap in the defensive line between the 9th and 10th Battalions, which the 7th Battalion was sent to fill. As the 2nd Brigade advanced, it prompted the 3rd Brigade to move towards Gun Ridge, unaware that Turkish forces had already prepared for a counter-attack around Scrubby Knoll since 08:00.

When the Australians reached the Lone Pine area of the plateau, they were met with devastating fire from Turkish machine guns and rifles. Troops advancing beyond Johnston's Jolly and Owen's Gully encountered similar resistance, followed by Turkish artillery. A Turkish counter-attack from Gun Ridge ensued, forcing the ANZACs into a dire situation. By 15:30, realizing the futility of advancing to Gun Ridge, McCay ordered his brigade to fortify their positions, extending from Owen's Gully to Bolton's Ridge.

Pine Ridge, a segment of the 400 Plateau, extends towards the sea in a curved fashion for about one mile. The terrain of Pine Ridge and the surrounding areas, including Legge Valley and Gun Ridge, was densely covered in thick gorse scrub, interspersed with stunted pine trees about eleven feet tall.

Several ANZAC units made their way to Pine Ridge. Lieutenant Eric Plant's platoon from the 9th Battalion was among the first to arrive. Captain John Whitham's company from the 12th Battalion advanced from Bolton's Ridge, inspired by the 6th Battalion's movement behind them. As the 6th Battalion reached the ridge and proceeded towards Gun Ridge, Lieutenant-Colonel

Walter McNicoll established their headquarters below Bolton's Ridge. The advancing 6th Battalion faced intense Turkish fire, suffering significant casualties.

At 10:00, a request for reinforcements from the 6th Battalion led to McCay dispatching half of the 5th Battalion for support. Meanwhile, the 8th Battalion was entrenched on Bolton's Ridge, except for two companies that advanced to engage a Turkish group approaching from the south. By noon, the 8th Battalion had secured its position on the ridge, with scattered elements of the 5th, 6th, 7th, and 9th Battalions in the vicinity, mostly concealed in the dense scrub. McCay, upon learning that the 6th Battalion needed more support to hold its position, sent his last reserves from the 1st Battalion and instructed the 8th Battalion to leave a company on the ridge and advance to support the 6th Battalion on the right. These dispersed units managed to maintain their positions through the afternoon until they observed a large force of Turkish troops moving over the southern section of Gun Ridge at 17:00.

Around 10:00, Kemal arrived with the 1st Battalion of the 57th Infantry Regiment between Scrubby Knoll and Chunuk Bair. From his vantage point, Kemal oversaw the landings. He directed an artillery battery to set up on the knoll and ordered the 1st Battalion to attack Baby 700 and Mortar Ridge from the northeast, while the 2nd Battalion encircled to attack Baby 700 from the west. The 3rd Battalion was initially held in reserve. At 10:30, Kemal informed II Corps of his attack plans.

By 11:30, Sefik reported to Kemal that the ANZACs had established a beachhead of approximately 2,200 yards, and planned an attack towards Ari Burnu in coordination with the 19th Division. Midday reports indicated that the 9th Division was fully engaged with British landings at Cape Helles and couldn't support Kemal's attack. Consequently, at 12:30, Kemal ordered two battalions of the 77th Infantry Regiment to advance between the 57th and 27th Infantry Regiments, and directed the reserve 72nd Infantry Regiment to move westward. Within thirty minutes, the 27th and 57th Infantry Regiments launched a counter-attack, backed by three artillery batteries. At 13:00, Kemal met with his corps commander Esat Pasha, persuading him of the need for a robust response to the ANZAC landings. Esat agreed, releasing the 72nd and 27th Infantry Regiments to Kemal's command. Kemal strategically positioned his regiments from north to south as the 72nd, 57th, 27th, and 77th. The Turkish forces opposing the landing numbered between ten thousand and twelve thousand troops.

At 15:15, Captain Joseph Lalor left the defense of The Nek to a newly arrived reinforcement platoon and moved his company to Baby 700, joining forces with a group from the 2nd Battalion led by Lieutenant Leslie Morshead. Tragically, Lalor was soon killed in action. The left flank of Baby 700, held by about sixty men from various units under the command of a corporal, had withstood five Turkish charges from 07:30 to 15:00. After their last stand, these Australians were instructed to retreat through The Nek. There, they encountered a company from the Canterbury Battalion, led by Lieutenant-Colonel Douglas Stewart. By 16:00, the New Zealand companies had established a defensive line on Russell's Top. The positions on Baby 700 included Morsehead's and Lalor's men on the left, survivors of the 2nd Battalion and some from the 3rd Brigade at Malone's Gulley, and a mixed group from the Auckland companies and various battalions on the right. Once Stewart's men were in place, he directed Morsehead to withdraw. During a Turkish artillery bombardment of The Nek, Stewart was killed, marking the onset of a Turkish counter-attack from Battleship Hill and the flanks.

At 16:30, the 72nd Infantry Regiment's three battalions arrived, attacking from the north. Concurrently, the Australian and New Zealand forces holding Baby 700 broke ranks, retreating to an improvised line stretching from Walker's Ridge in the north to Pope's Hill in the south. The defense at The Nek was then held by only nine New Zealanders, led by a sergeant, with three machine guns but no crew due to casualties. As more survivors from Baby

700 arrived, their numbers increased to around sixty.

Divisional headquarters, led by Bridges, began receiving distressing messages from the front lines. At just after 17:00, Lieutenant-Colonel George Braund on Walker's Ridge reported holding his position with potential for advancement if reinforced. At 17:37, Maclagen signaled a heavy attack, followed by a message at 18:15 from the 3rd Battalion indicating the 3rd Brigade was being pushed back. At 19:15, Maclagen urgently requested support from the 4th Brigade. Bridges responded by sending two hundred mixed-stragglers to reinforce Braund and promised additional battalions from the newly arriving New Zealand and Australian Division.

As dusk fell around 19:00, the Turkish assault reached Malone's Gulley and The Nek. The outnumbered New Zealanders held their fire until the Turks were close, then engaged in the dark, halting the advance. Despite their request for reinforcements, the supporting troops behind them were withdrawn, allowing the Turks to outflank them. Consequently, they retreated from Russell's Top into Rest Gully, taking their machine guns. This maneuver left the defenders on Walker's Ridge isolated from the rest of the ANZAC forces.

The Australians stationed on 400 Plateau had been enduring sniper and artillery fire, and witnessed Turkish forces fortifying positions on Gun Ridge. Around 13:00, a substantial force from the Turkish 27th Infantry Regiment was spotted advancing along the ridge-line from the south. They then veered towards 400 Plateau, moving in an extended formation. This counter-attack by the Turks compelled the forward Australian troops to retreat, suffering significant casualties from machine-gun fire. The Turkish assault effectively drove a divide between the Australian forces on Baby 700 and those on 400 Plateau, with those at Lone Pine retreating to the western slope of 400 Plateau under intense Turkish fire. By 14:25, the bombardment had become so intense that Indian artillerymen were forced to manually retreat their guns off the plateau to regroup on the beach.

Australian troops were variously positioned, with the 8th Battalion still centered around Bolton's Ridge in the south. Northward, the 6th and 7th Battalions, now both under the command of Colonel Walter McNicoll of the 6th, were intermingled on the southern sector of 400 Plateau. The 5th Battalion was further north, and the 10th Battalion covered the northern sector at Johnston's Jolly. All these battalions had suffered heavy losses and there was limited clarity on the exact locations of their troops.

At 15:30, the Turkish 77th Infantry Regiment, alongside the 27th Infantry, launched another counter-attack. Colonel James McCay, facing intense pressure, twice requested reinforcements at 15:30 and 16:45. Initially informed that only one battalion, the 4th, was available and being held in reserve, McCay communicated directly with Bridges, stressing the dire need for reinforcements. By 17:00, Bridges released the 4th Battalion, which McCay deployed to bolster the southern line along Bolton's Ridge, just in time to resist probing attacks from the 27th Infantry Regiment.

At 17:20, McCay reported to Bridges that many unwounded soldiers were retreating to the beaches. This was followed by an urgent request from Maclagen for artillery support on Gun Ridge due to a heavy attack on his left flank. Owen, at 18:16, reported a rapid retreat on the left flank. As dusk fell, Maclagen visited Bridges' headquarters, expressing his concern that a massed Turkish attack could be unstoppable. The arrival of nightfall saw a cessation of Turkish artillery, although sporadic small arms fire continued. The darkness provided a chance for the ANZACs to dig more substantial trenches and resupply with water and ammunition.

The day's last significant engagement occurred at 22:00, south of Lone Pine. A Turkish charge towards Bolton's Ridge met with heavy machine-gun fire from the 8th Battalion and engagement from the 4th Battalion. When the Turks closed in to about fifty yards, the 8th Battalion launched a bayonet counter-attack, causing the Turks to retreat. The ANZAC defense was bolstered by Royal Navy searchlights. Both sides, exhausted and heavily diminished, braced for further attacks, but their capacity for offensive operations had been severely weakened by the day's fierce battles.

By nightfall, approximately sixteen thousand men had landed, establishing an ANZAC beachhead. This beachhead stretched from Bolton's Ridge in the south, across 400 Plateau, to Monash Valley, with a break before resuming at Pope's Hill and then at the top of Walker's Ridge. Its length was under two miles, and its depth about 790 yards, with some areas so narrow that only a few yards separated the opposing forces.

That evening, General Birdwood visited the shore to assess the situation and was satisfied with the progress. Later, around 21:15, he returned to the beachhead following a request from his senior officers, who suggested considering an evacuation.

General Sir Ian Hamilton, upon consulting with naval commanders, concluded that evacuation was nearly impossible. He advised Birdwood to "dig in and stick it out." The exhausted and isolated survivors continued their struggle until April 28, when four battalions of the Royal Naval Division joined the corps.

On the Turkish side, by nightfall, the 2nd Battalion of the 57th Infantry was positioned on Baby 700, the 3rd Battalion, reduced to ninety men, held The Nek, and the 1st Battalion was on Mortar Ridge. South of these positions, the 77th Infantry was stationed, followed by the 27th Infantry opposite 400 Plateau, and the 72nd Infantry on Battleship Hill. The Turkish forces, similar to the ANZACs, faced their own challenges. The 57th Infantry was decimated, the 27th exhausted with high casualties, and the 77th had suffered desertions and was unfit for combat. The 72nd Infantry, mostly Arab conscripts, were poorly trained. The III Corps, engaged with both landings, had no reserves to offer. It wasn't until April 27 that the 33rd and 64th Infantry Regiments reinforced the Turkish forces. The ANZACs, unable to achieve their objectives, dug in, leading to a war of attrition reminiscent of the Western Front.

German commander Liman von Sanders credited the survival of the Turkish situation to the prompt and independent action of the 19th Division, led by Kemal, who emerged as a highly capable and imaginative officer. Kemal's leadership was exemplified by his order to the 57th Infantry Regiment, highlighting the sacrificial nature of their mission.

In the days that followed, both sides engaged in several unsuccessful attacks and counter-attacks. The Turks initiated the Second attack on Anzac Cove on April 27, followed by ANZAC attempts to advance on May 1/2. The Turkish Third attack on Anzac Cove on May 19 resulted in approximately ten thousand casualties, including around three thousand fatalities. Subsequent months saw only localized or diversionary attacks until the August 6 offensive in conjunction with the Landing at Suvla Bay, which achieved limited success. The Turks were unable to drive the Australians and New Zealanders back into the sea, and the ANZACs never broke out of their beachhead. Eventually, in December 1915, after eight months of grueling combat, the ANZAC forces evacuated the peninsula.

Third Attack on Anzac Cove

On April 25th, during the dawn of the Gallipoli Campaign, a pivotal moment in history unfolded. The Australian and New Zealand Army Corps (ANZAC), under the leadership of Lieutenant-General William Birdwood, made their historic landing at what would soon be known as Anzac Cove. The stakes were high, and the beachhead they secured was modest yet strategically crucial. It extended a mere 2 miles south to Chatham's Post, its depth never exceeding 750 yards. Amidst this narrow stretch, key positions like Quinn's and Courtnay's Posts stood, backed by steep cliffs and dangerously close to Turkish trenches.

The ANZAC's tenacity was soon tested. In April, a fierce Turkish counter-attack, led by the formidable Colonel Mustafa Kemal and his 19th Infantry Division, momentarily breached the ANZAC lines. This attack was a testament to the determination of both sides, with the Turks under the strategic guidance of the German officer Otto Liman von Sanders, transitioning to a defensive stance but still viewing the ANZAC beachhead as vulnerable enough to potentially drive the Allies back into the sea.

The Ottoman Turkish Army, often underestimated, proved to be a formidable adversary. By the time of the landings, they had strategically positioned artillery and were led by experienced commanders, veterans of the Balkan Wars. However, they faced challenges in their command structure, particularly at the NCO level.

In a bold move, Major-General Essad Pasha orchestrated an assault without preceding artillery bombardment to maintain the element of surprise. This attack, planned for May 19th, aimed to push the ANZAC defenders back into the sea. The signal for this massive offensive, involving around 42,000 men, was to be the detonation of a mine at Quinn's Post. However, fate had other plans, as the tunnel for the mine remained incomplete on the day of the attack.

The ANZAC Corps, now a formidable force of approximately 17,300 men and 43 artillery pieces, was strategically divided. The New Zealand and Australian Division held the northern half of the beachhead, while the 1st Australian Division guarded the south. The defensive perimeter was meticulously segmented into four sections. In the north, No.4 Section, was the domain of the New Zealand Mounted Rifles Brigade. Moving southward, No.3 Section was jointly defended by the 1st Light Horse Brigade and the 4th Australian Brigade. The 1st Australian Brigade took charge of No.2 Section, and the 3rd Australian Brigade anchored the defense in No.1 Section. Meanwhile, the 2nd Australian Brigade, slightly undermanned, stood ready in reserve at the junction of Shrapnel and Monash Valleys, poised to form a secondary defense line if needed. Adding to their strength, the New Zealand Infantry Brigade was dispatched to Cape Helles to bolster the British forces.

Unbeknownst to the ANZAC command, a significant Turkish offensive was brewing. Until May 16th, ANZAC intelligence underestimated the opposing forces, believing they faced only 15,000 to 20,000 troops. However, a revelation was about to unfold. On May 18th, a Royal Naval Air Service aircraft, initially tasked with directing naval gunfire, made a startling observation while flying back across the peninsula: Turkish troops densely packed the valleys opposite the ANZAC position. A second reconnaissance mission confirmed the gathering storm – a large influx of troops and equipment landing at Eceabat, alarmingly close to the ANZAC beachhead.

By late afternoon, the ANZAC divisions were alerted to the possibility of an imminent attack. The British battleship HMS Triumph, observing from offshore, reported significant Turkish troop and artillery movements.

As the night of May 18th deepened, a harbinger of the impending conflict echoed across the battlefield: a Turkish bomb exploded at Quinn's Post. This was followed by a brief but intense barrage of small arms fire. With all signs pointing to a massive Turkish assault, the ANZAC troops braced themselves. At 03:00, a half-hour earlier than usual, they stood to arms, hastily fortifying their positions with barbed wire and preparing for the battle that loomed just over the horizon.

The fierce battle began with an eerie quiet at No.2 Section, quickly shattered by the Australian 4th Battalion's observation of enemy movement and the glint of bayonets in the dark. The Turkish 5th Division, breaking with their usual battle tactics of bugle calls and war cries, advanced stealthily but was a mere 200 yards away from the Australian trenches. The Australians, particularly the 1st and 4th Battalions, responded swiftly, opening a lethal hail of gunfire on the encroaching Turks.

The Turkish 2nd and 16th Divisions, attempting to reinforce their compatriots, found themselves caught in a deadly crossfire. The 2nd Division, advancing from Johnson's Jolly, was particularly vulnerable as they moved diagonally across the 4th Battalion's front, facing intense rifle and machine-gun fire. The survivors either retreated or sought cover in Wire Gully, but the relentless waves of Turkish reinforcements met the same grim fate under the unyielding Australian barrage.

Meanwhile, near Lone Pine, Australian 2nd and 3rd Battalions had been strategically extending their trenches into no man's land. Their intention was to create a more advantageous firing position. However, at the time of the attack, a significant gap remained between the two extensions. It was through this gap that the Turkish 16th Division launched their assault. Initially protected by a gully from Australian fire, the 48th Infantry Regiment bravely advanced, but even their courage couldn't withstand the Australian firepower. Despite a jammed machine-gun, the Australians repelled wave after wave of Turkish attackers. Some Turks managed to reach the Australian trenches, but their success was short-lived. Australian artillerymen, faced with the proximity of the enemy, disabled their guns to prevent capture and joined the infantry in repelling the attackers.

The 16th Division's repeated assaults proved futile against the steadfast Australian defense. At Wire Gully, the Turks came close enough to destroy an Australian machine-gun with a grenade, momentarily advancing. However, this success was momentary as the Australian fire ultimately forced a Turkish retreat around 05:00, marking the end of a brutal and intense phase of the battle.

The intensity of battle escalated as the Turkish 16th Division launched a bold assault on the ANZAC 3rd Brigade in No.1 Section, stretching from Lone Pine southwards. Their approach, cutting through a wheat field in two distinct waves, was met with lethal precision by the Australian 10th Battalion. Only three Turkish soldiers managed to reach the trench, where they were quickly eliminated. As daylight broke, the retreating Turkish wounded and survivors were mercilessly targeted by the 11th Battalion's machine-gun, resulting in heavy casualties.

Further south, the independent 77th Infantry Regiment charged the 9th Battalion's trench. Here, too, the advancing Turks were systematically cut down by Australian fire, many falling just before the protective barbed wire of the trenches.

In No.3 Section, a different scenario unfolded. Unnoticed, a part of the Turkish 5th Division assembled below Courtnay's Post, defended by the 14th Battalion. At 04:00, they surged forward, launching grenades. The Australians, outnumbered, were forced to retreat as the Turks seized a portion of the post, gaining a vantage point to fire upon Monash Valley. It was here that Private Albert Jacka heroically led a counter-attack, eliminating several Turks and reclaiming the post, an act of bravery that earned him the Victoria Cross.

Near Quinn's Post, defended by the 15th Battalion and the 2nd Light Horse Regiment, the Turks initially focused on grenade attacks. However, around 03:30, they escalated to machine-gun and rifle fire. Despite their efforts, including a direct assault on the post, the Turkish attacks were repelled by the concentrated Australian fire, supported by neighboring positions and artillery.

On the opposite side of Monash Valley, the Turkish 5th and 19th Divisions targeted Pope's. The 1st Light Horse Regiment sentries initially engaged several hundred Turks moving down the valley. The ensuing attack on Pope's was met with a fierce response from the 1st and 3rd Light Horse Regiments, halting the Turkish advance with only three soldiers reaching the Australian lines before being neutralized.

In No.4 Section at Russell's Top, the Auckland Mounted Rifles faced a precarious situation, with incomplete trenches and unconnected saps heading towards The Nek. The attacking 19th Division Turks, employing hand grenades, faced the combined defense of the Auckland and Wellington Mounted Rifles. The Wellington's machine-guns provided devastating flanking fire, while the Aucklanders charged in a counter-attack, forcing the Turkish survivors to retreat.

Across the entire ANZAC defensive line, Turkish forces persisted in their attempts to advance, employing tactics of fire and maneuver. However, as the morning wore on, their momentum waned, and they shifted their focus to retreating to their own lines. During this period, the ANZAC troops, comprising both Australians and New Zealanders, maintained heavy fire on the withdrawing Turks, occasionally exposing themselves above the trenches. This return to the open led to the majority of ANZAC casualties as the Turks fired back.

It became evident to the ANZAC forces that the Turkish offensive had failed. However, a miscommunication at Turkish headquarters led to a belief that they had achieved some objectives. Consequently, at 05:00, Turkish commanders ordered a second wave of assaults, now reinforced with artillery support. The 2nd and 5th Turkish Divisions launched renewed attacks, but their altered approach, advancing at an angle, did little to improve their fate as they were once again decimated by ANZAC fire.

At No.1 Post in No.4 Section, the Canterbury Mounted Rifles spotted the Turks regrouping in Malone's Gully for another push against Russell's Top. The strategic position of the post enabled the Canterbury Mounted Rifles to use their machine-gun to strike the Turks from behind, effectively disrupting the assault. The Turks also launched multiple attacks on Quinn's Post, with one instance seeing a group of about thirty soldiers reaching the junction of Courtney's and Quinn's before being eliminated. This pattern of attack continued until around 10:00, when Allied observers noted a growing hesitancy among Turkish troops to leave their trenches.

Realizing the scale of the Turkish defeat, ANZAC commanders began considering their options. At 05:25, Lieutenant-General Birdwood, weighing the possibility of a counter-attack, advised against any move into Turkish artillery range. However, at 15:35, British General Headquarters instructed him to capitalize on the situation. Birdwood maintained that only a full-scale assault would be effective, deeming smaller operations futile.

In the northern sector, Major-General Alexander Godley of the New Zealand and Australian Division contemplated an attack. The Wellington Mounted Rifles were ordered to assault the Turkish trenches at The Nek, a daunting task given the exposed, coverless terrain across no man's land. Preparing for the assault, Captain William Hardham VC was appointed to lead a carefully selected mixed group from all three squadrons, to prevent the annihilation of any single squadron. However, upon consultation with Brigadier-General Andrew Russell, who highlighted the risks, the attack was prudently called off.

The remainder of the day saw continued Turkish artillery bombardment on the ANZAC positions. Information from a captured prisoner about an impending attack, coupled with the sustained bombardment, prompted the General Headquarters to order the recall of the New Zealand Infantry Brigade from Cape Helles back to Anzac Cove that night.

As the tumultuous day drew to a close at Gallipoli, the scale of the conflict became evident through the staggering amount of munitions used. The ANZAC forces had fired a total of 1,361 18-pounder rounds, 143 howitzer rounds, 1,410 smaller mountain artillery rounds, and an overwhelming 948,000 rounds from rifles and machine guns. The Turkish forces, while their exact figures remain unknown, suffered approximately 10,000 casualties, including 3,000 fatalities. The 5th Division bore the brunt of these losses, with even the less active 19th Division incurring over a thousand casualties. The aftermath was described by a Turkish soldier as a field of "countless dead." In contrast, the ANZACs suffered significantly fewer casualties, with 160 killed and 468 wounded. Among the Australian fatalities was Private John Simpson Kirkpatrick, remembered in Australian lore as "the Man with the Donkey" for his heroic acts during the campaign.

The following day, May 20th, was marked by a poignant turn of events. The horrific smell of decomposing bodies and the sight of numerous wounded soldiers stranded in no man's land led the New Zealand and Australian Division staff to propose a truce. An informal ceasefire ensued under the Red Cross and Red Crescent flags, allowing Turkish stretcher-bearers to recover the dead and injured. However, a brief misunderstanding occurred just after 19:00 when the 9th Battalion, suspecting a Turkish attack under the guise of the truce, opened fire, prompting a Turkish artillery response.

Reinforcements had arrived at the beachhead during the day, including the New Zealand Infantry Brigade and the 2nd and 3rd Light Horse Brigades. This buildup of forces preceded a more formal truce on May 24th. From 07:30 until 16:30, a ceasefire allowed both sides to bury their dead in a rare moment of shared humanity amidst the chaos of war. Private Victor Laidlaw of the 2nd Australian Field Ambulance described the surreal quietness and poignant scenes during the armistice in his diary, highlighting the contrast between the usual violence and this brief period of peace.

After the truce, the Turkish commanders reassessed their strategy, realizing the enormity of the task to capture the beachhead. Opting not to launch another major offensive, they left their depleted 16th and 19th Divisions to hold the line, withdrawing their other forces. The independent 77th Infantry Regiment also remained, covering the south.

Ultimately, the Turks never succeeded in capturing the ANZAC beachhead. By the end of 1915, the ANZAC forces were evacuated to Egypt. The Gallipoli Campaign, lasting 260 days, exacted a heavy toll on the British Empire forces, with 213,980 casualties, including 35,000 from the Australian and New Zealand Army Corps. This figure included 8,709 Australian and 2,721 New Zealand soldiers who lost their lives. Turkish casualties were estimated to be around 250,000, with approximately 87,000 dead, underscoring the campaign's tragic and costly nature for all involved.

August Offensive

In the shadow of Kocaçimentepe's imposing ridge, known to the Turks as the "Great Grass Hill" and to the British as "Hill 971," a pivotal battle was brewing. This strategic peak, part of the Sarı Bayır range, which means "Yellow Slope" in Turkish, dominated the landscape, culminating in the striking bluff known as "The Sphinx" that loomed over Anzac Cove.

At the helm of the Mediterranean Expeditionary Force was General Sir Ian Hamilton, armed with three fresh British New Army divisions untested in the flames of battle. His forces were later bolstered by two Territorial Army divisions, the 53rd and the 54th, along with the 2nd Mounted Division, a brigade of dismounted yeomanry.

The Suvla Bay landing was entrusted to the British IX Corps, led by Lieutenant-General Sir Frederick Stopford. Despite his retirement in 1909 and lacking any real battle command experience, Stopford's appointment was solely based on his seniority. His hesitancy during the landing's preparations cast doubts on his suitability for such a critical command.

Meanwhile, the Ottomans, bracing for a renewed offensive, dismissed any notions of the British abandoning the campaign, especially after Winston Churchill's revealing speech in Dundee, which vowed continuation regardless of the cost. This prompted a major reorganisation and expansion of the Ottoman Fifth Army to 16 divisions, strategically positioned across the Dardanelles and the Gallipoli Peninsula.

While the Ottomans anticipated a breakout from Anzac, they were uncertain of its direction. A new British landing was expected, but Suvla Bay was not considered a probable target, leading to a minimal defense force of just four battalions. The rugged Sari Bair range was also underestimated as a potential assault point by all but one Ottoman commander - Mustafa Kemal of the 19th Division at Anzac. His foresight and persistent efforts to fortify the area, however, were largely ignored by his superiors, resulting in a minimal reinforcement of the northern sector near Anzac.

Battle of Lone Pine

The Gallipoli campaign's early stages saw intermittent clashes near Lone Pine, a significant site that became the focus of intense fighting. On the morning of April 25, 1915, at around 7:00 a.m., Australian forces, having landed at Anzac Cove, advanced towards Lone Pine to neutralize an Ottoman artillery position targeting the beach. However, the Ottomans had already retreated to a nearby ridge, subsequently known as "Third Ridge" or "Gun Ridge" by the Australians.

During their push inland, the 6th Battalion of the Australian forces attempted to seize this ridge, crossing the expansive "Legge Valley". Their advance was thwarted around 10:00 a.m. when the Ottoman 27th Regiment launched a counteroffensive, aiming to reclaim the strategic 400 Plateau near Lone Pine. The Ottomans' aggressive push forced the Australians back to Pine Ridge, leading to significant casualties and a tactical withdrawal to Lone Pine, where they established a defensive foothold. Later, reinforced by New Zealand units, the Australians faced intense combat against the newly arrived Ottoman 77th Regiment. This marked the beginning of a prolonged stalemate characterized by trench warfare, with neither side gaining significant ground.

In early July 1915, Lieutenant General William Birdwood, commander of the Australian and New Zealand Army Corps, strategized an offensive to break the deadlock on the Gallipoli Peninsula. He envisioned an attack at Lone Pine as a diversion, drawing Ottoman focus from the main offensive led by British, Indian, and New Zealand troops targeting Sari Bair, Chunuk Bair, and Hill 971. The Australian 1st Infantry Brigade, about 3,000 strong and led by Colonel Nevill Smyth, was tasked with the Lone Pine operation. Despite reservations from Brigadier General Harold Walker, the division's commander, the operation was greenlit by General Sir Ian Hamilton, leading to meticulous planning for the challenging assault.

Facing the Australians at Lone Pine were two battalions from the Ottoman 47th Regiment, commanded by Tevfik Bey. With approximately 1,000 soldiers, half were positioned in the front trenches, while the rest held back in depth. Additionally, the 57th Regiment's battalion was in divisional reserve on "Mortar Ridge", and other Ottoman regiments, including the Arab battalion of the 72nd Regiment, held positions around Lone Pine.

The battlefront spanned a modest 160 yards with the opposing trenches separated by a mere 60 to 100 yards. The Australians, keen on minimizing the exposed ground to be traversed, dug several tunnels from a position known as The Pimple, aiming directly towards the Ottoman trenches. One of these tunnels was particularly crucial, planned to be opened in its entirety during the attack to create a direct communication trench for swift reinforcement movement, avoiding the perilous open ground.

For those who had to advance over this exposed terrain, the Australians devised a strategy for protection. Engineers set three mines to create craters that could offer temporary shelter. The preliminary artillery bombardment, spread over three days, escalated from a limited initial firing to an intense final hour of shelling, effectively severing much of the barbed wire defenses of the Ottomans.

At 2:00 p.m. on August 6, the Australians triggered the three mines, carving out protective craters in front of the Ottoman lines. This was followed, two and a half hours later, by a fierce bombardment involving Australian, British, and New Zealand artillery, targeting the Ottoman trenches. The naval gunfire from the British cruiser HMS Bacchante played a critical role, countering Ottoman artillery along Third Ridge. Most of the forward-positioned Ottoman troops, anticipating the assault, had already retreated into protective tunnels.

As the artillery softened the battlefield, the Australian assault formations began their movement towards The Pimple. Colonel Smyth established his brigade headquarters at Brown's Dip, about 200 meters from the frontline. Given the narrow front, the initial assault was organized in three waves, led by the 2nd, 3rd, and 4th Battalions. The 1st Battalion was held in reserve at Brown's Dip, ready to consolidate gains or repel counterattacks.

As the assault neared, the battalions positioned themselves along the frontline at The Pimple. Half of the force was to advance through the pre-dug tunnels, while the other half prepared for the more conventional 'over the top' approach. By 5:00 p.m., all units were in place, and as the artillery barrage concluded, the tunnels were opened for the final phase of the assault.

The first two waves of soldiers were equipped with 200 rounds of ammunition each, daily rations, and essential gear including gas masks. The third wave carried the same ammunition load but also bore entrenching tools for immediate defensive construction against expected Ottoman counterattacks. Supporting these infantrymen were four Vickers medium machine-guns per battalion, each supplied with 3,500 rounds, and a platoon dedicated to deploying the 1,200 grenades allocated for the attack. A small team of engineers was also assigned to perform demolitions as needed.

At 5:30 p.m., the Australian 1st Infantry Brigade launched a bold assault with an initial wave of 1,800 men surging forward. Meanwhile, the 2nd

Infantry Brigade provided crucial suppressing fire against Ottoman forces at Johnston's Jolly to the north, and the 3rd Infantry and 2nd Light Horse Brigades held their positions opposite Sniper's Ridge. The attackers split their approach: half advanced through the pre-dug tunnels, while the other half braved the open, perilous 100-meter stretch known as the "Daisy Patch," exposed to relentless Ottoman artillery and small arms fire.

From his vantage point, Ottoman commander Esad Pasa coordinated a counterresponse, ordering reinforcements and directing artillery fire. Remarkably, the first wave of Australian attackers suffered relatively light casualties, as many Ottoman defenders were still reeling from the artillery bombardment and hadn't returned to their firing positions.

Upon reaching the Ottoman trenches, the Australians encountered an unexpected obstacle: the trenches were fortified with pine logs, leaving no straightforward entry point. This detail had been overlooked in aerial reconnaissance. As the Ottoman soldiers recovered, they fired through specially crafted holes in the logs at point-blank range. The Australians responded with gunfire, grenades, and bayonet charges, some managing to enter the trenches through gaps or by lifting the heavy logs. Others advanced to the rear trenches, capturing about 70 Ottoman soldiers attempting to flee.

Several Australians reached The Cup, a critical position, but faced a robust Ottoman defense. Most of these attackers were either killed or captured. Inside the Ottoman trenches, the darkness and confined space created chaos. Initially hesitant to fire their rifles for fear of hitting their comrades, the Australians engaged in brutal close-quarters combat with bayonets and grenades.

Despite the challenging conditions, the Australians gradually established control over the trench line. Within half an hour, they secured the main Ottoman position and set up several defensive posts along the line. These included communication trenches on the flanks and a series of isolated but connected posts in the center.

The attack was a tactical victory for the Australians, who now occupied the main Ottoman line. As they fortified their position with sandbag barriers, the 1st Battalion, held in reserve, was moved up to reinforce the gains. Due to congestion in the tunnels, these reinforcements had to advance across the open ground that was still under heavy Ottoman fire from flanking positions. Despite this, the 1st Battalion successfully joined the assault battalions, and engineers from the 2nd Field Company began extending the tunnels towards the new Australian line, consolidating their position in anticipation of Ottoman counterattacks.

As the sun dipped below the horizon, shrouding the battlefield in darkness, a pivotal moment unfolded around 7:00 p.m. The silence of the night was shattered by the thunderous roar of the first Ottoman counterattack, led by a group from the 1st Battalion, 57th Regiment, under the fearless Major Zeki Bey. These brave souls had come to reinforce their comrades in the 47th Battalion, and what followed was nothing short of a harrowing clash of warriors.

The battleground resembled a chaotic labyrinth of trenches left behind by the Ottoman forces. In this claustrophobic maze, combatants hurled hand grenades at each other, creating a deadly dance of explosives. Some of these deadly projectiles ricocheted back and forth, adding an extra layer of tension to the already perilous situation.

The Australian soldiers held onto the remnants of the old Ottoman fire trench and had managed to establish footholds deeper within the enemy's lines. Desperate to maintain their grip on the position, they blocked the Ottoman communications trenches, resorting to grim measures, such as using the bodies of their fallen comrades as makeshift barricades.

In the midst of this ferocious battle, some casualties could not be evacuated due to the intensity of the fighting, the cramped quarters, and the sheer exhaustion of the men. They lay wounded at the bottom of the trench, a testament to the brutal nature of war.

Throughout that fateful night of August 6th into the early hours of August 7th, the Ottomans rallied their forces, bringing reinforcements from the 5th Division's 13th Regiment, led by Ali Riza Bey. These fresh troops marched from Kojadere, southeast of the area known to the Australians as "Scrubby Knoll." Meanwhile, the 9th Division, under the command of German Colonel Hans Kannengiesser, began its journey towards Lone Pine from a position situated between Helles and Anzac at Esad Pasa.

As the clock ticked past 8:00 p.m., the 15th Regiment from the 5th Division, under the leadership of Ibrahim Sukru, was thrust into the relentless fray. They advanced southward from their position near the Kurt Dere, close to Chunuk Blair.

The relentless struggle continued over the next three days, with the Ottomans launching wave after wave of desperate counterattacks in a bid to reclaim their lost ground. In total, three regiments were dispatched into the maelstrom of battle. Not to be outdone, the Australians also summoned reinforcements, bringing in soldiers from the 2nd and 3rd Infantry Brigades—the valiant 7th and 12th Battalions—to fortify the gains of the 1st Brigade.

August 7th saw the conflict evolve into a relentless exchange of hand grenades, as soldiers on both sides fought fiercely for every inch of territory. To ensure a steady supply of these lethal weapons, around 50 Australian soldiers toiled tirelessly at Anzac Cove, crafting makeshift grenades out of empty jam tins. Over 1,000 of these improvised grenades were dispatched to the 1st Infantry Brigade late in the day.

As the night of August 7th bled into the early hours of August 8th, the 47th

Regiment launched a determined counterattack. Though they suffered heavy casualties, including their regimental commander, Tewfik Bey, the attack failed to recapture the main front-line trenches. However, it did succeed in wresting back some ground in the north while pushing the Australians back slightly from The Cup.

As Ali Riza Bey took command of the 13th Regiment, the relentless grenade exchanges continued, casting a shadow over Lone Pine. The Ottomans were gearing up for a massive counterattack that would define the coming day.

In the morning, the remaining Australian positions that overlooked The Cup were abandoned. A momentary ceasefire ensued as both sides tended to their wounded and removed the fallen from the front lines. The toll of the battle had taken its toll on the 1st and 2nd Battalions, who had valiantly defended the heavily assaulted southern flank. They had suffered such staggering casualties that they were ordered to withdraw from the front lines. In their stead, the 7th Battalion assumed their positions, a changing of the guard that occurred late in the afternoon. Meanwhile, the 3rd, 4th, and 12th Battalions stood firm, maintaining their grip on the northern and central sections of the Australian line.

After 3:00 p.m., the Ottomans launched further assaults along the entire Australian front. As night descended, their focus shifted to the southern positions held by the 7th Battalion. Under the cover of darkness, the Ottomans managed to seize a portion of the Australian line. A fierce and brutal bout of hand-to-hand combat raged on into the early hours of August 9th, culminating in the Australians retaking their lost ground.

The Ottomans continued to rain down grenade attacks, and as the Australian trenches found themselves under fire from the Ottoman positions around Johnston's Jolly, a pivotal attack was launched at the junctions between the Australian battalions. The heart-pounding moment came when they broke through the center and reached the headquarters of the 1st Infantry Brigade, which had advanced forward from Brown's Dip after the initial gains. Here, the brigade commander, Smyth, rallied the defense, eventually driving the Ottomans back.

Around midday, the Ottomans mounted yet another assault, but their determination was met with staunch resistance and repulsion by the Australians. The positions on the southern Australian flank continued to endure a barrage of grenades, prompting the deployment of the 5th Battalion to relieve the beleaguered 7th. The 2nd Battalion, having enjoyed a brief respite, also moved forward, taking the place of the 4th Battalion with the support of a dismounted squadron from the 7th Light Horse Regiment. The stage was set for renewed conflict along the line.

However, the expected attack failed to materialize, and finally, late in the afternoon of August 9th, the Ottoman commanders abandoned their efforts to dislodge the Australians. The following day saw a lull in the fighting as both Ottomans and Australians worked to consolidate their positions, marking a temporary ceasefire in the relentless struggle for Lone Pine.

Battle of the Nek

In the pre-dawn hours of August 7, a daring and meticulously planned assault was set to unfold. Naval forces, positioned with deadly precision, prepared to unleash a fierce bombardment, their guns echoing across the sea. On land, the valiant soldiers of the 8th and 10th Light Horse Regiments, resolute and determined, gathered in a narrow trench, mere meters from the enemy. Their mission was clear: capture the Ottoman trenches, signal their triumph with vibrant marker flags, and stand as a beacon of success. To distinguish themselves in the chaos of battle, they adorned their uniforms with stark white armbands and patches, a silent testament to their courage and unity.

As dawn broke on that fateful day, the situation rapidly shifted. The plan, a complex web of synchronized attacks, began to unravel. The New Zealand forces, tasked with a critical maneuver to encircle the enemy, found their advance stymied, failing to secure their objective. This setback transformed the intended pincer movement into a desperate solo charge by the troops at the Nek. Despite this, hope flickered as the New Zealanders seized part of Rhododendron Spur, igniting a glimmer of possibility for the capture of Chunuk Bair. The commanders, Birdwood and Skeen, faced a pivotal decision. They chose to proceed with the attack on the Nek, now a diversion to aid their allies, while other forces launched simultaneous assaults on neighboring objectives.

Amidst this strategic chess game, another critical move was planned: a tunnel-based attack by Lieutenant Colonel Gordon Bennett's 6th Battalion against a key Ottoman position. This assault was crucial to neutralize the deadly Ottoman machine guns that threatened the Nek. Despite meticulous planning, this initial strike faltered, leaving the enemy's guns ominously intact. Undeterred, Birdwood adapted the strategy, ordering the 3rd Light Horse Brigade to advance, now as the critical right flank in the renewed push towards Chunuk Bair, linking arms with the New Zealand Infantry on Rhododendron Spur. In the face of adversity, the light horsemen stood ready to etch their names into the annals of history.

As the clock struck 4:00 AM, a symphony of destruction began. Field artillery and howitzers, positioned along the Anzac Cove beachhead, roared to life, unleashing a barrage of shells onto the Ottoman trenches at the Nek. The cacophony of war intensified as several warships, including a formidable destroyer, joined the fray, their guns thundering against the Nek and surrounding areas of Baby 700. This relentless assault crescendoed until 4:27 AM, the shells mostly falling beyond the first line of Ottoman defenses due to the trenches' close proximity.

Historian Charles Bean depicted this onslaught as the most intense since May 2, highlighting the ferocity of the bombardment. In contrast, another historian, Nick Carlyon, painted a different picture, critiquing the shelling as haphazard and ineffective, a sentiment echoed by an officer from the 9th Light Horse Regiment, who labeled it 'desultory' and a 'joke'.

A critical misstep soon became evident: a lack of coordination in timing. The field artillery abruptly ceased firing at 4:23 AM, while the naval guns continued their distant targeting. This premature halt in artillery support, a deviation from the original plan, was not compensated for by the local commanders. The troops, poised for assault, were left in limbo, uncertain if the bombardment would resume. It was later discovered that a crucial synchronization of watches between the artillery and assault officers had been overlooked.

This delay proved costly. Instead of immediately capitalizing on the bombardment's end, the attack was postponed until the scheduled time of 4:30 AM. This gave the Ottoman defenders, whose trenches had largely withstood the artillery fire, precious time to regroup and prepare for the impending attack.

As the clock marked the appointed hour, the first wave of 150 brave men from the 8th Light Horse Regiment, led by Lieutenant Colonel Alexander Henry White, courageously surged over the top. Tragically, they were immediately met with a devastating storm of machine gun and rifle fire. Within a mere 30 seconds, White and his men were cut down. A few managed to reach the Ottoman trenches, hurling grenades and raising marker flags in a fleeting moment of defiance. However, they were quickly overwhelmed by the prepared and resolute Ottoman defenders, their valiant effort engulfed by the unforgiving tide of battle.

As the tragedy of the first wave unfolded, the soldiers awaiting their turn in the second wave were struck by the grim reality of their mission. Historian Nick Carlyon argued that at this juncture, the assault should have been halted. Yet, driven by duty and without question, another 150 men of the second wave charged forward two minutes later, only to be met with the same merciless barrage of rifle and machine gun fire. Their brave attempt ended in devastation, with nearly all falling before even reaching the halfway point to the Ottoman trench.

This harsh outcome starkly contrasted with the simultaneous, albeit brief, attack by the 2nd Light Horse Regiment at Quinn's Post against the Ottoman "Chessboard" trench system. The first wave of this attack was decimated, with 49 of the 50 men becoming casualties. In this instance, the regiment's commander, who hadn't joined the first wave, was present to make the crucial decision to abort further attacks.

As the 10th Light Horse Regiment prepared for the third wave, the battlefield's chaos escalated with two Ottoman field artillery pieces opening fire into no man's land. Lieutenant Colonel Noel Brazier, leading the 10th, desperately sought to cancel the third wave. His search for Hughes, who had relocated to an observation post, led him instead to Antill. Antill, a dominant figure within Hughes' command and not fond of Brazier, believed him to be insubordinate for questioning orders. Reports had reached Antill of marker flags being sighted, indicating some level of success. These reports were later confirmed by the commander of the Turkish 27th Regiment after the war, who acknowledged that a few Australian soldiers had indeed reached the Ottoman trench and raised their flag, but were quickly killed.

Antill, however, did not verify the situation at the front or the current status of the marker flags. After a heated exchange with Brazier, he ordered the third wave to proceed without consulting Hughes. Brazier, unable to reach Godley at his headquarters on the beach, returned to the Australian position at Russell's Top. With a heavy heart and a sense of duty, he relayed the order to the waiting men, lamenting, "Sorry, lads, but the order is to go." The third wave, thus, was set into motion, stepping into a maelstrom of gunfire and history.

The third wave of the assault, launched at 04:45, met a swift and brutal end, mirroring the fate of its predecessors. In the wake of this devastation, Lieutenant Colonel Noel Brazier, determined to halt the carnage, once again approached Antill, this time joined by Major Allan Love, the 10th Light Horse Regiment's second-in-command. Despite their urgent pleas, Antill remained resolute, insisting the men advance. Brazier, seeking a decisive intervention, conferred with several majors before urgently seeking out Hughes, who finally called off the attack.

Amidst the chaos, the fourth wave of troops had already positioned themselves on the fire-step of the forward trench. In a muddled scene, the right side of the line prematurely charged, spurred by the momentum of battle before Hughes' cancellation order could be conveyed. The troops on the left hesitantly followed, with many adopting a more cautious approach, staying low and moving slowly, as noted by historian Charles Bean.

For a fleeting moment, Hughes considered deploying a detachment through Monash Valley to support the British offensive towards the "Chessboard". However, this plan was soon discarded.

In the grim aftermath, the ridge between Russell's Top and the Turkish trenches lay strewn with Australian soldiers - the fallen and the wounded, many of whom would remain there for the remainder of the war. Daylight attempts to retrieve the wounded were largely futile, the relentless heat exacerbating their suffering. Only a few who had fallen in sheltered positions could be rescued during the day. The majority had to endure an agonizing wait until nightfall, when the cover of darkness allowed stretcher bearers to retrieve some, and others to crawl back to safety.

Ultimately, 138 wounded soldiers were rescued. Among them, one who had suffered an ankle wound remarkably returned to Australian lines two nights later, one of the mere three who had reached the Ottoman firing line on the right. On the left, another Australian, Lieutenant E.G. Wilson, met his end from an Ottoman grenade after reaching the enemy trench.

Battle of Chunuk Bair

In a bold strategic move at Anzac, Major-General Alexander Godley's New Zealand and Australian Division planned an offensive against the Sari Bair range. This formidable task involved navigating through the challenging and sparsely defended terrain north of the Anzac perimeter. Strengthening this division were significant reinforcements: most of the 13th (Western) Division under Lieutenant-General F. C. Shaw, the 29th Indian Infantry Brigade, and the Indian Mountain Artillery Brigade, bringing the frontline infantry count to around 20,000.

The offensive was meticulously planned with two main assault columns. The Right Assaulting Column was to advance up Rhododendron Spur towards Chunuk Bair, while the Left Assaulting Column would split at Aghyl Dere. Half of this force would move across Damakjelik Spur and Azma Dere towards Abdul Rahman Spur, aiming to seize Hill 971. The other half would ascend Damakjelik Spur towards Hill Q. To eliminate potential delays, a Right Covering Force was assigned to secure Destroyer Hill, Table Top, Old No 3 Post, and Bauchop's Hill. Simultaneously, the Left Covering Force was tasked with reaching Walden Point, crossing Aghyl Dere, and capturing Damakjelik Bair.

The plan dictated that once the covering forces secured their objectives by 10:30 p.m., the assaulting columns would commence their advance at the same time, aiming to reach the ridge an hour before dawn. Upon capturing Hill Q and Hill 971, the Left Assaulting Column would entrench themselves, while the Right Assaulting Column consolidated their hold on Chunuk Bair and attempted to capture Battleship Hill. This effort would be supported by dawn attacks on the Nek and Baby 700 from Russell's Top by the 3rd Light Horse Brigade's dismounted Australian light horse, in conjunction with an assault on Chunuk Bair's summit by the New Zealand Infantry Brigade (led by Colonel Francis Johnston), traversing Rhododendron Spur, the Apex, and the Farm. Hill 971 was designated to be attacked by Gurkhas of the 29th Indian Brigade and Australians of the 4th Infantry Brigade.

On the Ottoman side, senior commanders underestimated the likelihood of an attack at Chunuk Bair, considering the rugged terrain unsuitable for such an offensive. However, Mustafa Kemal, the commander of the Ottoman 19th Division, presciently anticipated an attack, particularly recognizing the vulnerability of Chunuk Bair's peak. Despite his foresight, he faced challenges in convincing his superiors to significantly bolster the defenses in the area.

The strategic assault on Chunuk Bair was a complex operation, involving a challenging approach up Rhododendron Spur, a ridge extending from the beach to Chunuk Bair's peak. The Ottomans had fortified several key outposts along this spur - at Table Top, Destroyer Hill, and Old No. 3 Outpost near the beach, as well as Bauchop's Hill to the north. The New Zealand Mounted Rifles Brigade, comprising four understrength regiments, was tasked with neutralizing these outposts to pave the way for the main assault force.

The Auckland Mounted Rifles successfully overran Old No. 3 Outpost, while the Wellington Mounted Rifles took control of Destroyer Hill and Table Top. The Otago and Canterbury Mounted Rifles captured Bauchop's Hill, named after Lieutenant Colonel Arthur Bauchop of the Otagos, who tragically fell during the attack. The battle was intense; the Ottomans were well-prepared with machine guns and fortified trenches. In the aftermath, Ottoman wounded and prisoners faced brutal bayonet attacks. This phase of the operation resulted in approximately 100 casualties among the New Zealanders.

Despite the success in capturing the outposts, the mission fell two hours behind schedule, jeopardizing the plan to reach the summit before dawn.

The New Zealanders' advance initially took them through the valleys or 'deres' flanking Rhododendron Spur. After passing Table Top, they ascended onto the ridge, leaving about 1,000 yards to the summit. By 4:30 am, just before dawn, three battalions positioned on the north side of the spur were ready, stationed at a location known as "The Apex," merely 500 yards from the summit, which was lightly defended by around 20 Ottoman infantry at the time. However, the Canterbury battalion on the south side got lost and was delayed. Faced with this setback, Colonel Johnston, the overall commander of the assault, made the critical decision to wait for the last battalion, contravening the original orders that stipulated no halts.

Meanwhile, this attack on Chunuk Bair was a key component of a broader offensive. Concurrently, at 4:30 am, a supporting assault was planned at the Nek against Baby 700, intended to synchronize with the New Zealanders' push from Chunuk Bair towards the rear of the Ottoman trenches on Battleship Hill. Despite the delay in the New Zealand attack, the Battle of the Nek proceeded as planned, resulting in a tragic and heavy loss of life.

The fleeting window for a swift triumph at Chunuk Bair had closed. Following the failed assault at the Nek and the realization that Chunuk Bair was at risk of being overwhelmed, the Ottomans rapidly bolstered their defenses on the peak. By 7:30 AM, the New Zealanders were a mere 500 yards from the summit, but they were suddenly confronted with a significant influx of Ottoman and German reinforcements. The Ottoman 9th Division's commander, German Lieutenant-Colonel Hans Kannengiesser, had already arrived at the summit, orchestrating its defense. Close on his heels was Colonel Mustafa Kemal, the prescient Ottoman officer. He directed several regiments to fortify the area. A drastic change from just hours earlier, the peak now hosted approximately 500 reinforcements, in stark contrast to the mere 20 soldiers previously stationed there.

These reinforcements, however, did not escape the notice of Australian artillery observers. They managed to hinder the movements of the Ottoman forces, causing some to retreat down the summit for better cover.

In the harsh light of day, the New Zealanders, weary from their ascent and facing increasingly fierce resistance, saw their chances of assaulting the peak diminish rapidly. Colonel Johnston, assessing the situation, suggested waiting until nightfall for a renewed attack. Despite this, General Godley ordered an immediate assault.

Positioned 200 yards from the New Zealanders at the Apex was another key location, "The Pinnacle," which led directly to the summit. Off to the north side of the spur lay a small, sheltered area known as The Farm.

Responding to the order, the Auckland battalion launched an attack at 11:00 AM. Approximately 100 soldiers reached the Pinnacle, attempting to establish a foothold, but the cost was high. Around 300 men fell between the Apex and the Pinnacle. When Johnston instructed the Wellington battalion to continue the attack, its commander, Lieutenant Colonel William Malone, firmly opposed, refusing to send his men on what he saw as a futile mission. He asserted that his battalion would attempt to take Chunuk Bair, but only under the cover of darkness.

In 2018, New Zealand military historian Ian McGibbon revisited this episode, challenging the long-held belief that Colonel Malone defied a direct order for a daylight attack. According to McGibbon, both Malone and Johnston were in agreement against Godley's directive for the Auckland Battalion to attack in broad daylight, a decision Johnston had accepted with reluctance. The sole assertion of Malone's outright refusal came from NCO Charlie Clark in 1981. Malone had, in fact, clashed with Major Arthur Temperley, a British officer and Johnston's brigade major, who was junior to Malone.

Two assaults were undertaken before Godley finally halted the daytime offensive. The tragic result was hundreds of Anzac soldiers lying dead or wounded before the peak of Chunuk Bair.

On August 7, General Godley dedicated his efforts to crafting a new strategy for another offensive. Reinforcements were summoned, including the British 13th (Western) Division and units such as the 7th Battalion of The Gloucestershire Regiment and the 8th Battalion's pioneers from the Welch Regiment, commanded by Lieutenant-Colonel Bald. The Auckland and Canterbury Infantry Battalions were withdrawn from the attack plan, replaced by the Otago and Wellington Infantry Battalions, now at the forefront of the new assault strategy. A naval bombardment, lasting 45 minutes, was scheduled for 3:30 the following morning, supported by twelve machine guns providing cover fire for the troops.

Following this intense naval bombardment and a subsequent delay, the Wellington and Gloucester battalions managed to reach Chunuk Bair with minimal opposition. The bombardment had effectively dispersed most of the Ottoman defenders, the rocky terrain having prevented the establishment of deep entrenchments.

Defending Chunuk Bair proved to be a formidable challenge. The rocky landscape allowed for only shallow trenches, leaving the peak vulnerable to fire from both the main Ottoman line on Battleship Hill to the south and Hill Q to the north. If the initial offensive plans had succeeded, Hill Q would have been under Allied control. A battalion of Gurkhas, led by Allanson, briefly reached Hill Q the next day but couldn't provide support to the troops on Chunuk Bair.

By 5:00 AM, the Ottoman forces launched a counter-attack against the Wellington troops. The steep incline of the hill enabled the Ottoman soldiers to approach within 22 yards of the trenches undetected. The New Zealanders, entrenched there, fiercely resisted, using both their rifles and those of their fallen comrades, fighting until the rifle stocks were too hot to handle. When the Ottomans reached the trenches, the battle escalated to close-quarters combat with bayonets. Part of the New Zealand trench line was overrun, resulting in some prisoners being taken. Daylight only brought a slow trickle of reinforcements to the summit.

The conflict continued relentlessly throughout the day, ending with the trenches filled with fallen New Zealanders. Tragically, around 5:00 PM, Malone was killed by a stray artillery shell, potentially fired by Anzac artillery or a British ship.

Eventually, the Ottomans regained control of the eastern side of Chunuk Bair's summit, bolstered by reinforcements from the 8th Division from Helles. Recognizing the scale of the Allied offensive, General Otto Liman von Sanders, commander of the Ottoman forces in the Dardanelles, appointed Colonel Mustafa Kemal to oversee the defense of Suvla and Sari Bair.

As the night of August 8 set in, the combat gradually subsided, and the exhausted Wellington Battalion was finally relieved. Out of the 760 soldiers who had reached the summit, a staggering 711 were casualties. Despite Malone's initial resistance to a doomed charge following the Auckland Battalion on August 7, the outcome a day later was devastatingly similar. The New Army battalions also suffered heavily, with 417 casualties among the Welch pioneers and 350 among the Gloucesters, including the loss of all their officers. For the wounded, their ordeal was far from over, with some taking three days to journey from the higher areas of Rhododendron Spur to the beach, a distance of just over a kilometer.

Remaining at his headquarters near the beach, Godley was largely disconnected from the direct developments on the frontlines. His strategy for August 9 centered on capturing Hill Q. The assault was to be led by Brigadier-General Anthony Baldwin, commander of the 38th Brigade of the 13th Division. However, due to the chaotic nature of the battlefield, the composition of Baldwin's force was unorthodox. It included only one of his usual battalions, the 6th East Lancashires, alongside the 9th Worcestershires and 9th Warwicks from the 39th Brigade, and the 5th Wiltshires from the 40th Brigade, who were later redirected to Chunuk Bair.

Additionally, Baldwin's command encompassed two battalions from the 10th (Irish) Division, the 10th Hampshires and 6th Royal Irish Rifles of the 29th Brigade, most of whom had landed at Suvla on August 7.

The plan involved this mixed force ascending to Hill Q from the area known as The Farm. Concurrently, the New Zealanders positioned at Chunuk Bair and elements of General Herbert Cox's Indian Brigade would launch an assault on the hill from the right and left flanks, respectively.

However, the operation faced immediate setbacks. Baldwin's battalions, navigating through the darkness, lost their way and failed to find The Farm until after dawn, around 6:00 AM. The only unit that managed to reach Hill Q was Allanson's battalion of Gurkhas. Tragically, they experienced a fate similar to that of Colonel Malone, coming under fire from their own artillery, which led to their brief tenure on the hill.

As the offensive ground to a halt once again, the New Zealand forces on Chunuk Bair continued to withstand relentless Ottoman attacks throughout the day. With nightfall, the remaining New Zealand troops withdrew to the position known as the Apex. They were relieved by two New Army battalions: the 6th Battalion of the South Lancashire Regiment and portions of the 5th Battalion of the Wiltshire Regiment from Baldwin's original force.

On the morning of August 10th, Mustafa Kemal, demonstrating decisive leadership, launched a formidable Ottoman counter-attack. The capture of Chunuk Bair, the sole significant Allied success in the August offensive, was pivotal—if retaken by the Ottomans, it would signal a decisive shift in the battle. Kemal's strategy, while lacking in finesse, was remarkably effective: overwhelm the defenders with overwhelming numbers. He had already halted the advance of the IX Corps at Suvla with a dawn counter-attack on August 9th and, after conducting a reconnaissance of Chunuk Bair later that day, orchestrated an assault involving six battalions.

Approximately 2,000 Allied defenders were positioned on or near the summit of Chunuk Bair. Additionally, Baldwin's brigade, located at the Farm, comprised about 3,000 soldiers. The Ottoman forces rapidly overran the summit, overwhelming the Lancashire battalion stationed there, with a distressing number of casualties reported (510 soldiers missing). The Wiltshires, unarmed and ill-equipped, were scattered and overwhelmed. On the right flank, the Ottomans seized the Pinnacle, forcefully pushing back the New Army troops.

In the midst of this chaos, New Zealand machine gunners stationed at the Apex engaged fiercely, targeting the advancing Ottomans. However, in the confusion of battle, they could not distinguish between friend and foe, resulting in casualties among the New Army troops mixed within the Ottoman ranks. Reinforcements arrived as the Leinsters hurried to the Apex.

On the northern side of Rhododendron Spur, the Ottomans descended from Chunuk Bair to the Farm's small plateau, where they overran Baldwin's brigade. The Warwickshire battalion faced near annihilation, the 6th Royal Irish Rifles lost half of its men, and Baldwin himself was killed. The surviving troops retreated to Cheshire Ridge. Despite their success, the Turkish infantry, drained by the intense combat, withdrew to the main ridge. Consequently, the area around the Farm plateau became a contested no man's land.

Landing at Sulva Bay

In the summer of 1915, amidst the turmoil of World War I, a critical decision was made by the Dardanelles Committee in London, steering the course of the Gallipoli Campaign. Under the leadership of the renowned Lord Kitchener, a strategic move was made on June 7 to bolster the Mediterranean Expeditionary Force led by General Sir Ian Hamilton. This pivotal meeting led to the reinforcement with three fresh divisions from the New Army and two more from the Territorial Army, marking a significant escalation in the campaign.

The plan was audacious: to expand the beleaguered Anzac bridgehead, an idea initially envisioned by Lieutenant-General William Birdwood, commander of the Australian and New Zealand Army Corps. Birdwood's plan, proposed since May 30, was finally set into motion.

Yet, the challenges were formidable. Much like the initial Helles landing in April, which was hampered by limited space, the congested Anzac perimeter in July posed a logistical nightmare. There simply wasn't enough room to accommodate the influx of troops or maneuver them effectively in battle. Thus, a bold new strategy was conceived – a fresh landing at Suvla Bay, designed to unite with the Anzac forces.

This crucial Suvla operation was entrusted to the newly formed British IX Corps, consisting of units from the 10th (Irish) Division and the entire 11th (Northern) Division. Leadership fell to Lieutenant-General Sir Frederick Stopford, a choice that was met with skepticism. British military historian J. F. C. Fuller would later critique Stopford's lack of combat experience and generalship, pointing out his advanced age and retirement since 1909. Hamilton's preferred candidates, Lieutenant-Generals Julian Byng and Henry Rawlinson, were overlooked due to seniority issues.

On the 6th of August 1915, a major offensive was set to unfold during the Gallipoli Campaign, involving coordinated attacks at Helles (the Battle of Krithia Vineyard) and Anzac (the Battle of Lone Pine). The highlight of this plan was the ambitious Suvla landing, scheduled for 10:00 pm, following a breakout from Anzac towards the Sari Bair heights.

Initially, the 11th Division was to land south of Nibrunesi Point, avoiding the uncharted shoals within Suvla Bay itself. This was deemed safer for a nighttime landing. The 30th and 31st Brigades of the 10th Division were to follow the next morning. The IX Corps, under Lieutenant-General Sir

Frederick Stopford, aimed to capture the surrounding hills of the Suvla plain, strategic points that included Kiretch Tepe, Tekke Tepe, and the Anafarta Spur.

Stopford, initially confident in the plan he saw on July 22, soon wavered under the influence of his chief-of-staff, Brigadier General Hamilton Reed. Reed, an artillery veteran and Victoria Cross recipient from the Boer War, insisted on the necessity of artillery support for such assaults. Despite reconnaissance indicating no significant fortifications at Suvla, Stopford restricted the landing's objectives, and General Sir Ian Hamilton failed to intervene effectively. The resulting orders were vague, merely suggesting the capture of high ground "if possible."

In a deviation from the initial plan, Stopford and Reed advocated for landing the 34th Brigade directly within Suvla Bay. This operation was supported by a fleet of specialized, armored, self-propelled landing craft, led by Commander Edward Unwin, who had previously commanded the SS River Clyde during the V Beach landing at Cape Helles in April.

Meanwhile, the Ottoman commander, General Otto Liman von Sanders, anticipated a new landing but was uncertain of its location. British deception suggested a possible landing on the Asian shore, leading to a spread-out Ottoman defense. Consequently, Suvla was lightly defended by the "Anafarta Detachment," under Major Wilhelm Willmer, a Bavarian cavalry officer with limited resources and no machine guns.

When the Lone Pine attack commenced, Willmer had to dispatch one battalion as reinforcements. As a result, when the British began their Suvla landing, they faced merely 1,500 Ottoman soldiers, significantly outnumbered by the 20,000 British troops. Despite these odds, the Ottoman defense, including strategically positioned strong points and pickets, presented a formidable challenge to the British forces.

On the night of the Gallipoli Campaign's Suvla landing, the 32nd and 33rd Brigades of the 11th Division embarked on a significant and challenging operation. As they began landing at "B Beach" south of Nibrunesi Point, just before 10 pm, the 6th Battalion of The Yorkshire Regiment faced their first combat as a New Army unit. Their task was to seize the strategically important Lala Baba hill. Despite their valor and determination, the Yorkshires suffered severe losses, with almost all their officers either killed or wounded, and a third of their other ranks also fell.

Meanwhile, the 34th Brigade faced a troubled landing at "A Beach" within Suvla Bay. Misjudgments led the destroyers carrying the brigade to anchor too far south, resulting in the troops having to wade ashore in treacherous conditions, deeply submerged and disoriented. The 9th Battalion Lancashire Fusiliers, landing in utter darkness, found themselves trapped and under heavy fire between the beach and the nearby salt lake. They endured significant losses, including their commanding officer. The 11th Battalion, The Manchester Regiment, however, managed a more effective landing, fighting their way along the Kiretch Tepe ridge but at the cost of 200 casualties.

The overall landing operation was marred by chaos and confusion, exacerbated by the pitch darkness. Soldiers became disoriented, units got mixed up, and objectives remained elusive. When the moon rose, the illuminated British troops became easy targets for Ottoman snipers. The confusion was so rampant that initial attempts to capture Hill 10 failed simply because its location was unknown to the field officers. It was only after dawn that Hill 10 was located and captured, as the Ottoman defenders had withdrawn overnight.

Lieutenant-General Sir Frederick Stopford, commanding the operation, opted to oversee the landing from the relative safety of HMS Jonquil. However, as the night's events unfolded, Stopford retired to sleep, missing critical developments. It was not until Commander Unwin boarded the ship at 4 am on August 7th that Stopford was dissuaded from planning further landings in the challenging environment of Suvla Bay.

The Suvla landing unfolded under the watchful eyes of British war correspondent Ellis Ashmead-Bartlett, who observed the scene from the transport ship Minneapolis just after dawn. He noted the stark contrast between the ongoing intense fighting at Anzac and the relative quiet at Suvla, remarking on the apparent lack of effective command over the troops who were "suddenly dumped on an unknown shore." This observation was echoed in the blunt assessment of the British official history by Captain Cecil Aspinall-Oglander, a member of General Hamilton's staff, who described the situation in Suvla Bay as verging on chaos in broad daylight.

Amidst this disarray, the Royal Australian Naval Bridging Train, consisting of 300 engineers and construction specialists and representing Australia's sole contribution at Suvla, found themselves idle without orders for most of their first day. Only later in the afternoon were they tasked with constructing piers for the subsequent stages of the landing.

The day of August 7th saw little advancement. The arrival of two brigades from the 10th Division only compounded the confusion. Soldiers, suffering in the intense heat, grew increasingly desperate for drinking water. By evening, only two hills east of the salt lake had been captured, marking the only significant territorial gain for the day. In these initial 24 hours, IX Corps sustained 1,700 casualties, outnumbering the entire Ottoman force under Major Willmer. Willmer reported to General Von Sanders at 7 pm, noting the lack of aggressive action from the British.

Reacting to the situation, Von Sanders directed two divisions from Bulair, the Ottoman 7th and 12th Divisions under Feizi Bey, to reinforce the Suvla area.

Throughout August 7th, Lieutenant-General Stopford remained aboard

HMS Jonquil, failing to disembark. By the end of the day, the British command structure had effectively collapsed, highlighting a critical failure in leadership and coordination during this pivotal moment of the campaign.

Lieutenant-General Sir Frederick Stopford, seemingly content with the initial outcomes of the Suvla landing, communicated his satisfaction to General Sir Ian Hamilton on the morning of August 8th. He praised Major-General Hammersley and his troops for their efforts against formidable opposition and challenging conditions, signaling his intent to consolidate the positions they had gained, with no apparent plans for further advancement.

This stance was at odds with the urgent need for progress, especially given the British staff's estimation that Ottoman reinforcements from Bulair would arrive at Suvla by the evening of August 8th. Hamilton, already concerned about the slow pace and lack of initiative from Stopford and his subordinates, sent Captain Aspinall and Lieutenant-Colonel Maurice Hankey to Suvla to assess the situation firsthand and report back to the British Cabinet.

Upon arrival, Aspinall and Hankey initially misinterpreted the calm at Suvla as a sign of success, assuming the fighting had moved to the distant hills. However, they soon realized the front line was alarmingly close to the beach, and that Stopford was still aboard the Jonquil. Aspinall found Stopford in high spirits, content with the progress, despite not having secured the high ground.

Aspinall and Hamilton met on HMS Chatham, the flagship of Rear-Admiral John de Robeck, overseeing the landing fleet. It was not until the afternoon of August 8th that Hamilton fully grasped the situation at Suvla. Accompanied by Aspinall and Commodore Roger Keyes, he went to the Jonquil to confront Stopford, who had by then briefly visited shore to consult with Hammersley.

During this meeting, Stopford and Hammersley revealed their plan to advance on the morning of August 9th. However, Hamilton, recognizing the urgency, insisted on an immediate advance. Consequently, at 6:30 pm, the 32nd Brigade was ordered to march towards the Tekke Tepe ridge. The night march over unfamiliar and rough terrain proved challenging, and the brigade reached the vicinity of the summit only by 4 am the next day. Tragically, they arrived just after the Ottoman reinforcements and were met with a fierce bayonet charge. The brigade suffered catastrophic losses, and the few survivors scattered back towards the beach.

Ottoman reinforcements under Feizi Bey began arriving on the evening of August 8th, just as the British had anticipated. General Otto Liman von Sanders, eager to capitalize on the opportunity, pushed for an immediate attack. However, Feizi Bey argued against this, citing the troops' exhaustion and lack of artillery support. Dissatisfied, von Sanders replaced him with Mustafa Kemal, commander of the Ottoman 19th Division, who had already demonstrated his effectiveness at Chunuk Bair. Kemal took charge of the Anafarta section, extending from Suvla to Chunuk Bair.

Kemal, known for his aggressive tactics at ANZAC, now held the advantageous high ground at Suvla. He chose a defensive stance while focusing on the threat at Sari Bair ridge. By August 9th, the fighting intensified around Suvla, but the window for a swift British advance had closed. A poignant moment was observed by Ellis Ashmead-Bartlett, who described a harrowing scene where British wounded were trapped by flames on Scimitar Hill, a grim testament to the chaotic nature of the battle.

Meanwhile, British reinforcements continued to arrive, with the 53rd (Welsh) Infantry Division landing on the night of August 8th and the 54th (East Anglian) Division arriving on August 10th. However, effective command and control remained elusive. Lieutenant-General Sir Frederick Stopford's reasons for inaction, including his perception of Ottoman aggression, were seen as increasingly out of touch.

General Sir Ian Hamilton, recognizing the critical situation, communicated to Lord Kitchener that the IX Corps generals were unfit for their roles. Kitchener's response, sent on August 14th, emphasized the need for decisive and energetic leadership, reflecting his view that this was a "young man's war." He instructed Hamilton to replace any failing generals, offering to send replacements as needed.

Before Hamilton could respond, Kitchener made Lieutenant-General Julian Byng available to command IX Corps. On August 15th, Hamilton dismissed Stopford and temporarily replaced him with Major-General Beauvoir De Lisle of the 29th Division at Helles while Byng was en route from France. Major-General Hammersley was also dismissed. General Mahon, upset over De Lisle's appointment above him, resigned in protest, leaving his division during intense fighting at Kiretch Tepe. Additionally, the commander of the 53rd (Welsh) Infantry Division, Major-General John Lindley, voluntarily stepped down, further illustrating the turmoil within the British command structure during this critical phase of the Gallipoli Campaign.

While Lieutenant-General Sir Frederick Stopford was widely criticized for the failure of the Suvla operation, the ultimate responsibility for this fiasco extended beyond him. Lord Kitchener, then Secretary of State for War, played a crucial role in appointing Stopford, an older and inexperienced general, to a significant active corps command. Additionally, General Sir Ian Hamilton, who was in charge of the Mediterranean Expeditionary Force, accepted Stopford's appointment and subsequently failed to assert effective leadership over his subordinate. Hamilton's reflections in his diary on August 13, questioning whether he should have resigned rather than accept such appointments, came too late to alter the course of events. Stopford's removal was a contributing factor to Hamilton's own dismissal on October 15th.

Under the leadership of General de Lisle, the Suvla front underwent reorganization and reinforcement. This included the arrival of the seasoned

29th Division from Helles and the 2nd Mounted Division from Egypt, albeit without their horses. The campaign reached its zenith on August 21st with the Battle of Scimitar Hill, the largest confrontation of the entire Gallipoli Campaign. However, its failure led to a reduction in activity at Suvla, eventually culminating in the British evacuation in late December.

The conditions faced by the troops during the summer were horrendous, marked by extreme heat, swarms of flies, and poor sanitation. The situation worsened in November with torrential rainstorms and a subsequent blizzard, leading to the flooding of trenches and causing significant suffering among the soldiers. The harsh weather resulted in the drowning or freezing of 220 men, with an additional 12,000 cases of frostbite or exposure.

Notably, the Gallipoli Campaign also claimed the life of the renowned English physicist Henry Moseley, known for his groundbreaking work on atomic numbers. Moseley's promising scientific career was tragically cut short by a sniper's bullet in this battle.

In contrast to the campaign's overall mismanagement, the final withdrawal from Gallipoli was remarkably well-executed. The retreat was meticulously planned and implemented with a series of successful deceptions, preventing the Ottoman forces from realizing that a withdrawal was underway. This careful execution resulted in minimal losses and allowed for the successful evacuation of most artillery and equipment.

Following the battles on August 21st, the front lines at Suvla and Anzac stabilized, marking an end to significant territorial advances for the remainder of the Gallipoli Campaign. The troops, however, continued to engage in localized skirmishes and defensive actions, but no further large-scale offensives were launched.

The soldiers on these fronts faced severe hardships, largely due to inadequate preparation and training for the challenging conditions of the campaign.

The environment itself became an adversary; diseases spread by mosquitoes, the scarcity of fresh water, and the lack of adequate shelter severely affected the troops. These harsh conditions weakened the soldiers, diminishing their combat effectiveness and morale.

Moreover, the Allied forces' limited knowledge of the terrain placed them at a strategic disadvantage compared to their Ottoman adversaries, who were well-acquainted with the local landscape. This familiarity allowed the Ottoman forces to conduct successful ambushes and maintain a defensive advantage. Consequently, the Allied campaign at Suvla and Anzac witnessed a mix of successes and setbacks, heavily influenced by environmental challenges, tactical shortcomings, and the adversary's superior knowledge of the terrain.

Bibliography

Alexander, H. M. On Two Fronts: Being the Adventures of an Indian Mule Corps in France and Gallipoli. Heinemann, 1917.

Aspinall-Oglander, C. F. Military Operations Gallipoli: Inception of the Campaign to May 1915. Vol. I, History of the Great War Based on Official Documents by Direction of the Historical Section of the Committee of Imperial Defence, Heinemann, 1929.

Benninghof, Mike, Ph.D. Winter's Battle: An Infantry Attacks Campaign Study. Avalanche Press, Irondale, Alabama.

Boff, J. Haig's Enemy: Crown Prince Rupprecht and Germany's War on the Western Front. 1st ed., Oxford University Press, 2018.

Buttar, Prit. Germany Ascendant: The Eastern Front 1915. Osprey Publishing, Oxford, England, 2017.

Cameron, David Wayne. Shadows of Anzac: An Intimate History of Gallipoli. Big Sky Publishing, Newport, 2013.

Carlyon, Les. Gallipoli. Random House, Sydney, 2001.

Cassar, G. H. Hell in Flanders Fields: Canadians at the Second Battle of Ypres. Dundurn Press, 2010.

Cassar, G. Kitchener's War: British Strategy from 1914 to 1916. Brassey's, Washington, 2004.

Clayton, A. Paths of Glory: The French Army 1914–18. Cassell, London, 2003.

DiNardo, Richard L. Breakthrough: The Gorlice-Tarnow Campaign. Praeger, Santa Barbara, California, 2010.

Doughty, R. A. Pyrrhic victory: French Strategy and Operations in the Great War. Belknap Press, Cambridge, Massachusetts, 2005.

Edmonds, J. E. Military Operations France and Belgium, 1915: Battles of

Aubers Ridge, Festubert, and Loos. Vol. II, 1st ed., History of the Great War Based on Official Documents By Direction of the Historical Section of the Committee of Imperial Defence, Macmillan, London, 1928.

Schindler, John. Isonzo: The Forgotten Sacrifice of the Great War. Greenwood Publishing, 2001.

Stone, Norman. The Eastern Front 1914-1917. Penguin, 1998.

Strachan, H. The First World War: To Arms. Vol. I, Penguin Books, 2003.

Thompson, Mark. The White War: Life and Death on the Italian Front, 1915-1919. Faber & Faber, 2009.

Tucker, Spencer. The Great War, 1914–1918. Routledge, 2002 [1997].

www.ingramcontent.com/pod-product-compliance
Lightning Source LLC
Chambersburg PA
CBHW071302140726

47996CB00005B/1603